CW00738940

The
Sacred
Feminine
Through The Ages

PAULA MARVELLY

The Sacred Feminine Through The Ages

VOICES OF VISIONARY WOMEN ON POWER AND BELIEF

WATKINS
Sharing Wisdom
Since 1893

For Jean,
my beloved Mum

The Sacred Feminine Through the Ages
Paula Marvelly

First published as *Women of Wisdom* in the UK and USA
in 2005 by Watkins Publishing

This edition published in the UK and USA in 2024
by Watkins, an imprint of Watkins Media Limited
Unit 11, Shepperton House, 83–93 Shepperton Road
London N1 3DF

enquiries@watkinspublishing.com

A CIP record for this book is available from the British Library

ISBN: 9-7817-8-678-875-7 (Hardback)
ISBN: 9-7817-8-678-876-4 (eBook)

10 9 8 7 6 5 4 3 2 1

Typeset by Lapiz
Printed in the United Kingdom by TJ Books Ltd

www.watkinspublishing.com

CONTENTS

I, WOMAN, am that wonder-breathing rose
That blossoms in the garden of the King.
In all the world there is no lovelier thing,
And the learned stars no secret can disclose
Deeper than mine – that almost no one knows.
The perfume of my petals in the spring
Is inspiration to all bards that sing
Of love, the spirit's lyric unrepose.

Under my veil is hid the mystery
Of unaccomplished eons, and my breath
The Master-Lover's life replenisheth.
The mortal garment that is worn by me
The loom of Time renews continually;
And when I die – the universe knows death.

"The Mystic Rose"
Elsa Barker

PROLOGUE

In her seminal book, *A Room of One's Own*, discussing the nature of female fiction in relation to the meaning of existence, Virginia Woolf urges women everywhere to pick up their pen and write:

> What is meant by "reality"? It would seem to be something very erratic, very undependable – now to be found in a dusty road, now in a scrap of newspaper in the street, now a daffodil in the sun. It lights up a group in a room and stamps some casual saying. It overwhelms one walking home beneath the stars and makes the silent world more real than the world of speech – and then there it is again in an omnibus in the uproar of Piccadilly. Sometimes, too, it seems to dwell in shapes too far away for us to discern what their nature is. But whatever it touches, it fixes and makes permanent. This is what remains over when the skin of the day has been cast into the hedge; that is what is left of past time and of our loves and hates. Now the writer, as I think, has the chance to live more than other people in the presence of this reality. It is his business to find it and collect it and communicate it to the rest of us.[1]

Since time immemorial, women have indeed sought to convey their interpretations of reality, whether it be through mythological stories, sacred poetry, philosophical treatises or simply heartfelt letters, in an attempt to describe the feminine mysteries of the universe and the holiness of our natural state.

Exploring the spiritual testimony of many remarkable women – some lesser known as well as those more renowned – we embark on a fascinating voyage from the beginning of recorded history up to the present time, charting the agonies and ecstasies of their respective beliefs, whether Jewish, Christian, Sufi, Hindu, Buddhist, Taoist or without any religious affiliation at all.

Furthermore, presented as an anthology of excerpts set within a contextual narrative, we honour these exceptional women in their quest for emancipation, equality and the expression of their most intimate moments: Mesopotamian priestess Enheduanna, Egyptian pharaoh Hatshepsut, Greek lyrist Sappho, Medieval polymath Hildegard of Bingen, Christian mystic Julian of Norwich, Transcendentalist Emily Dickinson and Sweet Mother Mirra Alfassa, to name but a few.

In this completely revised second edition, an additional chapter on Virginia Woolf has also been included, bringing our investigation into the modern age. Interestingly, in another of her compelling essays, *How Should One Read a Book?*, Virginia suggests that to bring a text to life, the author and reader should enter into a state of holy communion.

On that humble yet rousing note, let our journey begin . . .

CHAPTER ONE
MESOPOTAMIA AND PRIESTESS ENHEDUANNA

You of the bountiful heart
You of the radiant heart
I will sing of your cosmic powers

From the very first Indigenous tribespeople to the end of Stone Age society, humankind intuited life and the very universe itself as a personification of the great primordial Mother Goddess. Everything was seen as her manifestation: birds and beasts, mountains and meadows, rivers and seas. The changing seasons, experienced just as much in the abundance of the late-summer harvest as in the devastation of winter storm, were all aspects of her infinite expression.

The shapeshifting faces of the moon were also associated with the life cycles of the Mother. Birth, transformation and death, as well as woman's menstrual cycle, were synonymous with the moon's recurring phases – waxing (the maiden), full (the pregnant mother) and waning (the wise old woman). Similarly, the moon's final phase, where its features are hidden in shadow, symbolized the underlying consciousness, the omnipresent totality of the universe, in which everything else was contained.

The recurrence of goddess and lunar iconography, which can be charted between the great cultures from Old Europe to the Indus Valley – specifically statues of fertile goddesses and painted female images in caves and on pottery – reveals how the divine feminine was perceived and worshipped in such a way. However, the advent of the Bronze Age (3300–1200 BCE) saw momentous changes that profoundly affected this state of affairs. The discovery of bronze, an alloy of tin and copper, was to provide not only more powerful and flexible tools for farming but also weapons of defence and killing, used to protect and win land to accommodate an ever-growing population.

Mesopotamia, the land between the Euphrates and Tigris rivers, incorporating Sumer, Assyria, Babylonia and the Akkadian Empire, had principally been an agricultural community living in accord with nature. Worshipping a universal Mother Goddess, the Mesopotamians lived a relatively peaceful existence up until this point. However, invading migratory warriors – Aryan tribes from the steppe lands between the Dnieper and Volga Rivers north of the Black and Caspian Seas, as well as Semitic tribes from the Syro-Arabian Desert – soon violated their societal harmony, imposing patriarchal customs and ideas of their own.

The perpetual fear of violence and subordination to marauders subsequently brought about a profound shift in the mindset of human beings. Survival and the quest for individual power became the primary focus of life, with the notion of the "hero" passing tests of strength and courage starting irrevocably to emerge.

More importantly, death was no longer seen as part of a recurring phase in the natural rhythm of the universe but rather it was the end, a complete finality, with no hope of rejuvenation or rebirth. This limiting and fearful world view inevitably caused a split in humankind's harmonious relationship with the natural world and all of sentient life.

This resulted in the immanent, all-forgiving Mother Goddess being systematically replaced by the emergence of a transcendent, judgemental Father God, personified by a pantheon of celestial deities who were separate from and above the manifest world. Where there once had been harmony, sustenance and peace, there was now discord, degeneration and war. And with the decline in the veneration of the sacred feminine, inevitably the position of women in society also started to deteriorate – where they had once been held in high matriarchal regard, they were now increasingly reduced to the subordination, and even possession, of men.

Thankfully, one idol worshipped by the Mesopotamians reconciled these ruptured, dualistic components of the masculine and feminine principles, melding them back into a unified, equalitarian whole. Inanna, the Sumerian goddess of the moon (known as Ishtar in neighbouring Babylonia) embodied the waxing and waning world within her very being. Reminding her devotees through the myths told about her that life is a process filled with many trials and triumphs, she also symbolized the independent power of women.

Inanna is represented pictorially as a goddess with wings, flanked either side by two owls. Many stories feature her, including the famous legend of her descent into the underworld, where her widowed sister Queen Ereshkigal reigns supreme. Inanna tells the gatekeeper that she desires to witness the funeral rites of her recently deceased brother-in-law. However, her sister fears Inanna secretly wants to usurp her of her powers, and so strips her sister of garments and jewellery that are symbolic of her sovereignty, until finally sacrificing her by suspending her from a hook. For three days Inanna hangs like a carcass, while all fertility on earth withers away.

Ninshubur, Inanna's trusted advisor and servant, manages to obtain help from Enki, the god of wisdom, who secures Inanna's release. Once she is returned to earth, all of nature's vitality is mercifully restored. In a story that echoes the later Greek myth of Persephone, who is similarly carried off by Hades to the underworld, Inanna's tale is rich in psychological metaphor, particularly in relation to the unconscious realms of the human psyche, and the pattern of life portrayed as an eternal dance of darkness and light. Such is the educational power of mythology – although not true literally, it embodies relatable, eternal truths about human nature and the ultimate meaning of existence.

In an epoch that saw the invention of writing, such legends and stories surrounding the sacred feminine were finally given a recorded voice. In fact, the very first named writer in world history was a woman. Enheduanna (2285–2250 BCE), meaning "High Priestess of Heaven", was appointed to serve Nanna, the moon god, at the temple of Ur by her father King Sargon of Akkad. Despite her religious duties, Enheduanna soon turned her devotion and literary skills to Nanna's daughter, the goddess Inanna.

Composed in wedge-shaped characters inscribed on clay tablets called cuneiform and discovered during excavations between the two great World Wars in Ur by the British archaeologist Sir Leonard Woolley, Enheduanna's poems resonate passionately with her veneration of the

Mother Goddess. In 42 attributed temple hymns and three stand-alone poems, Enheduanna's words are suffused with the confidence and self-awareness of a powerful, all-knowing woman, reasserting the noble position of the sacred feminine in the cosmos.

Using her position at the temple as upholder of the Mesopotamian concept of Me ("wisdom"), Enheduanna presents her metaphysical vision of the world, particularly through her verse addressed specifically to Inanna: "Inanna and Ebih", "Lady of Largest Heart" and "The Exaltation to Inanna".

The first poem tells the story of a battle between the moon goddess and a defiant mountain called Ebih, who fails to show Inanna proper respect. Asserting her self-worth and independence, the poem is a rallying cry of an impassioned female warrior:

Inanna
   child of the Moon God
a soft bud swelling
her queen's robe cloaks the slender stem
on her smooth brow she paints
fire beams and fearsome glint

fastens carnelian [semi-precious stone]
blood-red and glowing
around her throat

and then her hand clasps
the seven-headed mace
she stands as in youth's prime
her right hand grasps the mace

5

steps, yes she steps her narrow foot
on the furred back
of a wild lapis lazuli bull

and she goes out
white-sparked, radiant
in the dark vault of evening's sky
star-steps in the street
through the Gate of Wonder[1]

Enheduanna's next poem, "Lady of Largest Heart", is a series of intense and emotional epithets in praise of Inanna's feminine nature – her power and charisma, her wisdom and immortality, her rejuvenating, bountiful love:

she wears
the carved-out ground plan
of heaven and earth [...]

YOU mistress of the powers of heaven
YOU unequalled in the earth around you
YOU exalted all on your own
    heaven and earth cannot gird your fame [...]

to have a husband   to have a wife
to thrive in the goodness of love
are yours Inanna[2]

Indeed, the sacred practice of performing sexual intercourse in temples devoted to Inanna was an important ritual in Mesopotamia, as making love within holy precincts was believed to infuse divine energy back into nature, so increasing the yield of summer crops as well as the autumn harvest.

In her third and most celebrated poem, "Exaltation to Inanna", Enheduanna sings of her goddess' greatness and the glory of her celestial being, leaving us in no doubt of her everlasting devotion to the Universal Mother:

mistress of the scheme of order
great Queen of queens
babe of a holy womb
greater than the mother who bore you
You all knowing
You wise vision
Lady of all lands
life-giver for the many
faithful Goddess
worthy of powers
to sing your praise is exalted

You of the bountiful heart
You of the radiant heart
I will sing of your cosmic powers

***

truly for your gain
you drew me toward
my holy quarters
I
the High Priestess
I
Enheduanna[3]

7

During Sir Leonard Woolley's excavations, a calcite disc was also unearthed depicting the priestess accompanied by loyal attendants. Identifiable by her tiered, ornamental robe and elaborate headdress, Enheduanna's face is shown in profile as she raises her eyes up to her beloved Inanna.

Mesopotamia retained the image of the great Mother Goddess in the form of Ninhursag ("Lady of the Mountains") for centuries long after Enheduanna's day. Sadly, the advent of the Iron Age (1200–600 BCE) and rise of patriarchal attitudes saw the emergence of the Babylonian creation myth, *Enuma Elish* ("When on High"), which recounts the story of the conquest and murder of Tiamat, the primordial Mother Goddess of the sea, by the god Marduk, her great-great-great-grandson.

Furthermore, the *Code of Hammurabi* – a collection of 282 laws inscribed on a stone pillar discovered by French archaeologists in 1901 while excavating the ancient city of Susa in modern-day Iran – consolidated Mesopotamian legislation, explicitly laying out the status of women. Although they were allowed certain legal and economic rights in society, the code categorically stated that authority within the household belonged to their husbands, meaning that women were effectively the disposable property of their spouse.

It is not surprising, therefore, that long after she had died, Enheduanna's poetry was sung in the temples devoted to Inanna and Ishtar throughout Mesopotamia – a powerful female voice re-establishing harmony in the universe and the rightful place of the sacred feminine.

CHAPTER TWO
ANCIENT EGYPT AND QUEEN HATSHEPSUT

I shall be eternal like an undying star...

In the neighbouring lands of ancient Egypt, another powerful woman was carving out her destiny in spite of all the odds. Born into the royal household, Pharaoh Queen Hatshepsut embodied many of the qualities associated with the goddess mythology of this formidable African state.

Dating back as far as 3100 BCE and lasting up until the birth of Jesus, the ancient Egyptian civilization was one of the most sophisticated cultures in the known world. As society expanded and became more structured and patriarchal, creation mythology describing the origins of the cosmos inevitably started to evolve. Like Mesopotamia, we hear again of a watery chaos. In one story the "great flood" is called Nu, a primordial male energy, which gives birth to the god Atum, who then masturbates the celestial pantheon into life.

However, an older tradition describes the heavenly sea as feminine, and the place from which the Primordial Mother manifests in the form of Hathor, a great anthropomorphic cow, her ever-flowing rain-milk nourishing and sustaining the entire universe. As she swims in the ocean of her divine being, she carries the sun god Re between her magnificent horns.

Hathor is also personified as a beautiful woman and many temple poems were written in her honour:

All hail, jubilation to you, O Golden One …
Sole ruler, Uraeus [Egyptian cobra] of the Supreme Lord
*   himself!*
Mysterious One, who gives birth to the divine entities,
forms the animals, models them as she pleases, fashions
*   men …*
O Mother! … Luminous One who thrusts back the darkness,
who illuminates every human creature with her rays,
Hail Great One of many names …[1]

One of the Golden One's many monikers was Maat, the goddess of truth, order and cosmic harmony, similar to the universal principle of Me in Mesopotamia. Pictorially, Maat wears an ostrich feather on her head, often with wings on her arms that are used to counterbalance the scales of justice measuring the purity of men and women's hearts upon their respective deaths, to determine if they may continue their journey to the afterlife.

Also representative of the feminine aspect of consciousness and married to the god, Thoth, she pervades the entire universe:

… Maat is in every place that is yours … You rise with Maat,
you live with Maat, you join your limbs to Maat, you make
*   Maat*

rest on your head in order that she may take her seat on your
forehead.
You become young again in the sight of your daughter Maat,
you live from the perfume of her dew.
Maat is worn like an amulet at your throat, she rests on
your chest,
the divine entities reward you with Maat, for they know
her wisdom...
Your right eye is Maat, your left eye is Maat...
your flesh, your members are Maat...
your food is Maat, your drink is Maat...
the breaths of your nose are Maat...
you exist because Maat exists,
and she exists because you exist.[2]

Another important Egyptian goddess ubiquitously worshipped was Isis, Queen of Heaven, Earth and the Underworld, depicted as a beautiful woman, again with soaring wings, as well as identifying with the star of Sirius.

Many myths feature her story, but the most important links Isis with her brother, the god Osiris. Gestating simultaneously in the womb of their mother, the sky goddess Nut, the siblings form an inseparable bond leading to their eventual marriage. In a fit of jealousy, their other brother, Seth, murders Osiris and dismembers his body, scattering it across the land. Devastated, Isis gathers up the pieces and with the final part – Osiris' penis – she impregnates herself, subsequently giving birth to their son Horus, the god of kingship.

Akin to the mythological lore surrounding Inanna, hymns to Isis immortalize her sacred beauty and her power to restore eternal life:

I play the sistra before
your beautiful face,
Isis, Giver of Life, residing in
the Sacred Mound,
Eye of Re who has no equal
in heaven and on earth.
Great of love, mistress of women,
who fills heaven and earth with
her beauty …[3]

Together with its rich tradition of mythological folklore, Egypt is especially renowned for its illustrious line of pharaoh kings. As gods incarnate on earth, they would pledge to rule justly and wisely in exchange for the harmonious flow of the seasons and the annual inundation cycle of the Nile. Over the centuries, a small number of women also assumed the royal role, one in particular being responsible for one of the longest periods of peace and prosperity that Egypt ever witnessed.

Hatshepsut, meaning "foremost among noblewomen", ruled between roughly 1479 and 1458 BCE during the 18th dynasty. The eldest daughter of King Thutmose I and his consort Queen Ahmose, at the age of 12 she was married to her half-brother King Thutmose II, and initially shared the throne with him, acting as his Queen Consort and bearing him two daughters. Surviving statues of Hatshepsut in her youth show a beautiful woman with an oval face, almond-shaped eyes and a rather prominent nose.

The premature death of her husband, leaving no male primogenital heir, inspired Hatshepsut to proclaim the title of Regent and then, ultimately, Pharaoh for herself. In similar tradition to the male rulers before her, hieroglyphs in the Temple of Amun-Re (the union of Amun, god of the wind, and Re, god of the sun) at Karnak leave autobiographical details of her reign:

I have done this with a loving heart for my father,
    Amun;
Initiated in his secret of the beginning,
Acquainted with his beneficent might,
I did not forget whatever he had ordained.
My majesty knows his divinity,
I acted under his command;
It was he who led me,
I did not plan a work without his doing.[4]

Commissioned by Hatshepsut, the obelisk inscription asserts her spiritual right to rule, for, as she explicitly states, it was not her will but the will of the king of the gods.

Despite her divine blessing, somewhat bizarrely, Hatshepsut starts to be portrayed in artwork and sculpture as male, presumably in a further attempt to endorse her royal status. Although Egyptian society at the time was overall quite liberal toward women, its structure was predominantly patriarchal, with official and religious offices controlled mainly by men.

So, unlike the pronounced sensuality of later, more illustrious Egyptian queens such as Nefertiti and Cleopatra, Hatshepsut was now portrayed as a handsome man dressed in male clothing and sporting the traditional pharaoh's false beard. The obelisk inscription also verifies her new gender-appropriated status:

13

I swear, as I am loved of Re,
As Amun, my father, favours me,
As my nostrils are refreshed with life and dominion,
As I wear the white crown,
As I appear with the red crown,
As the Two Lords have joined their portions for me,
As I rule this land like the son of Isis,
As I am mighty like the son of Nut,
As Re rests in the evening bark,
As he prevails in the morning bark,
As he joins his two mothers in the god's ship,
As sky endures, as his creation lasts,
As I shall be eternal like an undying star,
As I shall rest in life like Atum –
So as regards these two great obelisks,
Wrought with electrum by my majesty for my father Amun,
In order that my name may endure in this temple,
For eternity and everlastingness . . .[5]

Hatshepsut reigned for more than 20 years, eventually being usurped by her nephew-stepson Thutmose III. Interestingly, after her death, significant attempts were made to delete her memory from the history of Egypt – her temples and monuments were desecrated, her portraits and cartouches vandalized, and details of her rule omitted from the official list of kings. Thankfully, the legacy of this female pharaoh was recorded by the early third-century BCE priest and historian, Manetho, though it took modern scholarship to verify her identity unequivocally.

In 1920, famous Egyptologist Howard Carter was part of a team of archaeologists who excavated one of Hatshepsut's earliest chosen tomb sites, situated high up on the face of a cliff in mountains near Luxor. Although the tomb was later abandoned by Hatshepsut as a burial chamber, the lid of the excavated sarcophagus was found to be inscribed with a prayer to Nut, goddess of the sky:

> The King's Daughter, God's Wife, King's Great Wife, Lady of the Two Lands, Hatshepsut, says, "O my mother, Nut, stretch thyself over me, that thou mayest place me among the imperishable stars which are in thee, and that I may not die."[6]

Hatshepsut's actual mummy was finally discovered in 2006 by Egyptologist Zahi Hawass, who reinvestigated the identity of an anonymous, embalmed corpse from a tomb (KV60) in the nearby Valley of the Kings, which had originally been unearthed by Howard Carter in 1903. A CT scan revealed an obese, middle-aged woman with very bad teeth. Hatshepsut's body was formally verified by matching a loose tooth from a box of artefacts that bore her cartouche with the corresponding hole left behind in her gum.

Needless to say, it is an inglorious end to a formidable reign and yet, perhaps, the definitive proof of her existence is testament to the fact that, despite all attempts to obliterate her from the annals of history, her legacy endures both in body and in spirit for all time.

CHAPTER THREE
HINDUISM AND SAGE VAK

I spread through all the worlds:
And touch this heaven with my eminence.

As well as the great empires of Mesopotamia and Egypt in the West, another great civilization was emerging in the north-west Indian subcontinent in the East, in the Indus Valley. In fact, the recently unearthed cities of Harappa and Mohenjo-daro show evidence of a race of people dating back as far as 3300 BCE. Like the Mesopotamians and Egyptians, they too had their own sophisticated mythology that explained the nature of creation – an omnipresent absolute Being in which manifested the phenomenal world.

Over time, the Indus Civilization developed a complex religious system, which we now know broadly as Hinduism ("Hindu" being a derivative of "Sindhu", a major river in northern India). Various oral classifications and sects subsequently developed explaining the nature of the universe – undifferentiated consciousness was known as Brahman (and later also as Purusha); the creative spirit was known as *maya* (and later as Prakriti). Interestingly, undifferentiated consciousness was also referred to as Siva, the divine masculine principle, with the creative spirit as Shakti, the divine feminine principle.

Between roughly 1500 and 1200 BCE, various priests and poets, including the relatively unknown female sage Vak, started to transcribe Hindu mythology into written Sanskrit by compiling four distinct texts or Vedas, meaning "knowledge": the Rigveda (composed of hymns), the Yajurveda (worship rituals), the Samaveda (melodies and chants) and the Atharvaveda (prayers and spells).

It is the Rigveda, comprising ten books, that contains the mystical wisdom of Advaita Vedanta ("the nondual philosophy contained at the end of the Vedas"). In the final book, the beginning of creation is laid bare:

Then, neither the non-Real nor the Real existed.
There was no sky then, nor the heavens beyond it.
What was contained by what, and where, and who sheltered it?
What unfathomable depths, what cosmic ocean, existed then?

Then, neither death nor deathlessness existed;
Between day and night there was as yet no distinction.
That ONE, by Its own power breathlessly breathed.

In the beginning, darkness lay wrapped in darkness;
All was one undifferentiated sea.
Then, within that one undifferentiated Existence,
[Something] arose by the heat of concentrated energy.

What arose in That in the beginning was Desire,
[Which is] the primal seed of mind.
The wise, having searched deep within their own hearts,
Have perceived the bond between the Real and the unreal.

They [the wise] have stretched the cord of their vision
  [to encompass the Truth],
And they have perceived what is higher and lower:
The mighty powers [of Nature] are made fertile
By that ONE who is their Source . . .[1]

As in Mesopotamia and Egypt, Vedic literature in India is replete with reverential references to the Mother Goddess and the sacred feminine – Aditi (the primal goddess and mother of all the gods), Saraswati (goddess of creativity and learning), Prithvi (goddess of the earth) – with their worship supported by the discovery of terracotta figurines throughout the Indus Valley.

Many of the *rishis* (Hindu saints or sages) involved in compiling the Vedas were men; however, several poems are believed to have been written by women. Out of ten identified, one woman in particular, who conveyed the perennial philosophy more profoundly than any other of her female counterparts was Vak, a mystic in her own right.

Coincidentally sharing the same name as the goddess of learning, she was the daughter of the *rishi* Ambhrina, although little else is known of her life. In the tenth book of the Rigveda, Vak's words are still chanted today as a devotional song – the "Devisukta" – in praise of the Mother Goddess:

I am the queen, the bestower of riches,
  I was the first to know among the holy ones;
Me, the gods put in many places,
  Making me enter and dwell abundantly.

By me, whoever eats food, and whoever sees,
  Whoever breathes, and whoever hears what is said,
They dwell in me, though they know it not;
  Listen, O wise, to thee I say what is true.

Verily I myself speak all this,
  What is welcome to the gods and men;
Whoever I love I make strong,
  I make him a Brahma [god of creation], a sage and a seer.

I spread out the bow of Rudra [god of roaring wind] for him
  To slay the unbeliever with his arrow;
I make strife among the people;
  I pervade all the earth and heaven.

I give birth to the father on the head of all this;
  My source is in the midst of waters in the sea;
Thence I spread through all the worlds;
  And touch this heaven with my eminence.

It is I who blow as the winds blow,
  Taking hold of all the worlds,
Past heaven and past this earth
  I have by greatness become such.[2]

As time moved on, the core nondualist teaching would be crystallized even further, finding expression in the Upanishads (which means "sitting with" a teacher), and forming the philosophical appendages to each Veda. Of the 108 identified, the core Upanishads were mainly composed during the first millennium BCE, their common motif being non-attachment to *maya* (the creative spirit) and the merging of the *atman* (individual self) with Brahman (universal consciousness).

Although the authorship of the Upanishads is largely unknown, many speak of feminine wisdom. Collectively known as the Shakta Upanishads, the eight minor texts eulogize the form of the goddess, with none so beautifully expressed as in the Devi Upanishad:

Great goddess, who art thou?

She replies: I am essentially Brahman [the Absolute].
From me has proceeded the world comprising Prakriti [material substance] and Purusha [cosmic consciousness], the void and Plenum [matter].

I am [all forms of] bliss and non-bliss.
Knowledge and ignorance are Myself...

I am the entire world.
I am the Veda as well as what is different from it.
I am unknown.
Below and above and around am I.[3]

However, it is the Brihadaranyaka Upanishad, the "Upanishad of the Great Forests", that speaks of the wisdom of two real women: Gargi, daughter of the sage Vachaknu, and Maitreyi, wife of the sage Yajnavalkya. Both come to the realization of universal Brahman through their perseverance in discovering the ultimate Truth. Gargi does so through her repeated questioning of Yajnavalkya at a philosophical congress held by King Janaka; and Maitreyi upon Yajnavalkya's departure to the forest for a life devoted to ascetic contemplation. This is relayed in a crucial passage outlining the nature of immortality:

"Maitreyi!" said Yajnavalkya, "Lo, verily, I am about to go forth from this state. Behold! Let me make a final settlement for you and that Katyayani [Yajnavalkya's second wife]."

Then said Maitreyi: "If now, sir, this whole earth filled with wealth were mine, would I be immortal thereby?"

"No," said Yajnavalkya. "As the life of the rich, even so would your life be. Of immortality, however, there is no hope through wealth."

Then said Maitreyi: "What should I do with that through which I may not be immortal? What you know, sir – that, indeed, tell me!"

Then said Yajnavalkya: "Ah! Lo, dear as you are to us, dear is what you say! Come, sit down. I will explain to you. But while I am expounding, do you seek to ponder thereon."

Then said he: "Lo, verily, not for love of the husband is a husband dear, but for love of the Soul [atman] a husband is dear.

"Lo, verily, not for love of the wife is a wife dear, but for love of the Soul a wife is dear.

"Lo, verily, not for love of the sons are sons dear, but for love of the Soul sons are dear.

"Lo, verily, not for love of the wealth is wealth dear, but for love of the Soul wealth is dear.

"Lo, verily, not for love of Brahmanhood is Brahmanhood dear, but for love of the Soul Brahmanhood is dear.

21

"Lo, verily, not for love of Kshatrahood [courage] is Kshatrahood dear, but for love of the Soul Kshatrahood is dear.

"Lo, verily, not for love of the worlds are the worlds dear, but for love of the Soul the worlds are dear.

"Lo, verily, not for love of the gods are the gods dear, but for love of the Soul the gods are dear.

"Lo, verily, not for love of the beings are beings dear, but for love of the Soul beings are dear.

"Lo, verily, not for love of all is all dear, but for love of the Soul all is dear.

"Lo, verily, it is the Soul that should be seen, that should be hearkened to, that should be thought on, that should be pondered on, O Maitreyi. Lo, verily, with the seeing of, with the hearkening to, with the thinking of, and with the understanding of the Soul, this world – all is known."[4]

The Vedic period was a time when women essentially had equal rights overall. However, as society expanded and became more sophisticated during the Upanishadic era, women's position in society came increasingly under the governance of their male counterparts.

Texts such as the first century CE *Manusmriti* ("Laws of Manu"), a collection of instructions written by Brahmin priests on how to order one's daily affairs, do in fact endorse the sacredness of the female form:

Women must be honoured and adorned by their fathers, brothers, husbands and brothers-in-law, who desire [their own] welfare.

Where women are honoured, there the gods are pleased; but where they are not honoured, no sacred rite yields rewards.[5]

And yet, it also states that if a wife is barren or dishonourable, or merely displeases her husband, she may be superseded at any time – a rule that does not appear to apply to her husband.

More disturbingly, at around this time, the act of *sati*, whereby a widow would throw herself on her husband's funeral pyre in an act of selfless devotion, started to become more and more widespread throughout the Indian subcontinent. Initially, self-immolation was voluntary, but it soon became a mandatory custom. Over the centuries, various attempts were made to outlaw this heinous practice. However, it was only as recently as 1987 that the Prevention of Sati Act came into force, forbidding women from committing suicide either by the will of others or by their own hand.

It is hard to reconcile India's contradictory attitudes – on the one hand honouring the sacred feminine principle, while on the other endorsing the violation of mortal women. And yet the ascendancy of the digital age has enabled the flow of knowledge, particularly surrounding human rights, to permeate feudal customs and educate primitive societies, thereby empowering all women, not just in Asia but all around the globe.

CHAPTER FOUR
JUDAISM AND QUEEN OF SHEBA MAKEDA

Wisdom is sweeter than honey,
brings more joy than wine . . .

So far, the likes of Enheduanna, Hatshepsut and Vak have only been recognized in recent times, their legacies finding appreciation through the rise of interest in women's studies and feminism. However, one woman whose reputation required little championing was Makeda, the illustrious Queen of Sheba, who is even mentioned in the Old Testament at a time when the earliest monotheist religion was dawning in the West.

Around the beginning of the second millennium BCE, a small group of people, led by Terah and his son Abraham, set out from Enheduanna's birthplace, the Mesopotamian city of Ur, and travelled northward across the Euphrates River to Haran in modern-day Iraq. Here it is said that Abraham heard God speaking directly to him – saying that if his followers obeyed His commandments and settled in the "Promised Land" of Canaan in the south, they would become His "chosen people". Abraham immediately agreed to this covenant and the Judaic religion was born.

Charted through the Hebrew Bible or Tanakh, the descendants of Abraham lived as nomads in Canaan for several hundred years, paying reverence to their Father God, Yahweh. However, archaeological evidence shows widespread worship of a Mother Goddess personified as Astarte, a conglomerate of her Mesopotamian and Egyptian goddess ancestors. Typically wearing a horned headdress reminiscent of Hathor, and surrounded by lions, she is associated with war and royal power, together with love and sexuality.

As time progressed, the developing Judaic code laid out in the Torah (the first five books of the Hebrew Bible) meant that women became increasingly excluded from formal religious studies and worship in the synagogue. Nonetheless, against all the odds the suppressed spirit of the sacred feminine still managed to retain its voice in a collection of 15 texts written in Greek, known as the Apocrypha, meaning "hidden books", called as such because they had been excluded from the orthodox canon of Jewish literature.

Here, Astarte resurfaces under a new guise in the form of Hokhmah, meaning "wisdom". Similar in concept to Me in Mesopotamia and Maat in Egypt, Hokhmah is at the very heart of the Apocrypha. One text in particular, titled The Book of Sirach (also known as Ecclesiasticus and found in the Catholic and Orthodox Bibles), was written by Ben Sira, a Jew living in Egypt in the second century BCE, who speaks of the immanent feminine principle of the universe:

The sand of the sea, the drops of rain,
  and the days of eternity – who can count them?
The height of heaven, the breadth of the earth,
  the abyss, and wisdom – who can search them out?
Wisdom was created before all other things,
  and prudent understanding from eternity.
The root of wisdom – to whom has it been revealed?
  Her subtleties – who knows them?
There is but one who is wise, greatly to be feared,
  seated upon his throne – the Lord.
It is he who created her;
  he saw her and took her measure;
  he poured her out upon all his works,
upon all the living according to his gift;
  he lavished her upon those who love him.[1]

Sadly, Ben Sira lacked the courage of his convictions, going on to support the split in gender relations by declaring, "From a woman sin had its beginning, and because of her we all die."[2] It would appear that he forgot, paradoxically, that it is she who is the bestower of all life.

During this period in history a formidable ruler emerges, who venerated both wisdom and the sacred feminine. Solomon, King of Israel – a unified kingdom between Assyria and Egypt – lived in approximately 1000 BCE and has been accredited with writing over 3,000 proverbs and 1,000 songs. His name meaning "peace", Solomon was born to King David and Bathsheba and was famed for his wealth and hundreds of wives. Although his life was devoted to the service of Yahweh, he also paid reverence to the divine goddess Astarte, with her image even adorning Solomon's Temple in Jerusalem.

He was reputedly the author of the Wisdom of Solomon, a further book of the Apocrypha, though the modern academic consensus is that it was composed by his contemporaries in his honour. Whoever its author is, the king eulogizes the feminine form of knowledge:

Wisdom is radiant and unfading,
and she is easily discerned by those who love her,
and is found by those who seek her.
She hastens to make herself known to those who desire her.
One who rises early to seek her will have no difficulty,
for she will be found sitting at the gate.
To fix one's thought on her is perfect understanding,
and one who is vigilant on her account will soon be free
    from care,
because she goes about seeking those worthy of her,
and she graciously appears to them in their paths,
and meets them in every thought.[3]

For Solomon, her presence becomes an intoxicating vision of the Beloved:

I loved her and sought her from my youth;
I desired to take her for my bride,
and became enamoured of her beauty.
She glorifies her noble birth by living with God,
and the Lord of all loves her.
For she is an initiate in the knowledge of God,
and an associate in his works.
If riches are a desirable possession in life,
what is richer than wisdom, the active cause of all things?[4]

In the Book of Proverbs, also attributed to Solomon and included in the Old Testament, the king again praises the omniscient feminine:

Does not wisdom call,
*   and does not understanding raise her voice?*
On the heights, beside the way,
*   at the crossroads she takes her stand;*
beside the gates in front of the town,
*   at the entrance of the portals she cries out:*
"To you, O people, I call,
*   and my cry is to all that live.*
O simple ones, learn prudence;
*   acquire intelligence, you who lack it.*
Hear, for I will speak noble things,
*   and from my lips will come what is right;*
for my mouth will utter truth;
*   wickedness is an abomination to my lips.*
All the words of my mouth are righteous;
*   there is nothing twisted or crooked in them.*
They are all straight to one who understands
*   and right to those who find knowledge.*
Take my instruction instead of silver,
*   and knowledge rather than choice gold;*
for wisdom is better than jewels,
*   and all that you may desire cannot compare with her.*
I, wisdom, live with prudence,
*   and I attain knowledge and discretion.*
The fear of the Lord is hatred of evil.
Pride and arrogance and the way of evil
*   and perverted speech I hate.*
I have good advice and sound wisdom;

I have insight, I have strength.
By me kings reign,
  and rulers decree what is just;
by me rulers rule,
  and nobles, all who govern rightly.
I love those who love me,
  and those who seek me diligently find me."[5]

As a great lover of the feminine form, both in its abstract principle and its physical being, it is therefore no surprise that when Solomon encountered a queen of outstanding beauty and intelligence, he immediately fell passionately in love with her, wanting to possess her as his own. Numerous legends abound about the life of this powerful female figure throughout Arabia, Persia, Ethiopia and Israel, but there is little doubt of her title – she was the Queen of Sheba, known as Makeda by the Ethiopians and Bilqis by the Arabians, meaning "Great One".

Fanciful tales of Islamic, Arabian and Jewish origin about her life involve magic carpets, teleportation and talking birds. However, more realistic portraits appear in the Old Testament, the Qur'an and the Ethiopian Bible, the Kebra Nagast ("Glory of Kings"). Born of royalty in the latter half of the 11th century BCE in the kingdom of Sheba (or Saba), modern-day Yemen, she succeeded her father to the throne upon his death when she was only 15. It is said that she possessed exquisite beauty, although several accounts testified that she had a deformed foot in the shape of a hoof.

The kingdom of Sheba, which some historians believe also incorporated the territories of Ethiopia and parts of Egypt, was a wealthy country, famous for its precious stones and exotic spices. Links had already been long established between Sheba and its neighbours, trading frankincense and myrrh up the Incense Road along the Rea Sea into the land of Israel. Like all great nations, the people of Sheba had their own pantheon of gods and goddesses, which included worship of the universal Mother Goddess as Astarte.

As Sheba's ruling queen, Makeda was also renowned for her love of wisdom personified as a female deity. Although she did not write verse herself, Makeda is given voice in the Kebra Nagast:

Wisdom is
sweeter than honey,
brings more joy
than wine,
illumines
more than the sun,
is more precious
than jewels.
She causes
the ears to hear
and the heart to comprehend.

I love her
like a mother,
and she embraces me
as her own child.
I will follow
her footprints
and she will not cast me away.[6]

When she learned of Solomon's wise reputation, Makeda immediately set off to Jerusalem with 797 camels laden with precious gifts to seek him out for herself. The King of Israel was overjoyed at her arrival at court and immediately gave her a luxurious apartment and showed her around his palace. However, Makeda had not come to stand in awe of his wealth; she had presented herself to hear his wise counsel and proceeded to challenge him with philosophical questions and riddles.

Over the following six months, Makeda conversed daily with Solomon on all manner of subjects. In spite of being overcome by his profound insight, she eventually felt it was time to return to her own country. However, Solomon could not bear to let her go, begging her to remain with him as his principal consort. After she refused his offer, Solomon secretly devised a plan to seduce her by ordering a lavish feast full of spicy foods, after which he asked Makeda to rest in his royal apartments. She agreed on the condition that he must not attempt to have her by force, to which Solomon consented. He also set a condition of his own – that she must not take anything from the palace without his permission – to which she also gave her word.

In the middle of the night, with a raging thirst, Makeda got up to pour herself a glass of water. Solomon, who had only been pretending to sleep, immediately asked her if she were not breaking their agreement – what, after all, is more precious than the liquid of life? She acquiesced and demanded to be released from her promise. This meant that Solomon was similarly released from his and, subsequently, they consummated their relationship. A child was later conceived through their union. Named Menelik, he would go on to become King of Ethiopia upon his mother's death.

Again, the Kebra Nagast relates details of Makeda's union with Solomon and her ensuing pregnancy:

I fell
because of wisdom,
but was not destroyed:
through her I dived
into the great sea,
and in those depths
I seized
a wealth-bestowing pearl.

I descended
like the great iron anchor
men use to steady their ships
in the night on rough seas,
and holding up the bright lamp
that I there received,
I climbed the rope
to the boat of understanding.

While in the dark sea,
I slept,
and not overwhelmed there,
dreamt: a star
blazed in my womb.

I marvelled
at that light,
and grasped it,
and brought it up to the sun.
I laid hold upon it,
and will not let it go.[7]

One of the most beautiful love poems dating from this period is the Song of Songs. Although there is no firm evidence to support it, the sacred marriage text is ascribed to Solomon, with Makeda the object of his desire. Interestingly, despite its intoxicating blend of mysticism and sexual ecstasy, the Song of Songs finds a place both in the Hebrew Bible and the Old Testament:

> *Let him kiss me with the kisses of his mouth –*
> *For thy love is better than wine.*
> *Thine ointments have a goodly fragrance,*
> *Thy name is as ointment poured forth;*
> *Therefore do the maidens love thee.*
> *Draw me, we will run after thee.*
> *The king hath brought me into his chambers;*
> *We will be glad and rejoice in thee,*
> *We will find thy love more fragrant than wine.*
> *Sincerely do they love thee.*[8]

Through their sexual union, Solomon and Sheba merge into the bliss of their sacred devotion:

> *I am a rose of Sharon,*
> *A lily of the valleys.*
>
> *As a lily among thorns,*
> *So is my love among the daughters.*
>
> *As an apple tree among the trees*
>   *of the wood,*
> *So is my beloved among the youths.*

I delight to sit in his shadow
And his fruit is sweet to my taste.
He brought me to the banqueting house,
And his banner of love was over me.

Stay me with flagons, comfort me with apples;
For I am lovesick.
His left hand is under my head,
And his right hand doth embrace me.[9]

And, in reverence to the universal Mother Goddess, the two lovers are nourished in the bosom of the divine feminine:

O that thou wert as my brother,
that sucked the breasts of my mother!
When I should find thee without, I would kiss thee;
Yea, and none would despise me.

I would lead thee, and bring thee
Into my mother's house,
That thou mightest instruct me;
I would cause thee to drink of spiced wine
Of the juice of my pomegranate.

His left hand should be under my head,
And his right hand should embrace me.[10]

Like Enheduanna, Hatshepsut and Vak before her, Makeda remains essentially an enigmatic character, and her full biography is sketchy at best. Nonetheless, whatever her identity, her memory is a powerful example of a passionate woman with a thirst for experiencing a profound and meaningful life.

Lamentably, for the following two millennia, rabbinic literature presented women as lowly beings, specifically in relation to menstruation, miscarriage and childbirth. It would not be until the Middle Ages in Europe, within the Kabbalistic tradition, that the voice of the Judaic goddess would re-emerge in the form of Shekhinah, the sacred feminine.

CHAPTER FIVE
ANCIENT GREECE AND LYRIST SAPPHO

Come to me again now, release me
from my agony, fulfil all
that my heart desires . . .

One civilization where the nondualist teaching came into its own and whose metaphysical legacy formed the basis of Western thinking was ancient Greece. Indeed, many Greek philosophers during the first millennium BCE were conversant with an immanent mystical power through the influence of cultural links with Egypt, Mesopotamia and the Indus Valley. Goddess mythology also played an important part in the psyche of the populace, specifically through the poetry of the Lesbian poet Sappho, whose laments about love still echo down through the centuries to this day.

One wise individual, whose perennial philosophy became the cornerstone of Greece's Golden Age, was the martyred sage Socrates. Born in 469 BCE in Athens, he championed what became known as the Socratic Method – deconstructing philosophical argument in order to arrive at one, unchanging Truth, which he called the "Good". Although he never wrote a single word, his teaching was immortalized by his devoted disciple Plato.

Born slightly later than his mentor in 427 BCE, Plato venerated Sappho, calling her the Tenth Muse, in reference to the Nine Muses believed to be the source of artistic knowledge embodied within Greek culture. He was also instrumental in spreading the teachings of Socrates by establishing an academy just outside the city walls of Athens as a place for philosophical enquiry.

In Book VII of *The Republic*, Plato's seminal work on the nature of a just city-state, he describes Socrates' famous metaphor of the "Analogy of the Cave", which illustrates the difference between the world of shadows and the reality of universal consciousness. In *Symposium*, another of Plato's celebrated and arguably more accessible works, the nature of love is discussed at a dinner party, presented by Diotima, a Mantinean priestess. Expounding the essence of beauty, she demonstrates how falling in love can lead to a love of the Divine:

"The correct way," she said, "for someone to approach this business [the pursuit of love] is to begin when he's young by being drawn towards beautiful bodies. At first, if his guide leads him correctly, he should love just one body and in that relationship produce beautiful discourses. Next he should realize that the beauty of any one body is closely related to that of another, and that, if he is to pursue beauty of form, it's very foolish not to regard the beauty of all bodies as one and the same. Once he's seen this, he'll become a lover of all beautiful bodies [. . .] After this, he should regard the beauty of minds as more valuable than that of the body, so that, if someone has goodness of mind even if he has little of the bloom of beauty, he will be content with him, and will love and care for him, and give birth to the kinds of discourse that help young men to become better [. . .]

"After practices, the guide must lead him towards forms of knowledge, so that he sees their beauty too [. . .] [He] will be turned towards the great sea of beauty and gazing on it, he'll give birth, through a boundless love of knowledge, to many beautiful and magnificent discourses and ideas [...] [This], Socrates, is the ultimate objective of all the previous efforts [. . .] [This] beauty always *is* and doesn't come into being or cease; it doesn't increase or diminish [. . .] It will appear as in itself and by itself, always single in form; all other beautiful things share its character but do so in such a way that, when other things come to be or cease, it is not increased or decreased in any way nor does it undergo any change."[1]

Greek cosmology abounds with references to immortal beauty, personified as a pantheon of female deities responsible for giving life to the manifest world. Gaia, the primordial Mother Goddess, was first to be revered and worshipped, specifically by priestesses at Delphi. Often depicted as a buxom woman emerging from the earth, there are many poems written in her honour, including the celebrated Homeric "Hymn to Gaia":

O universal mother, who dost keep
From everlasting thy foundations deep,
Eldest of things, Great Earth, I sing of thee;
All shapes that have their dwelling in the sea,
All things that fly, or on the ground divine

Live, move, and there are nourished – these are thine;
These from thy wealth thou dost sustain; from thee
Fair babes are born, and fruits on every tree
Hang ripe and large, revered Divinity!

  The life of mortal men beneath thy sway
Is held; thy power both gives and takes away!
Happy are they whom thy mild favours nourish,
All things unstinted round them grown and flourish.
For them, endures the life-sustaining field
Its load of harvest, and their cattle yield
Large increase, and their house with wealth is filled.
Such honoured dwell in cities fair and free,
The homes of lovely women, prosperously;
Their sons exult in youth's new budding gladness,
And their fresh daughters free from care or sadness,
With bloom-inwoven dance and happy song,
On the soft flowers the meadow-grass among,
Leap round them sporting – such delights by thee
Are given, rich Power, revered Divinity.

  Mother of gods, thou wife of starry Heaven,
Farewell! be thou propitious, and be given
A happy life for this brief melody,
Nor thou nor other songs shall unremembered be.[2]

Hellenic mythology includes many other illustrious female deities. The goddess of wisdom and warfare, Athena – often with the epithet, Pallas – appears most famously in Homer's *Odyssey*, the epic tale of Odysseus' journey home from the Trojan Wars. Depicted carrying a spear and wearing a helmet, Athena guides her male protégé through a series of tests in his voyage of self-discovery and mastery. The opening lines of the Homeric "Hymn to Athena" reiterate both her dazzling charm and wise counsel:

Pallas Athena
I shall sing,
the glorious goddess
whose eyes gleam,
brilliantly inventive,
her heart relentless,
formidable maiden,
guardian of cities...[3]

Other prominent female deities include Artemis (goddess of the moon and hunting), Demeter (goddess of the harvest), Hecate (goddess of sorcery) and Hera (goddess of marriage and queen of the gods). However, there is one goddess who eclipses all others in the hierarchy of divine beings: Aphrodite, "the Golden One". The tale of the "Judgement of Paris", from Ovid's *Metamorphoses*, relates how the Trojan prince chooses Aphrodite over Hera and Athena, believing her to be the fairest of them all. (His reward is Helen, Queen of Sparta, which comes at the heavy price of triggering the Trojan Wars.)

Immortalized in Sandro Botticelli's *Birth of Venus* (the Roman name for Aphrodite), where she rises out of the sea at Paphos in Cyprus standing nude in a giant scallop shell, she is goddess of love and beauty. The Homeric "Hymn to Aphrodite" heralds her captivating form:

Golden crowned, beautiful
awesome Aphrodite

is who I shall sing,
she who possesses the heights
of all
sea-wet Cyprus
where Zephyros [god of the west wind] swept her
with his moist breath
over the waves
of the roaring sea
in soft foam.

In their circles of gold
the Hours [goddesses of time and the seasons] joyously
received her
and wrapped
the ambrosial garments around her.
On her immortal head
they laid a crown of gold
that was wonderfully made
and in
the pierced lobes of her ears
they hung
flowers of copper
from the mountains
and precious gold . . .[4]

Given the extent to which goddesses were revered and honoured in Hellenistic culture, it is difficult to reconcile this with the way in which ordinary women were treated in daily life. Excluded from participating in civic democracy, they were generally perceived as irrational creatures, lacking morality and sound intelligence.

Sadly, Hesiod's *Theogony* (composed circa 700 BCE) perpetuates such misogynistic thinking through its story of Pandora, who, in the manner of Eve, is blamed for violating man's harmonious existence. The first woman on earth, Pandora is given a sealed box by the gods and told never to open it. But her curiosity finally overwhelms her and she lifts the lid, allowing innumerable plagues and sorrows to escape into the world.

And so it was into this contradictory atmosphere of attitudes that Sappho, writer and priestess, was born on the island of Lesbos, off the coast of modern Turkey, in approximately 600 BCE. It is said that she later married and had a daughter called Cleis.

We only know scant amounts of Sappho's work because most of it – up to nine papyrus rolls – was allegedly destroyed in the fire at the Great Library of Alexandria. The only remaining evidence of her writing comes to us either through quotations in various books passed down from era to era or on the surviving parts of papyri that were miraculously unearthed at the end of the 19th century in the ancient town of Oxyrhynchus in Egypt.

There are many complex interpretations of Sappho's verse. Some commentators have focused on stories surrounding her tragic love for Phaon, a ferryman, and her apparent suicide; others have concentrated on her sexuality and the perceived female homoerotic elements in her work. Whether or not she endorsed lesbianism we can never know, but of one thing we can be in no doubt – her poetry is the celebration of sexual love.

Translated from Greek, Sappho's poems are in the genre of the lyric, with her "Sapphic" meter inspiring many subsequent generations of poets. Infused with intense erotic desire, she implores her patron muse, the immortal goddess of love, to help her in her quest to find her beloved:

Shimmering,
> *iridescent,*
>> *deathless Aphrodite,*
child of Zeus, weaver of wiles,
>> *I beg you,*
do not crush my spirit with anguish, Lady,
but come to me now, if ever before
you heard my voice in the distance
and leaving your father's golden house
drove your chariot pulled by sparrows
swift and beautiful
over the black earth, their wings a blur
as they streaked down from heaven
>> *across the bright sky –*

and then you were with me, a smile
playing about your immortal lips
as you asked,
> *what is it this time?*
>> *why are you calling again?*
And asked what my heart in its lovesick raving
most wanted to happen:
>> *"Whom now*
should I persuade to love you?
Who is wronging you, Sappho?
She may run now but she'll be chasing soon.
She may spurn gifts, but soon she'll be giving.
She may not love now, but soon she will,
>> *willing or not."*

43

Come to me again now, release me
from my agony, fulfil all
that my heart desires, and fight for me,

fight at my side, Goddess.[5]

During a period in history when the segregation of the sexes in public life was widespread, it is little wonder that Sappho alludes predominantly to the society of women and the figure of the goddess – her solace, her inspiration, her guide:

down from the mountain top
and out of Crete,
come to me here
in your sacred precinct, to your grove
of apple trees,

and your altars
smoking with incense,

where cold water flows babbling
through the branches,

the whole place
shadowed with roses,
sleep adrift down
from silvery leaves
an enchantment

horses grazing in a meadow
abloom with spring flowers
and where the breezes blow sweetly,
here, Cypris,

delicately in golden cups
> *pour nectar*
> *mixed for our festivities.*[6]

Throughout her work, Sappho employs all the imagery and symbolism recurrent with a sacred deity blessed with a bountiful nature – the sea, roses, the moon:

from Sardis
often turning your mind here

we thought you were like a goddess
> *everyone looked at you*
she loved the way you moved in the dance

now among the women of Lydia

as at sunset the rose-fingered moon
> *outshines all stars, spreading her light*
over the salt sea, the flowering fields,

and the glimmering dew falls, roses
> *bloom amid delicate starflowers*
chervil and sweet clover . . .[7]

Sappho understands the alchemy between lovers, their agonies and ecstasies along the path of love, yet she has faith that Aphrodite will always eventually bring the heart's desire:

Lucky bridegroom,
the marriage you have prayed for has come to pass
and the bride you dreamed of is yours . . .

Beautiful bride,
to look at you gives joy; your eyes are like honey,
love flows over your gentle face ...

Aphrodite
has honoured you above all others[8]

Over two millennia later, Sappho herself would embody the figure of an ideal muse for many 19th-century painters, such as the Pre-Raphaelites Simeon Solomon and Lawrence Alma-Tadema, as well as the Neo-Classicist John William Godward. Similarly, in modern times, she has become the towering inspiration for students of women's studies and feminists alike. As Sappho herself predicted:

The Muses have made me happy
in my lifetime

and when I die
I shall never be forgotten[9]

CHAPTER SIX

INDIAN BUDDHISM AND MOTHER OF THE BUDDHA MAHAPAJAPATI

I have reached the state where everything stops.

In the ancient city of Kapilavastu (in modern-day Nepal), a child named Siddhartha Gautama of the Shakya clan was born to a king, Suddhodana, and his wife, Maya, in around 563 BCE. Unfortunately, his mother died a week after the delivery and so her sister, Mahapajapati Gotami, also married to Suddhodana, raised the infant as her own. At the time of Siddhartha's birth, it was said that a holy man predicted the boy would eventually either rule the world or renounce it forever.

To ensure that his son would grow up to be a great king, Suddhodana surrounded him with luxury and splendour – the boy wanted for nothing. At the age of 16, Siddhartha married the princess Yashodhara, and together they had a son, Rahula. All was seemingly well until Siddhartha reached the age of 29. Travelling one day outside the palace gates, he encountered four aspects of human life that he had never witnessed before – a person riddled with sickness, an old man, an ascetic and a rotting corpse. Profoundly shocked by the experience, Siddhartha decided right then and there to find the meaning of the transitoriness of existence. And so he renounced his wealth and family and, taking nothing with him, set off to find spiritual liberation.

After six years on a futile path of intense study and extreme austerities, Siddhartha Gautama, the Buddha, became enlightened while sitting in Bodh Gaya under a bodhi tree. He realized the ineffable Truth of all existence – that his essential being transcended the ocean of samsara (the endless cycle of rebirth) and was at one with undifferentiated Mind:

From this state of limited consciousness, I appear once again to be a separate form within samsara; but from the state of expanded awareness, all of samsara is a manifestation of myself. I am a single, undifferentiated Mind, yet I shine forth, like the radiant beams of the Sun, as a universe of countless living beings, all made of my light. All beings are united in me, for I am their consciousness, their form, their very being. Never are there any separate selves; that is only an illusion produced by the limiting of consciousness. All are but players in the outflowing radiance of the one Being. These transient forms live but for a moment, but I, One, live forever. Though I appear as many, I am forever One, forever serene.[1]

In a time period when the mystical tradition of the Vedas and Upanishads was being subverted by a priestly class into a ritualistic religion steeped in superstition and dogma, the "Enlightened One" set out to brush away the many and varied descriptions of undifferentiated consciousness, including goddess mythology, all of which tried to objectify the formless state.

Instead, he put greater emphasis on the actual *experience* of nonself, without the need to define it in words. In fact, it is said that often, when the Buddha was asked to comment on many metaphysical arguments about the nature and origin of the universe, he would simply remain silent – what is the point, he would later argue, when knowledge of oneself is not even known?

Travelling to Sarnath, Uttar Pradesh, the Buddha gave what has now come to be known as the "Sermon of the Turning of the Wheel of Law", in which he expounded his core teaching, the "Four Noble Truths": that there is suffering; that there is a cause of suffering (owing to the false belief in the illusory ego); that there is a remedy to suffering (enlightenment); and that there is a cessation of suffering through the destruction of ignorance. (This is attained through the practice of the "Noble Eightfold Path", consisting of right understanding, right thought, right speech, right action, right livelihood, right effort, right mindfulness and right concentration.)

The Buddha, also known as Tathagata, meaning "one who has arrived [at the Truth]", subsequently established a sangha or order of monks, called *bhikkhus*, where the Dharma – the Buddhist doctrine on the nature of reality – was taught. However, the Buddha's initial attitude to the ordination of women was to refuse them admission into the monastery. Various theories abound regarding his decision, including that he believed the monks would be adversely affected by their female presence.

Even Mahapajapati, Siddhartha's own aunt and foster mother, was repeatedly rebuffed by the Buddha when she was so inspired by the transformation in her son that she wanted to be similarly initiated into the supreme knowledge. Allegedly, it took the intervention of a senior monk, the Venerable Ananda, to resolve the crisis:

Now at one time the Buddha was staying among the Shakyans at Kapilavatthu [Kapilavastu] in the Banyan Monastery. Mahapajapati Gotami went to the place where the Buddha was, approached and greeted him, and, standing at a respectful distance, spoke to him: "It would be good, Lord, if women could be allowed to renounce their homes and enter into the homeless state under the Dharma and discipline of the Tathagata."

"Enough, Gotami. Don't set your heart on women being allowed to do this."

[A second and a third time Pajapati made the same request in the same words and received the same reply.] And thinking that the Blessed One would not allow women to enter into homelessness, she bowed to him, and keeping her right side towards him, departed in tears.

Then the Blessed One set out for Vesali [Vaishali]. Pajapati cut off her hair, put on saffron-coloured robes, and headed for Vesali with a number of Shakyan women. She arrived at Kutagara Hall in the Great Grove with swollen feet and covered with dust. Weeping, she stood there outside the Hall.

Seeing her standing there, the Venerable Ananda asked, "Why are you crying?"

"Because, Ananda, the Blessed One does not permit women to renounce their homes and enter into the homeless state under the Dharma and discipline proclaimed by the Tathagata."

Then the Venerable Ananda went to the Buddha, bowed before him, and took his seat to one side. He said, "Pajapati is standing outside under the entrance porch with swollen feet, covered with dust, and crying because you do not permit women to renounce their homes and enter into the homeless state. It would be good, Lord, if women were to have permission to do this."

"Enough, Ananda. Don't set your heart on women being allowed to do this."

[A second and a third time Ananda made the same request in the same words and received the same reply.]

Then Ananda thought: The Blessed One does not give his permission. Let me try asking on other grounds.

"Are women able, Lord, when they have entered into homelessness, to realize the fruits of stream-entry, once-returning, non-returning and arahantship [one who is free from cravings]?"

"Yes, Ananda, they are able."

"If women then are able to realize perfection, and since Pajapati was of great service to you – she was your aunt, nurse, foster mother; when your mother died, she even suckled you at her own breast – it would be good if women could be allowed to enter into homelessness."

"If then, Ananda, Pajapati accepts the Eight Special Rules, let that be reckoned as her ordination."[2]

The Buddha acquiesced but there were conditions – the Eight Special Rules (not to be confused with the Noble Eightfold Path) were additional precepts that only women had to adhere to. These included the first rule, which stated that a nun, a *bhikkhuni,* even of a hundred years' standing, should bow down before a monk ordained even for just one single day; and the final rule, which expressed that admonition of monks by nuns was strictly forbidden, a rule that was not applicable the other way around. Regardless, Mahapajapati accepted these stipulations, eventually going on to establish a sangha of her own sisters and becoming known as the Great Mother of the Buddhist tradition.

It is difficult for us to appreciate the cultural context of the Enlightened One's refusal, and what was actually said between them will always remain speculation at best. However, despite her undoubted frustration, this did not prevent Mahapajapati's veneration of her foster son for initiating her into the Dharma.

As a consequence, and in an act of selfless gratitude, Mahapajapati composed poetry and songs, together with other ordained nuns, in the Buddha's honour. Collectively known as the *Therigatha* ("Theri" meaning "women elders" and "gatha" meaning "stanza"), they were initially passed down through successive generations orally, until the 73 poems were finally written down in Pali in the first century BCE. Later, the fifth-century CE Buddhist commentator Dhammapala prefixed each poem with a narrative story, including a short biography of every nun.

The profound simplicity of the nuns' individual experience, originally written in stanzas of four verses, each of eight syllables, is compelling beyond measure.

Unlike the impassioned cries of Enheduanna and Sappho, the nuns of the *Therigatha* coolly recount their visionary wisdom in keeping with their Buddhist values, their discerning voices ever mindful yet detached. Indeed, the sensory aspects of worldly experience are positively shunned throughout their inspired renditions, as is physical beauty, a trait highly regarded by the Mesopotamians and ancient Greeks.

Given the diversity of their social status before ordination – widows, single women, prostitutes – the sisters' literary insights were testament to the fact that enlightenment was for all, not just their male counterparts or even the upper echelons of the caste system. Their humble tales of ploughing fields, lighting lamps and bathing feet remind us that nirvana (the blissful state beyond the cycle of rebirth in which suffering ceases) may be found by anyone, simply in the here and now.

Within her own verse, Mahapajapati reveals the powerful, understated wisdom she has realized:

Homage to you Buddha,
best of all creatures,
who set me and many others
free from pain.

All pain is understood,
the cause, the craving is dried up,
the Noble Eightfold Way unfolds,
I have reached the state where everything stops.

I have been
mother,

son,
father,
brother,
grandmother;
knowing nothing of the truth
I journeyed on.

But I have seen the Blessed One;
this is my last body,
and I will not go
from birth to birth
again.

Look at the disciples all together,
their energy,
their sincere effort.
This is homage to the buddhas.

Maya gave birth to Gautama
for the sake of us all.
She has driven back the pain
of the sick and dying.[3]

It is said that Mahapajapati lived to be 120 years old, with miracles reputedly occurring around her upon her demise. During a life of devotion and service, her eminent position in the Order afforded her many disciples – it is believed there were up to 500 nuns under her care – whom she guided to realize the ultimate Truth.

Also included in the *Therigatha* is the illustrious nun, Patacara. Renowned for her charisma and brilliance in teaching, she too oversaw the spiritual welfare of up to

30 women. Utterly bereft from having suffered a series of personal disasters, including the deaths of her parents, husband and two children, she had sought the help of the Enlightened One to alleviate her torment.

Despite feeling compassion for the broken woman, the Buddha explained that no one could help her because mental pain was part of everyday existence. Instead, he instructed her simply to recover her presence of mind by following the path of the Middle Way – avoiding both deprivation and indulgence. Upon taking this advice, her turmoil ended and she was initiated into the sangha.

Patacara's poem recounts her later experience of total enlightenment. Through its vivid immediacy, we almost hold our breath in anticipation of her ultimate breakthrough:

When they plough their fields
and sow seeds in the earth,
when they care for their wives and children,
young brahmins find riches.

But I've done everything right
and followed the rule of my teacher.
I'm not lazy or proud.
Why haven't I found peace?

Bathing my feet
I watched the bathwater
spill down the slope.
I concentrated my mind
the way you train a good horse.

Then I took a lamp
and went into my cell,
checked the bed,
and sat down on it.
I took a needle
and pushed the wick down.

When the lamp went out
my mind was freed.[4]

At the other end of life's spectrum of mystical experience is the poetry of Khema, who was chief consort of King Bimbisara, an Indian emperor. It was said that such was her physical beauty, her complexion was like molten gold. The Buddha would often preach in the royal household, but Khema was initially uninterested in listening to discourses on the transitoriness of the body, being vain and conceited by nature. However, when she heard about the loveliness of the Buddha's own hermitage grove, she was intrigued to see it for herself.

Upon her arrival, the Buddha manifested the image of a goddess, whose beauty far surpassed even Khema's own. Then the image changed to an elderly woman with grey hair, wrinkled skin and decaying teeth. The message of the image was obvious – Khema immediately understood the nature of impermanence and the folly of being attached to physical matter, becoming enlightened there and then.

Her poem in the *Therigatha* recalls the subsequent loathing she had for the body and its sensual delights. Tempted by Mara, the embodiment of death and evil, she transcends the physical world through honouring the sacred Truth:

[Mara:]
Come on, Khema!
Both of us are young
and you are beautiful.
Let's enjoy each other!
It will be like the music of a symphony.

[Khema:]
I'm disgusted by this body.
It's foul and diseased.
It torments me.
Your desire for sex
means nothing to me.

Pleasures of the senses are
swords and stakes.
The elements of mind and body
are a chopping block for them.
What you call
delight
is not delight for me.

Everywhere the love of pleasure
is destroyed,
the great dark
is torn apart,
and Death,
you too are destroyed.
Fools,
who don't know things
as they really are,
revere the mansions of the moon

and tend the fire in the wood
thinking this is purity.

But for myself,
I honour the Enlightened One
the best of all
and, practising his teaching,
am completely free from suffering.[5]

Immediately afterwards, Khema left King Bimbisara to live as a nun, becoming one of the Buddha's most esteemed female disciples.

Another celebrated Buddhist sister included in the *Therigatha* is Kisagotami. Of illustrious connections, her mother's brother was Suddhodana, the father of the Buddha, making Siddhartha Gautama her cousin. Having married, she bore a son who died while still an infant, and his death had such a devastating effect on her that she completely lost her mind. In her inconsolable state, she cradled the lifeless child in her arms and wandered from house to house in the hope of finding medicine that would bring him back from the dead.

On her travels, an old man redirected her to the Buddha. Taking pity on her, the Enlightened One told her he could indeed bring her son back to life on the condition she brought back a mustard seed from the home that had never experienced death. Innocently, she set off to accomplish the task but soon, the light of truth finally dawned upon her – no house in this world is free from mortality. And so, after burying her son in the forest, Kisagotami asked the Buddha for ordination.

Her subsequent poetry details the wisdom of a woman formerly burdened with misery yet now released from the sorrows of life:

The Sage looked at the world
and said –
with good friends
even a fool can be wise.

Keep good company,
and wisdom grows.
Those who keep good company
can be freed from suffering.

We have to understand suffering,
the cause of suffering,
its end,
and the Eightfold Way –
these are the Four Noble Truths.

The Guide of a restless,
passionate humanity has said –
to be a woman is to suffer.
To live with co-wives is suffering.
Women can give birth
and, becoming depressed,
cut their throats.
Beautiful young women eat poison,
but both will suffer in hell
when the mother-murdering foetus
comes not to life [...]

I have practised the Great
Eightfold Way
straight to the undying.
I have come to the great peace,
I have looked into the mirror
of the Dharma.

The arrow is out.
I have put my burden down.
What had to be done has been done.

Sister Kisagotami
with a free mind
has said this.[6]

Despite accepting women into the sangha and acknowledging their spiritual attainments, the Buddha continued to have doubts about their presence in the monastery right up until his own death at 80 years old. Confiding in Ananda, he remarked:

"If . . . women had not received permission to renounce their homes and enter into homelessness under the dhamma [Dharma] and discipline proclaimed by the Tathagata, then would the pure religion . . . have lasted long, the good law would have stood for a thousand years. But since . . . women have now received that permission, the pure religion . . . will not last so long, the good law will now stand fast for only five hundred years. Just . . . as houses in which there are many women but few men are easily violated by robber burglars; just so . . .

under whatever dhamma and discipline women are allowed to renounce their homes and enter into homelessness, that religion will not last long. And just . . . as when the disease called mildew falls upon a field of rice in fine condition, that rice does not continue long; just so . . . under whatever dhamma and discipline women are allowed to renounce their homes and enter into homelessness, that religion will not last long . . . And just . . . as a man in anticipation builds an embankment to a great reservoir, beyond which the water should not overpass, just even so . . . have I laid down these Eight Chief Rules for the *bhikkhunis*, not to be disregarded throughout their whole life."[7]

It is hard to imagine why a wise teacher, advocating a philosophy so free from ideology, retained such a prejudiced position. Interestingly, his prophesy in one sense was to come true – by the fifth century CE, the sangha of nuns had, to all intents and purposes, dwindled and died out completely. It would take the pioneering work of Ayya Khema in the 20th century to establish Parappudua Nuns' Island in Sri Lanka and a thriving community of Buddhist women.

As the centuries passed after the Enlightened One's death, the pure Buddhist teaching essentially split into two "vehicles": Theravada (also known as Hinayana) Buddhism in southern India, which believes in a personal and final enlightenment; and Mahayana Buddhism, in northern India, which believes that an individual may choose to remain in samsara and reincarnate out of compassion for others, assisting them on their own spiritual path.

Inevitably, as a result of this philosophical fissure, a complex Buddhist mythology would also emerge over the coming millennia, including the re-deification of the sacred feminine as a mythological goddess. This is precisely what the Buddha had not wanted, and yet perhaps it does serve to rebut the negative perception of women and reaffirm their equal ability to realize Universal Mind.

CHAPTER SEVEN

GNOSTICISM AND DISCIPLE MARY MAGDALENE

Walk forth,
and announce the gospel of the Kingdom.

By the time Christianity became a fully fledged monotheist religion in the West, the image of the goddess was subsumed beneath a swathe of patriarchal dogma. Nonetheless, the figure of Mary, mother of Jesus, continues the lineage of the archetypal sacred feminine, and her ubiquitous form over the centuries is testament to her position both in the cosmic order and the human psyche.

With her more traditional name "Maria" taking its etymological root from the Latin *mare* meaning "sea", Mary is often depicted wearing an elaborate sea-blue robe. She is also hailed as the Great Mother, Queen of Heaven and a living conduit of divinity:

Hail, Mary,
full of grace,
the Lord is with you.
Blessed are you among women
and blessed is the fruit of your womb, Jesus.

Holy Mary,
Mother of God,
pray for us sinners,
now and at the hour of our death.[1]

The Eastern Orthodox Church duly revered Mary, as well as generally holding women in high regard. However, Catholicism was less accommodating of the female gender, believing woman to be the carrier of ancestral sin created by Eve, her lustful forebear, and finding full expression in the figure of Mary Magdalene, the companion of Jesus.

Misogynistic interpretations of the Christian message were further reinforced by St Paul in the sixth decade CE in his correspondence to the Church at Corinth. First, he outlines his views on women in general:

> Wives, be subject to your husbands as you are to the Lord. For the husband is the head of the wife just as Christ is the head of the church, the body of which he is the Saviour. Just as the church is subject to Christ, so also wives ought to be, in everything, to their husbands.[2]

Next, in terms of woman's ability to honour the Saviour in public, Paul is in absolutely no doubt:

> ... women should be silent in the churches. For they are not permitted to speak, but should be subordinate, as the law also says. If there is anything they desire to know, let them ask their husbands at home. For it is shameful for a woman to speak in church.[3]

Finally, in a breathtaking statement of patriarchal propaganda, he adds:

> I desire, then, that in every place the men should pray, lifting up holy hands without anger or argument; also that the women should dress themselves modestly and decently in suitable clothing, not with their hair braided, or with gold, pearls, or expensive clothes, but with good works, as is proper for women who profess reverence for God. Let a woman learn in silence with full submission. I permit no woman to teach or to have authority over a man; she is to keep silent. For Adam was formed first, then Eve; and Adam was not deceived, but the woman was deceived and became a transgressor. Yet she will be saved through childbearing, provided they continue in faith and love and holiness, with modesty.[4]

When we consider the apostles' accounts of Christ's teaching, not only is there no mention of the shameful legacy of Adam's companion but we also discover he found fellowship with women and even prostitutes, professing the kingdom of heaven resides within all, no matter what their gender and status in the world.

In fact, several religious sects espousing the Saviour's egalitarian message and emphasizing an esoteric truth for everyone were to flourish around the Mediterranean during this time. Referred to as Gnostics, from the Greek word *gnostikoi*, meaning "those who have knowledge", they drew their wisdom from the mystical traditions of Egypt, India and ancient Greece.

Originally, very little was known about the extent of their influence on early Christian society. It was not until the middle of the 20th century that two important discoveries were made, which have fundamentally altered our perception of the religious ideas prevalent during the early decades of the first millennium.

Between 1946 and 1951 (and even as recently as 2017 and 2021), the Dead Sea Scrolls – a collection of Hebrew, Aramaic and Greek manuscripts – were discovered in a series of caves in Jordan, on the north-west shore of the Dead Sea in Khirbet Qumran. The 900 or so intact or reconstructed codices, originally written on leather, papyrus and even forged copper, include hymn books, biblical commentaries and copies of books from the Old Testament.

However, of much greater importance was the discovery of a large clay jar in 1945 under a cliff, near the town of Nag Hammadi in Upper Egypt. Inside were 13 papyrus leather-bound books containing 52 texts. Written in Coptic (the last stage of the ancient Egyptian language) roughly one and a half millennia ago, they are translations of earlier texts written in Greek. They are known collectively as the Gnostic Gospels and bring to light the extent to which the mystical teachings existed during this period. Focusing on a diverse range of subject matter, they include creation mythology, discussions on the nature of reality, the lives of the apostles, the teachings of Jesus and issues concerning the sacred feminine.

One of the most striking examples comes from the enticingly titled Gnostic text, *The Thunder: Perfect Mind*, which speaks about the all-encompassing power of the Infinite through a female voice:

For I am the first and the last.
I am the honoured one and the scorned one.
I am the whore and the holy one.
I am the wife and the virgin.
I am [the mother] and the daughter.
I am the members of my mother.
I am the barren one,
  and many are her sons [...]
I am the mother of my father
  and the sister of my husband,
  and he is my offspring [...]
I am the silence that is incomprehensible
  and the idea whose remembrance is frequent.
I am the voice whose sound is manifold
  and the word whose appearance is multiple.
I am the utterance of my name.[5]

And in the Gnostic text *Trimorphic Protennoia* ("Three Formed First Thought"), the same voice speaks of her immanent presence:

I am the Invisible One within the All. It is I who counsel those who are hidden, since I know the All that exists in it. I am numberless beyond everyone. I am immeasurable, ineffable, yet whenever I [wish, I shall] reveal myself of my own accord. I [am the head of] the All. I exist before the [All, and] I am the All, since I [exist in] everyone.

I am a Voice [speaking softly]. I exist [from the first. I dwell] within the Silence [that surrounds every one of] them. And [it is] the [hidden Voice] that [dwells within] me, [within the] incomprehensible, immeasurable [Thought, within the] immeasurable Silence.[6]

Many other texts are expressed through a female voice in the form of Sophia, the Greek word for "wisdom", but it is the discovery of the *Gospel of Mary Magdalene* that has done much to reassert women's rightful position within the hierarchy of the Christian teachings and restore the reputation of one of its most infamous souls.

In 1896, a fifth-century CE papyrus written in Coptic, containing the text of the *Gospel of Mary Magdalene* along with a handful of other Gnostic manuscripts, was bought in Cairo by a German scholar. Although it was not in the Nag Hammadi discovery, it is included in the library canon and known as the Berlin Codex. Whether or not Mary composed the original document herself, we can only speculate.

In fact, many myths and legends surround Mary Magdalene. Believed to have come from Magdala on the western shore of the Sea of Galilee, she is often described negatively in the Canonical Gospels, traditionally perceived as a prostitute possessed of seven demons and evil spirits. However, whatever her status, she was the first human being to witness the resurrected Christ.

What is also clear within the text itself is that Jesus initiates Mary into the mystical knowledge, revealing that everything in the universe returns to its "roots", the eternal Good of all:

"... What is matter?
Will it last forever?"
The Teacher answered:
"All that is born, all that is created,

all the elements of nature
are interwoven and united with each other.
All that is composed shall be decomposed;
everything returns to its roots;
matter returns to the origins of matter.
Those who have ears, let them hear."[7]

The opening sequence of Mary's Gospel sounds more akin to a passage from the Upanishads rather than a more conventional Christian homily. The Teacher then goes on to speak of the nature of existence and the ultimate reality of the universe, explaining that it is by detaching oneself from the physical world that one can find inner tranquility:

"Attachment to matter
gives rise to passion against nature.
Thus trouble arises in the whole body;
this is why I tell you:
'Be in harmony…'
If you are out of balance,
take inspiration from manifestations
of your true nature…"[8]

Salvation comes from being free of all our desires and identifications – this is the truth that shall set us all free. The Teacher then instructs Mary that heaven is not a place located in a distant land, far away in the future. It is present, in the here and now. It is, in fact, within:

"Peace be with you – may my Peace
arise and be fulfilled within you!
Be vigilant, and allow no one to mislead you

by saying:
'Here it is!' or
'There it is!'
For it is within you
that the Son of Man dwells.
Go to him,
for those who seek him, find him.
Walk forth,
and announce the gospel of the Kingdom."[9]

Regarding the concept of original sin, the Teacher offers a revelatory perspective:

"There is no sin.
It is you who make sin exist,
when you act according to the habits
of your corrupted nature;
this is where sin lies…"[10]

In other words, there is nothing inherently bad within the human temperament – it is the indulgence of the senses that causes problems. As the Teacher concludes:

"This is why the Good has come into your midst.
It acts together with the elements of your nature
so as to reunite it with its roots."[11]

The *Gospel of Mary Magdalene* is one of the most radical and timeless expositions of the nondual teaching. And yet these profound words are uttered by a woman! Indeed, Peter the apostle challenges Mary on this very issue:

"How is it possible that the Teacher talked
in this manner with a woman
about secrets of which we ourselves are ignorant?
Must we change our customs,
and listen to this woman?
Did he really choose her, and prefer her to us?"[12]

It is the apostle Matthew who leaps to her defence:

"Peter, you have always been hot-tempered,
and now we see you repudiating a woman,
just as our adversaries do.
Yet if the Teacher held her worthy,
who are you to reject her?
Surely the Teacher knew her very well,
for he loved her more than us."[13]

As the only discile to be at both Christ's crucifixion and resurrection, it is little wonder that Mary Magdalene is also known as the "Apostle of Apostles".

Despite its historical and spiritual significance, there are still Christians who fail to acknowledge the *Gospel of Mary Magdalene*'s contribution to New Testament teaching, let alone to the canon of wisdom literature as a whole. In modern times, it has taken the medium of film and Garth Davis' sympathetically stunning biography – featuring Rooney Mara as Mary and Joaquin Phoenix as Jesus – to elevate Mary Magdalene to the status she rightly deserves in the public eye.

Perhaps the only way forward is to put aside religious contention and simply abide by the powerful words of

Mary's Gospel itself, when she states that the only true way to hear the words of the wise is to remain steadfastly silent:

"Henceforth I travel toward Repose,
where time rests in the Eternity of Time;
I go now into Silence."
Having said all this, Mary became silent,
for it was in silence that the Teacher spoke to her.[14]

CHAPTER EIGHT
CHINESE BUDDHISM AND NUN HUI-HSÜ

You invite me to a week-long feast of food,
But the feast of meditation has no end.

By the time Buddhist teaching had started to flourish along the Silk Road into the far reaches of the Asian continent and the Far East beyond, the inevitable fragmentation of the Buddha's message was already taking effect, just as he had predicted. However, a scattering of Chinese Buddhist sisters held fast to the Enlightened One's message, their wisdom distilled in similar manner to the *Therigatha* before them, in a collection of written biographies, including poetry by Hui-hsü, a humble nun on the brink of death.

The socioreligious context in which they existed was predominantly the Mahayanan school of Buddhism, which adopted many creation myths from Hindu and Chinese cosmology to explain the nature of reality and the origins of the universe. In the *Visuddhimagga*, written by the fifth-century CE Ceylonese philosopher Buddhaghosa, the beginning of the world is seen as part of a recurring cycle where existence manifests out of a watery void, destroys itself and then arises once more:

Now after the lapse of another long period, a great cloud arises. And first it rains with a very fine rain [...] After the water has thus been massed together by the wind, it dwindles away, and by degrees descends to a lower level [. . .] This water is sweet, and as it wastes away, the earth which arises out of it is full of sap, and has a beautiful colour, and a fine taste and smell, like the skimmings on the top of thick rice-gruel.

Then beings, who have been living in the Heaven of the Radiant Gods, leave that existence [...] and are reborn here on earth.[1]

Of far greater importance is a text composed in India from a slightly earlier period, sometime between the first and third centuries CE, known as the *Lotus Sutra*. Containing the final teaching of the Buddha, the original Sanskrit version speaks of Avalokitesvara, the celestial male bodhisattva of compassion. Interestingly, in its Chinese translation, the bodhisattva of compassion is female, personified by the Mother Goddess, Kuan-yin, meaning "one who listens to the cries of the world". She is often depicted with a thousand heads and arms, which she uses to tackle the laments and woes of the entire cosmos.

In the famous 25th chapter of the *Lotus Sutra*, an unnamed female deity extols the virtues and deeds of Kuan-yin, imploring all to worship her:

Inexhaustible Knowledge, the Bodhisattva Mahasattva Kuan-yin's magnificent spiritual powers are like this. If living beings are intensely passionate and yet they always revere the Bodhisattva Kuan-yin, they will be able to give up their desire. If they are intensely hateful yet they always revere the Bodhisattva Kuan-yin, they will give up their hatred. If they are greatly disillusioned yet they always revere the Bodhisattva Kuan-yin, they will give up their disillusionment.[2]

Like her goddess counterparts from ancient Greece and Mesopotamia, Kuan-yin also descends to hell to comfort the dead. Reciting Buddhist scriptures, the underworld is transformed into a paradise, all instruments of torture are turned into lotus blossoms and its inhabitants are blessed with everlasting peace and happiness.

Worshipped principally by women as the harbinger of life and childbearing, Kuan-yin is often depicted wearing a long white robe and sitting on a lotus flower cradling a child in her lap. Akin to Inanna, Isis and Mary before her, Kuan-yin is the immortal Goddess of Heaven and Earth, the creative spirit of the universe:

A mind perfected in the four virtues,
A gold body filled with wisdom,
Fringes of dangling pearls and jade,
Scented bracelets set with lustrous treasures,
Dark hair piled smoothly in a coiled-dragon bun,
And elegant sashes lightly fluttering as phoenix quills,
Her green jade buttons
And white silk robe
Bathed in holy light;
Her velvet skirt
And golden cords
Wrapped by hallowed air,
With brows of new moon shape
And eyes like two bright stars,

Her jadelike face beams natural joy,
And her ruddy lips seem a flash of red.
Her immaculate vase overflows with nectar from year to year,
Holding sprigs of weeping willow green from age to age.
She disperses the eight woes;
She redeems the multitude;
She has great compassion;
Thus she rules on the T'ai Mountain,
And lives at the South Sea.
She saves the poor, searching for their voices,
Ever heedful and solicitous,
Ever wise and efficacious.
Her orchid heart delights in green bamboos;
Her chaste nature loves the wisteria.
She is the merciful ruler of Potalaka Mountain,
The living Kuan-yin from the Cave of Tidal Sound.[3]

Even though Kuan-yin was venerated widely, yet again we witness the strange anomaly found within cultures of the period – namely that, while the immortal sacred feminine was duly honoured in abstract form, an essentially misogynistic attitude toward mortal women prevailed in daily life.

It was the first-century BCE scholar, Liu Xiang, who did much to reinforce patriarchal attitudes in his sexist tract, *Lieh Nü* ("Biographies of Exemplary Women"), in which he outlines the subordinated lives of 125 female "role models", particularly mothers. Its impact was such that it became a standard work for the deportment and behaviour of all women throughout China. Through the voice of Meng Mu, Liu Xiang writes:

Now the proper conduct of a woman is found in her skill in preparing the five foods, fermenting wine, caring for her husband's parents, and making clothes and that is all. A woman's duty is to care for the household and she should have no desire to go abroad. The *Book of Changes* says, "She provides sustenance and avoids going out." The *Book of Songs* says, "For her no decorations, no emblems; her only care the wine and food." This means that it does not belong to the woman to determine anything herself but she has the three obediences. Therefore, when young, she has to obey her parents; when married, she has to obey her husband; when her husband is dead, she obeys her son. This is proper etiquette . . .[4]

Is it any wonder that many women sought sanctuary from the burdens of domestic drudgery and male control? Against the backdrop of the political and sociological upheavals of third-century CE China and the collapse of the ruling Han Dynasty, many women took Buddhist vows, like the *bhikkhuni* of India, to escape their obediences and the wretchedness of everyday life.

One specific document meticulously details the lives of Chinese nuns from this period. The *Pi-ch'iu-ni chuan* ("Lives of the Nuns"), compiled by Shih Pao-ch'ang in approximately 516 CE, contains the distilled biographies of 65 women. Entering the monastery often as a young child and remaining there until an old age, the nuns' commitment to the Buddhist Dharma is both powerful and exemplary. As Shih Pao-ch'ang says himself in his preface:

These nuns then, whom I hereby offer as models, are women of excellent reputation, paragons of ardent morals, whose virtues are a stream of fragrance that flows without end.[5]

Moreover, his mission in collating the stories of the nuns' lives is to offer the world a testament to dedicating one's existence to the pursuit of the Dharma:

The first Buddhist nun in the world was Mahapajapati, [the Buddha's own stepmother]. [From the time of Mahapajapati] nuns throughout the succeeding generations have ascended the stages of the Buddhist path and realized the fruits of spiritual practice. These illustrious examples of the religious life are like the sun passing through the sky, shedding light and warmth on all.[6]

The issue concerning women's rights in relation to the sangha, having already been raised in the Buddha's time by Mahapajapati herself (see Chapter 6), is discussed again in the biographies. In the life of Chu Ching-chien, the matter is addressed head on:

"Because the scripture speaks of the two terms, *monk* and *nun*, can it be that the rules for each group are different?"

Fa-shih said, "Foreign Buddhists say that nuns have five hundred rules to follow as compared to fewer for monks [five hundred being a Chinese expression meaning a great many], and that must be the difference. I asked the instructor about this, and he said that the rules for nuns are highly similar and only slightly different from the monks' regulations, but, if I cannot get the complete texts of these rules, then I certainly cannot bestow on women the obligation to observe them. A woman aspiring eventually to become a nun may, however, receive the ten fundamental precepts from the Assembly of Monks only, but, without a [female] monastic instructor to train her on the practice of all the rules, a woman has no one on whom to rely [for that training which prepares her to accept the obligation to observe all the rules of monastic life]."[7]

Unperturbed, many of the nuns, therefore, decided not to place their inspiration in the direct teachings of the Buddha but to find instruction instead from the story of the bodhisattva Kuan-yin.

Indeed, the biography of K'ang Ming-kan relates how the young nun initially asks a monk to give her the fundamental Buddhist precepts but is directed elsewhere:

He granted her request and also presented her with a copy of the *Bodhisattva Kuan-shih-yin Scripture*, which she then practised chanting day and night without pause.[8]

Another nun, Fa-sheng, is also blessed with a vision of Kuan-yin after falling seriously ill:

The illness grew worse, and on the evening of the night of the new moon, the last day of the month, as she lay asleep [Amita Buddha] the Tathagata appeared in the air together with his two bodhisattva attendants [Kuan-shih-yin on the left and Ta-shih-chih on the right], with whom he discussed the two types of Buddhism [namely the Mahayana, or Great Vehicle, and the Hinayana, or Small Vehicle]. Suddenly [Amita Buddha] with his entire entourage soared over in a fragrant mist, descending to visit the sick woman. Rays of light gleamed, filling the whole convent for all to see. When everyone came to Fa-sheng to ask about the light, she explained what it was, and as soon as she had finished speaking, she died.[9]

The manner of dying is taken very seriously in Buddhism, as an auspicious death signifies holiness and the attainment of nirvana. Rather alarmingly, the practice of committing suicide by burning oneself alive was also highly revered and a nun would typically carry this out on the night of either the half or full moon.

The biography of Shan-miao is one particularly disturbing example – after wrapping herself in cloth soaked in oil and setting herself alight, she summons her fellow sisters to tell them the following:

Each of you must diligently make the effort to perfect your spiritual life because the cycle of birth and death is a fearsome thing. You must seek to escape it, taking heed not to fall into further transmigration. I have previously abandoned this body as a worship offering to the Buddha twenty-seven times, but it is only this time that I shall attain the first fruit [whereby I am no longer liable to rebirth in the woeful destinies of hell, hungry ghosts or animals].[10]

A more benign, key practice for the Chinese nuns is meditation. In the life of Fa-hsiang, Shih Pao-ch'ang documents how she encourages another nun, Hui-su, to excel in her contemplative discipline:

> Later, the nun Hui-su, whom the others thought to be hopeless, sponsored a seven-day meditation session. On the third night Hui-su sat down in meditation with the rest of the assembly, but she did not get up again with the others. When they observed her they saw that she was rigid like wood or stone. When they tugged at her, she did not move. Some said that she had died, but three days later she got up and was her usual self. It was only then that the whole assembly recognized Hui-su's extraordinary accomplishment in meditation, and for the first time they became aware of Fa-hsiang's profound insight and ability [to recognize the spiritual capacities of others].[11]

It is in the biography of another nun, Hui-hsü (not to be confused with Hui-su) whose secular surname is Chou, that Shih Pao-ch'ang writes of the only woman in his *Lives* to have composed her own poetry. High-minded and aloof in character, it is said that she resembled a man rather than a woman in her physical appearance. As a young child, she was already abstaining from eating meat, observing the fasts and being resolute in her determination to maintain her chastity. At 18, she renounced the householder life to take up residence in the Three-Storey Convent of Ching

Province on the Yangtze River. Renunciants and laity alike all admired her devoted practice to monastic discipline.

Her holy reputation spreading far and wide, she was also a frequent visitor to the sovereign palace, where she initiated members of the court into the art of meditation, inspiring many ladies of the royal family to make a commitment to Buddhist practice.

She always kept to a strict diet, and a vegetarian meal was prepared in her honour during the final days of her life when she was suffering from a mysterious illness. Picking up a brush and piece of paper at the end of the festivities, she wrote:

Worldly people who know me not
Call me by my worldly name of Old Chou.
You invite me to a week-long feast of food,
But the feast of meditation has no end.[12]

As the early centuries of the first millennium CE passed, elements of Chinese and then Japanese Buddhism would similarly place greater emphasis on meditative practice. Subsequently, specific esoteric exercises developed, known as Chan in China and Zen in Japan, with the final "goal" being the state, or non-state, of *satori* – the sudden and transformative experience of enlightenment.

The key understanding of both teachings was that mystical knowledge was gained through transmission from master to pupil. This would be through either the imparting of koans or verbal paradoxes, the use of shock tactics such as being beaten with a stick or simply sitting in silence with the master.

The Tang Dynasty Buddhist scholar-monk Guifeng Zongmi, in his work *The Complete Explanation of the Source of Chan*, observes how the fifth-century CE Indian teacher Bodhidharma tries to convey this point in a passage reminiscent of the relationship between Mary Magdalene and Jesus:

> When Bodhidharma came to China, he saw that most Chinese students did not grasp the truth of Buddhism. They merely sought it through interpretation of textual terminology and thought of the changing phenomena all around them as real activity. Bodhidharma wished to make these eager students see that the finger pointing at the moon is not the moon itself. The real Truth is nothing but one's own mind. Thus, he maintained that the real teaching must be transmitted directly from one mind to another, without the use of words.[13]

Inevitably, the mystical teaching that filtered into Japan, and eventually evolved into Shinto, developed its own exoteric mythology on the nature of reality and the birth of the cosmos. The sacred feminine thus re-emerges and finds expression in the eighth-century CE creation myth *Kojiki* in the form of the goddess Amaterasu, meaning "great divinity illuminating heaven". Despite being worshipped unconventionally as the sun and not the lunar planet, she represents the changing phases of nature, akin to her mythical forebears:

Immaculate as the sacred tree,
Her spirit pure and clear,

She lights the far corners
  Of Heaven and earth –
The Great Kami [god] of the Sun

This Way is the way
  Of the Great Sun Kami,
Whose radiance from above
  Lightens the very bounds
Of Heaven and earth.[14]

It would be remiss not to mention the legacy of the Chinese philosopher Confucius (551–479 BCE), and his metaphysical vision founded on the concepts of balance and harmony, with specific delineation of the feminine principle. He recognized that, akin to the Vedic relationship between Brahman and *atman*, the universe was pervaded by an omnipresent, benevolent energy, *li*, manifesting as *chi* in the individual self. He also believed that heaven, *ch'ien*, embodied the male principle, with the earth, *k'un*, embodying the female. Despite stating that they coexist in complementary opposition, he believed heaven to rule over the earth, a view borne out by his misogynistic attitudes toward women in general.

Given that Confucianism became the philosophical basis for the structure of Chinese society as we know it, a patriarchal hierarchy became the norm. It has only been in recent times, with the opening of the Asian continents to Western sociological influences, as well as advances in human rights within China itself, that women have finally been given greater individual freedom and the respect they rightfully deserve.

CHAPTER NINE

SUFISM AND MYSTIC RABIA AL-ADAWIYYA

Each lover is alone, in secret, with the one he loves.
And I am here too: alone, hidden from all of them –
With You.

As the centuries were passing, many shades and nuances of the mystical teaching were appearing in different parts of the world, as we have already seen – the impassioned reverence of the Mesopotamians and Egyptians; the insightful gnosis of the early Christians; the cool logic of the Indians and Buddhists. Now a new interpretation of the Truth was emerging in Arabia, with more emphasis on devotion, revealed by the angel Gabriel to the Prophet Muhammed (570–632) in his sacred book, the Quran.

Islam, the exoteric expression of the religion of the Muslim people, would draw from Jewish and Christian sources and develop a distinct revelation of its own, having the effect of unifying a diversified collection of tribes throughout the Arabian continent. Moreover, the esoteric message at the very heart of the Islamic teaching speaks of the Absolute, the unchanging omnipresent consciousness, accessible to those who earnestly seek the Beloved in the form of Allah, the Eternal Source.

Nevertheless, while the Quran addresses both men and women who have faith in the teaching, Surah IV, titled "The Women", raises contentious issues surrounding women's position in the household and their character, with references to the need for righteousness and obedience, and, if falling short of such noble virtues, how they should be admonished. Even today, extreme fundamentalist imams have delivered lectures upon the "appropriate" punishment of women, including the barbaric act of stoning them to death.

Mercifully, the core Islamic teaching has evolved into a purer expression known as Sufism. Several explanations abide as to the word's derivative, possibly coming from either the Arabic word *suf*, meaning "wool", and referring to the coarse woollen mantles that Sufis wore to set themselves apart from the rest of the community, or *safa*, meaning "pure".

Whatever its etymological root, the Sufi way is the personal path of love through the secret mysteries hidden in the human heart. Developing fully in the eighth century, Sufism has as its goal unity with the Creator – once the soul has renounced the world of its trappings and purged the ego of its desires, it is free to seek union with the Divine in an everlasting mystical marriage.

One of the greatest exponents of Sufism is the poet Ibn Arabi (1165–1240), who was born in Spain but lived his life in Damascus. In his seminal work, *Fusus al-Hikam* ("Bezels of Wisdom"), which he intended to be a summary of his vast collection of writings, he redresses the balance of the spiritual role of women and the nature of the sacred feminine:

Thus it is that Muhammad's love for women derives from the divine love and because God *gives to everything He has created* what is its due [...]

He places women first because they are the repository of passivity, just as the Universal Nature, by its form, comes before those things that derive their being from her. In reality, Nature is the Breath of the Merciful in which are unfolded the forms of the higher and lower Cosmos ...[1]

The first Sufis were lone men, seeking God in isolation. However, the most prominent Sufi, revered even above her male counterparts, was the female poet Rabia al-Adawiyya. Information about her life is scant at best, with her story coming to us primarily through her 13th-century biographer Attar in his famous work, *Tadhkirat al-Awliya* ("Biographies of the Saints"). Speaking of Rabia, he says:

That one set apart in the seclusion of holiness, that woman veiled with the veil of religious sincerity, that one on fire with love and longing, that one enamoured of the desire to approach her Lord and be consumed in His glory, that woman who lost herself in union with the Divine, that one accepted by men as a second spotless Mary – Rabia al-Adawiyya, may God have mercy upon her. If anyone were to say, "Why have you made mention of her in the class of men?", I should say ... "God does not look upon the outward forms ..."[2]

Born in Basra (717–801), the youngest of four daughters in a poor Muslim family, she was given the name "Rabia", meaning the "fourth girl". At her birth, it is said that the Prophet Muhammed appeared to her father in a dream, prophesying that his daughter would become a glorified mystic. And yet, despite such auspicious beginnings, a famine caused the death of her parents while she was still very young. Separated from her sisters, homeless and vulnerable, she was captured and sold into slavery.

According to legend, Rabia suffered innumerable hardships, including attempted sexual assault when out one day attending to her chores. Back home in the service of a merciless master, her spirit at its lowest ebb, she knelt down one evening in prayer and asked God to deliver her from a life of servitude. It is said that a lamp appeared hovering above her head, filling the house with radiance and awakening her master, who was left stupefied by what he had witnessed. Fearing the wrath of the Lord, he set Rabia free the very next morning, and she travelled into the desert, finally ensconcing herself in a secluded cave.

The precise moment when Rabia started composing poetry is only speculation, and whether it is actually written by her is also unclear. Nevertheless, the timeless beauty of the work is unmistakably imbued with the nondualist message of the mystics:

O God,
Whenever I listen to the voice of anything You have made –
The rustling of the trees
The trickling of water
The cries of birds
The flickering of shadow
The roar of the wind
The song of the thunder,

I hear it saying:

> *God is One!*
> *Nothing can be compared with God!*[3]

Exquisitely succinct and almost in the manner of Zen poetry, Rabia's devotional verse beautifully encapsulates being at one with nature and living in the moment – observations so easily unnoticed in the typical hubbub of daily life.

In fact, the worship of God in Sufism, known as *dhikr* (meaning "remembrance"), is both a practice and a mystical experience. After the initial calling to embark on a journey to "non-being", either through contact with a sheikh (authorized teacher) or through the grace of an inner whisper, the progress of the seeker is charted by a series of stages or "stations", through which the soul acquires certain qualities that enable it to ascend higher and higher to its final goal – the revelation of divine love.

Rabia knew only too well the bittersweet taste of the voyage to self-surrender, coupled with the rewarding fruit of God's intimacy at the journey's end:

> *In love, nothing exists between breast and Breast.*
> *Speech is born out of longing,*
> *True description from the real taste.*
> *The one who tastes, knows;*
> *The one who explains, lies.*
> *How can you describe the true form of Something*
> *In whose presence you are blotted out?*
> *And in whose being you still exist?*
> *And who lives as a sign for your journey?*[4]

Annihilation of the self is complete. After negation of the ego, all is unveiled to be the loving totality of the Lord:

Serving girl:
"It's Spring, Rabia –
Why not come outside,
And look at all the beauty God has made!"

Rabia:
"Why not come inside instead, serving girl
And see the One who made it all –
Naked, without veil."5

Throughout her long life, Rabia was reputedly offered money, gifts and many proposals of marriage, but she refused them all, citing the need for humble solitude:

My peace, brothers, is in my aloneness
Because my Beloved is alone with me there – always.
I've found nothing to equal His love,
That love which harrows the sands of my desert.
If I die of desire, and He is still unsatisfied –
That sorrow has no end.

To abandon all He has made
To hold in my hand
Proof that He loves me –
This is the name of my quest.6

And on the specific issue of becoming a man's wife:

Marriage has to do with being –
But where can this being be found?
I should belong to you? What makes you think
I even belong to myself?
I am His – His![7]

For Rabia, her only interest is her love for God – an exclusive, all-consuming passion that burns up every other earthly commitment:

I have two ways of loving You:
A selfish one
And another way that is worthy of You.
In my selfish love, I remember You and You alone.
In that other love, You lift the veil
And let me feast my eyes on Your Living Face.
That I remember You always, or that I see You face-to-face –
No credit to me in either:
The credit is to You in both.[8]

It is said that Rabia would stay up all night in silent prayer and meditation, long after her companions had retired:

O God, the stars are shining;
All eyes have closed in sleep:
The kings have locked their doors.
Each lover is alone, in secret, with the one he loves.
And I am here too: alone, hidden from all of them –
With You.[9]

At the time of Rabia's passing in her 80s, her only worldly possessions were a reed mat, an earthenware jug and a bed of felt. As is the case with many lives of the saints, her friends and followers allegedly heard her voice from beyond the grave, decrying that she had attained to that which she had beheld.

With her memory living on through her hagiographers and poetry, Sufism itself was gaining ground in its influence, attracting men and women to its mystical heart. Many other Sufi poets would emerge to carry on its devotional message, but none were so revered as the teacher Jalal al-Din Rumi (1207–73), who is arguably the most sublime composer of mystical love poetry the world has ever known.

Founder of the Mevlevis, the Sufi order of whirling dervishes, Rumi beautifully conveys the ecstatic yearning for union between lover and Beloved:

> When men and women become one, Thou art that One; when the units are wiped out, lo, Thou art that Unity.
> Thou didst contrive this "I" and "we" in order to play the game of worship with Thyself,
> That all "I-s" and "thou-s" might become one soul and at last be submerged in the Beloved.[10]

Drunk on love, all is One. And yet Rumi also understood the particular nature of the divine feminine:

> *The Prophet said that woman prevails over the wise […]*
> *Woman is a ray of God; she is not just the earthly beloved.*
> *She is creative: you might say she is not created.*[11]

Admired as much as Rumi for being a devotional poet, Rabia al-Adawiyya is, unsurprisingly, still referred to as the "Doorkeeper of the Heart" centuries later. Transcending all earthly ties, her inner self annihilated in the Source, she gains immortal life:

> *O God,*
> *Another Night is passing away,*
> *Another Day is rising –*
> *Tell me that I have spent the Night well so I can be*
>   *at peace,*
> *Or that I have wasted it, so I can mourn for what is lost.*
> *I swear that ever since the first day You brought me back*
>   *to life,*
> *The day You became my Friend,*
> *I have not slept –*
> *And even if You drive me from Your door,*
> *I swear again that we will never be separated –*
> *Because You are alive in my heart.*[12]

CHAPTER TEN

TANTRIC BUDDHISM AND LAMA YESHE TSOGYAL

I seem a separate entity
Because you do not know me.
Therefore find my source and root!
And from within, awareness will arise ...

In addition to the Greater and Lesser Vehicles of the Buddhist teaching, yet another school would emerge in northern India in the fifth century called Vajrayana or Tantric Buddhism, which included many shamanistic practices and the worship of the Mother Goddess. Unlike the more purist approaches of Mahayana and Theravada, Tantra focuses on sensual activity as well as visionary experience as a means to realizing the Truth. Moreover, the cultivation of psychic powers is an essential component of the Tantric path, and the female lama Yeshe Tsogyal was one of its chief exponents.

Deriving from the Sanskrit root *tan*, meaning "to expand", Tantra is essentially the union of the pure universal Absolute of the masculine principle, Siva, with the creative spirit of the feminine principle, Shakti.

Despite acknowledging that all is One, experience of apparent duality takes centre stage. So, unlike in the abstract Advaita philosophy of the Upanishads, Tantra focuses on the expression of reality through the direct utilization of emotion, as well as the physical and psychic energies of the body–mind.

In fact, cultivating Shakti, specifically through self-enquiry, devotion or kundalini yoga (a spiritual discipline involving chanting, breathing exercises, physical poses and even sexual practices) is synonymous with acquiring inner wisdom or Prajna.

Buddhist texts known as the Prajnaparamita ("The Perfection of Knowledge"), used in both the Mahayana and Vajrayana schools, outline the need to focus on refining wisdom as a prerequisite for enlightenment. Akin to Inanna, Isis and Sophia, wisdom is characterized as feminine, as eulogized in the *Rahulabhadra Prajnaparamita*:

Homage to Thee, Perfect Wisdom,
Boundless, and transcending thought!
All Thy limbs are without blemish,
Faultless those who Thee discern.

Spotless, unobstructed, silent,
Like the vast expanse of space;
Who in truth does really see Thee
The Tathagata perceives.

As the moonlight does not differ
From the moon, so also Thou
Who aboundst in holy virtues,
And the Teacher of the world [...]

To all heroes who of others
Have the welfare close at heart
Thou a mother, who does nourish,
Who gives birth, and who gives love.

Teachers of the world, the Buddhas
Are Thine own compassionate sons;
Then art Thou, O Blessed Lady.
Grandam thus of beings all

All th'immaculate perfections
At all times encircle Thee,
As the stars surround the crescent,
O Thou blameless holy one!

Those in need of light considering,
The Tathagatas extol
Thee, the Single One, as many,
Multiformed and many-named.[1]

Additionally, in the Buddhist text *Ashtasahasrika Prajnaparamita*, one of the Buddha's wisest male devotees, Sariputra, speaks of the nature of the sacred feminine:

The perfection of wisdom gives light, O Lord. I pay homage to the perfection of wisdom! She is worthy of homage. She is unstained, and the entire world cannot stain her. She is a source of light, and from everyone in the triple world she removes darkness, and leads them away from the blinding darkness caused by defilements and wrong views.

In her we can find shelter. Most excellent are her works. She makes us seek the safety of the wings of enlightenment.[2]

Crossing the Himalayas into the Tibetan Empire, there is a particularly revered female deity or *dakini* known as Tara, a name deriving from the Sanskrit word for "star". Presented in the *Tara Tantra* composed by the late 16th-century lama Taranatha, who chronicled the history of Tibetan Buddhism, it speaks of Tara's incarnation as a woman and how she is offered the form of a man in reward for her spiritual insight, to which she scoffs:

In this life there is no such distinction as "male" and "female", neither of "self-identity", a "person" nor any perception [of such], and therefore attachment to ideas of "male" and "female" is quite worthless. Weak-minded worldlings are always deluded by this [. . .] There are many who wish to gain enlightenment in a man's form, and there are but few who wish to work for the welfare of sentient beings in a female form. Therefore may I, in a female body, work for the welfare of beings right until samsara has been emptied.[3]

Individuals paying homage to Tara are guided across the sea of samsara to the shore of eternal life by her radiant being. Like many of her goddess counterparts, Tara can take on myriad forms, the most popular being the Green Tara, Mother of all the Universe, as well as the White Tara, the bodhisattva of compassion, who is still greatly revered in modern-day Tibet:

Lady whose eyes flash like lightning,
heroine, TARE, TUTTARE [To you, I prostrate always],
born from the corolla of the lotus
of the Buddha's face: to you I bow.
Lady whose face is like the circle
of the full autumn moon,
lady who grasps a lotus flower
with the gift-bestowing gesture,
homage to you!

From the cage of this world TUTTARE!
Pacifying defilements with SVAHA! [Hail!]
With OM by your very essence
opening the gate of Brahma: to you I bow.
Protecting the entire world
from the eight terrors,
Blessed Lady, mother of all,
homage to Tara, the mother![4]

With over 20 variations of Tara existing in a multitude of vibrant colours – Yellow, Blue, Orange and even Black – their images often adorn ceremonial banners in temples, as well as being the focus of mandalas used as a visual aid to help cultivate thoughts of loving kindness and attain spiritual enlightenment.

One of the founding lamas of Tibetan Buddhism was Padmasambhava ("Lotus Born"), also known as Guru Rinpoche, who brought Vajrayana to Tibet in the eighth century upon the invitation of its king, Trisong Detsen, during a time of great political upheaval. Being of the Tantra school, Padmasambhava's teachings focused on the way oneness differentiates into duality, playing itself out into complementary opposites. However, he never lost sight of the underlying unity of creation, and in his immortal work, *The Yoga of Knowing the Mind and Seeing the Reality, Which Is Called Self-Realization*, he writes:

> Although the wisdom of nirvana and the ignorance of samsara illusorily appear to be two things, they cannot truly be differentiated. It is an error to conceive them as other than one.[5]

At the time, King Trisong Detsen was married to a 16-year-old girl called Yeshe Tsogyal, who was one of his many wives living in the harem. Having no interest in worldly affairs, Yeshe Tsogyal soon sought the company of Padmasambhava to receive his spiritual instruction; in no time, she excelled to such an extent that she became his foremost Tantric disciple. Understandably, this precipitated a scandal at the king's palace and she was banished from court.

The biography of Yeshe Tsogyal, *Lady of the Lotus Born*, was composed as a *terma* or Dharma treasure – a spiritual text that is concealed in a sacred site to be discovered by future generations, so preserving the teaching's lineage. Yeshe Tsogyal recounted her story to a scribe, who wrote it down in old Tibetan symbolic script on sheets of yellow paper, which were then sealed up and hidden away to be rediscovered many years later by the *terton*, or treasure finder, Taksham Samten Lingpa in the 17th century.

Yeshe Tsogyal (757–817), meaning "victorious sea of wisdom", was born in Tibet and legend recounts that, upon her birth, the sky was full of rainbows, sweet music and lotus blossoms. It is also said that her mother Getso had been visited nine months earlier by a goddess, who had announced that the Buddha would reincarnate as her daughter.

Despite her auspicious entry into the world, Yeshe Tsogyal's early adulthood was full of suffering and hardship, similar to Rabia al-Adawiyya's life (see Chapter 9). Recalling this period of her existence, she observes:

> ... I am a timid woman and of scant ability; of lowly condition, the butt of everyone. If I go for alms, I am set upon by dogs; if food and riches come my way, I am the prey of thieves; since I am beautiful, I am the quarry of every lecherous knave; if I am busy with much to do, the country folk accuse me; if I don't do what they think I should, the people criticize; if I put a foot wrong, everyone detests me. I have to worry about everything I do. That is what it is like to be a woman! How can a woman possibly gain accomplishment in Dharma? Just managing to survive is already hard enough![6]

Her fears and experience were not unique. Despite the Vajrayana teachings expounding equality of the masculine and feminine principles, everyday life, even as the wife of a royal king, was fraught with patriarchal attitudes, resulting in very few female practitioners during this period.

Meanwhile, Padmasambhava had been reflecting upon how to help propagate the Buddhist message. Being trained in Tantra, he knew he must take a suitable pupil and consort. At the court of King Trisong Detsen, upon the first sight of Yeshe Tsogyal, he allegedly exclaimed:

Emaho! [How wonderful!]
The Secret Mantra is called "secret"
Not because it harbours any defect.
But rather it is hid
From narrow minds upon the lower paths [...]

By sensual desire I am utterly unstained,
The fault of carnal longing is unknown to me.
But in the practice of the Secret Mantra
The presence of a woman is required.
She must be faithful, of good lineage,
And pure in her samaya [commitment to the Tantric guru].
She must be fair and excellently wise,
Skilled, and graced with qualities of mercy,
Unreserved in open-handed giving,
A perfect wisdom dakini indeed.[7]

And so, for the purposes of spiritual enlightenment, Padmasambhava initiated Yeshe Tsogyal into Vajrayana Buddhism.

Throughout her long life, she would travel around Tibet and neighbouring Nepal, staying in caves and monasteries, helping those striving for spiritual perfection. Such was her holiness, she is accredited with raising the dead, defeating demons and even controlling the elements of nature. Of her master, whether separated from or by his side, she says:

All the teachings of the Buddha were present in the precious Master Padmasambhava. He was like a vessel filled to overflowing. And after I had served him long in the three ways pleasing to a teacher [to render practical service, both physical and verbal, and to make material offerings], all that he possessed he gave to me, the woman Yeshe Tsogyal. He poured it out as from one vase to another. My mind at ease in Dharma, I understood the differences between the nine vehicles and was able to distinguish true doctrine from false. Knowing the secret of the karmic law of cause and fruit, I conceived a desire for that truly unsurpassable teaching that totally transcends karma.[8]

And of Yeshe Tsogyal, Padmasambhava is similarly in no doubt of her perfected wisdom:

In the supreme body of a woman you have gained accomplishment;
Your mind itself is Lord; request him for empowerment and blessing.
There is no other regent of the Lotus Guru.[9]

Moreover, he goes on to praise Yeshe's achievements:

Yogini seasoned in the Secret Mantra!
The ground of Liberation
Is this human frame, this common human form –
And here distinctions, male or female,
Have no consequence.
And yet if bodhichitta [the desire to attain Buddhahood] graces it,
A woman's form indeed will be supreme![10]

The importance of finding an authentic teacher is a significant aspect of Tibetan Buddhism, and it is for this reason that Yeshe Tsogyal speaks at great length about the relationship between herself and Padmasambhava. When it is time for her master to leave his mortal body, she is utterly beside herself with sorrow and yet Padmasambhava is having none of it, initiating Yeshe Tsogyal into the highest level of insight:

> *Nothing will surpass this, Mistress Tsogyal!*
> *Padmasambhava's compassion neither ebbs nor flows;*
> *The rays of my compassion for Tibet cannot be severed.*
> *There I am in front of anyone who prays to me –*
> *Never will I separate from those with faith.*[11]

As the remaining veils of illusion fall away, Yeshe Tsogyal stands stupefied:

> It was like waking in the morning from a dream [...]
> Thereupon I gained a fearless confidence: the nest of hope and fears fell to nothing, and the torment of defiled emotions was cleared away. I experienced directly that the Teacher was inseparable from myself...[12]

Yeshe Tsogyal was entrusted with carrying on the work of spreading the Tantric teaching far and wide. Attracting dozens of followers, she established many monasteries and lay communities, yet her mission was not without its trials. Once, on retreat in a cave in the Tibetan mountains, she was attacked and raped by a gang of reprobates. But, in an extraordinary act of compassion, instead of berating them for their violation, she took the opportunity to initiate them into the Dharma.

When it comes to her own departure from the world, Yeshe Tsogyal records the wisdom that she first received from her beloved master:

Meditate upon the Teacher as the glow of your awareness.
When you melt and mingle mutually together,
Taste that vast expanse of nonduality.
There remain.

And if you know me, Yeshe Tsogyal,
Mistress of samsara and nirvana,
You will find me dwelling in the heart of every being.
The elements and senses are my emanations,
And emanated thence, I am the twelvefold chain of co-
    production:
Thus primordially we never separate.

I seem a separate entity
Because you do not know me.
Therefore find my source and root!
And from within, awareness will arise;
The great and primal Wisdom will be all-pervading.
Bliss of the natural state will gather like a lake,
And Higher Insight, fishes' eyes of gold, will grow and spread.
Nurture this production of experience and bliss,
And on the wings of such perfected virtuosity,
You will make the crossing to the other shore.[13]

In her biography, Yeshe Tsogyal also speaks of her encounter with Mandarava, another of Padmasambhava's consorts, who was a young princess from India. Yeshe Tsogyal requests to be initiated even further into the highest knowledge, but Princess Mandarava reassures her thus:

> *Accomplished in the Secret Mantra,*
> *Dancer in the sky,*
> *Wonder-worker who dissolved her impure form*
> *Into the sphere of purity,*
> *You drank the nectar of the teachings*
> *Of the Lotus-Born*
> *And gathered all their essence –*
> *Great Mother, Wisdom that has gone beyond,*
> *Is this not yourself?*
>
> *Entering the path wherein the truth*
> *Of all phenomena is seen,*
> *You utterly forsook the eight preoccupations of this life*
> *And, practising austerities, lived upon essential substance,*
> *Overcoming all phenomenal existence.*
> *Tsogyal, ever-young, immaculate, to you I bow!*[14]

Buddhist art portraying Padmasambhava will often depict the Tantric master flanked either side by Princess Mandarava and Yeshe Tsogyal, his two principal consorts, adorned with resplendent green haloes around their respective heads.

It is believed that Yeshe Tsogyal reincarnated as Machig Labdron (1055–1153), who is best known for creating the Chod ritual, a Tantric technique in which practitioners mentally cut up their body into pieces, offering them to the Buddhist deities as an aid to transcending attachment to physical matter. In *The Dedication of the Illusory Body in Sacrifice*, Machig Labdron's teaching is outlined:

This illusory body, which I have held to be so precious,
I dedicate [in sacrifice] as a heaped-up offering,
Without the least regard for it, to all the deities that
  constitute the visualized assembly;
May the very root of self be cut asunder.[15]

And in a further text, *The Yogic Dance which Destroyeth Erroneous Beliefs*, Machig Labdron encourages her devotees, having mentally mutilated their outward form, to infuse their inner being with the power of the sacred feminine:

Now visualize thyself as having become, instantaneously,
The Goddess of the All-Fulfilling Wisdom,
Possessed of the power of enlarging thyself to the vastness of
  the Universe,
And endowed with all the beauties of perfection;
[Then] blow the human thigh-bone trumpet loudly,
And dance the Dance which Destroyeth Erroneous Beliefs.[16]

In the modern age, when conventional religious faith has been on the decline for decades, the unprecedented spread of Buddhism throughout the West has paradoxically enabled both men and women to re-evaluate the meaning of their existence through meditation and mindfulness practice. Additionally, the plight of the Tibetan people under Chinese oppression has given new life to the mythological stories featuring *dakinis* and female lamas, such as Yeshe Tsogyal and Machig Labdron, inspiring all to stand firm in their ethical and spiritual beliefs.

CHAPTER ELEVEN
HINDUISM AND POET ANDAL

O famed and expert God of Love,
Take note of the penance I undergo –

Back in India, a new class of writing was emerging, which would convey the unified vision of Advaita Vedanta in a more accessible format. Unlike the directly revealed Truth of the Vedas and Upanishads, referred to as *sruti*, meaning "heard", this new body of orally transmitted literature is known as *smriti*, meaning "remembered", and has the added distinction of being teachings popularized through concrete examples, such as myths, legends and the lives of great saints, within the context of historical events. Into this burgeoning literary atmosphere was born the Rajasthani poet Andal, who wrote some of the most beautiful love poetry ever composed.

The most important universal texts of this period were the Puranas, simply meaning "ancient", which have a central theme of stories featuring Hindu goddesses. Composed by a variety of sages and poets between approximately 400 and 1400 CE, there are 18 principal Puranas. In the *Devi Mahatmya* section of the *Markandeya Purana*, the goddess figure is eulogized in her immanent being:

O Goddess, you are insight, knowing the essence of all scripture, you are Durga, a vessel upon the ocean of life [that is so] hard to cross, devoid of attachments [. . .] Slightly smiling, spotless, like the orb of the full moon, as pleasing as the lustre of the finest gold [is your face].[1]

Indeed, Durga is one of the most revered deities in the Puranas, who is created by the gods to slay Mahishasura, the buffalo demon. Like the warrior aspect of her Greek counterpart Athena, she is the powerful goddess of warfare who rides a lion with a garland of skulls hanging around her neck. In one hand she holds a severed head, while in the other a lotus blossom, symbolizing the opposing forces of good and evil in the cosmos.

Durga gives birth to Kali from the spot between her eyebrows, right in the midst of battle. A goddess of similarly terrifying demeanour, Kali's mission is to save the world:

In such a way, then, does the divine goddess, although eternal, take birth again and again to protect creation. This world is deluded by her; it is begotten by her; it is she who gives knowledge when prayed to and prosperity when pleased. By Mahakali is this entire egg of Brahma pervaded, lord of men.[2]

The Hindu trinity of primal gods – Brahma the creator, Vishnu the preserver and Siva the destroyer – are all graced with the presence of their goddess consorts. Saraswati, who first appeared in the Rigveda as the goddess of creativity and learning, now re-emerges in the Puranic era as the consort of Brahma and the personification of wisdom.

Represented pictorially as sitting on a lotus wearing a white sari, Saraswati holds the sacred scripture in one hand (representing *jnana* yoga, the path of knowledge) and a lotus blossom (*padma*) in the other, with her third and fourth hands playing the Indian veena (representing *bhakti* yoga, the path of devotional love). Her four hands are also representative of the four aspects of the human psyche, namely: *manas* (the mind), *buddhi* (the intellect), *ahamkara* (the ego), and *chitta* (the heart).

In the *Padma Purana*, she is reverentially honoured:

Devi Saraswati, the protectress of the universe [. . .] is adorned with white jewels, to Her [. . .] gods and demons offer their salutations as also the sages and Her praise the Rishis always sing.

Whoever chants this hymn to Devi Saraswati, the sustainer of the universe, at dawn, noon and at dusk attains all knowledge.[3]

The second god of the Hindu trinity, Lord Vishnu, is the preserver of the universe and is married to Lakshmi, goddess of power, beauty and prosperity, who is typically seated on a red lotus with a garland of red lotuses around her neck. In the myth of the "Churning of the Ocean Milk" as told in the *Vishnu Purana*, Lakshmi emerges from the sea wreathed in blossoms, representing the *sattvic* or tranquil state of mind. Of Lakshmi (here called Sri) and Vishnu's relationship, the Purana says:

The eternal Sri, loyal to Vishnu, is the mother of the world. Just as Vishnu pervades the universe, O excellent Brahmin, so does she. Vishnu is meaning;

Sri is speech. She is conduct; [. . .] [Vishnu] is behaviour. Vishnu is knowledge; she is insight. He is Dharma; she is virtuous action.

Vishnu is the creator; Sri is creation. She is the earth and [. . .] [Vishnu] earth's upholder. The eternal Lakshmi is contentment, O Maitreya; the blessed lord is satisfaction.[4]

The final goddess of the trinity is Parvati, who is married to Siva, lord of destruction. Being the crystallized form of Shakti, Parvati represents the celebration of the sacred feminine in its mortal form.

As the nourishing, life-giving Source and typically depicted in brightly coloured saris, drenched in garlands and holding lotuses, Parvati is born into the world to seduce Siva. However, she does not win him over through her feminine wiles despite being of unsurpassed beauty; rather, she does so through her commitment to the nondual teachings and devotion to spiritual practice. Disguising himself as a matted-haired ascetic, Siva decides to test Parvati until he is satisfied as to her purity and steadfastness:

"I have tested you, blameless woman, and find you firmly devoted to me. I came to you in the form of a *brahmacarin* [spiritual practitioner] and said to you many things, all out of desire for your own welfare. I am profoundly pleased with your special devotion. Tell me what your heart desires! There is nothing you do not deserve! Because of your *tapas* [spiritual practice], I shall be your servant from this moment on. Due to your loveliness, each instant without you lasts an age. Cast off your modesty! Become my wife forevermore! Come, beloved. I shall go to my mountain at once, together with you."

Parvati became overjoyed at hearing these words of the lord of the gods and abandoned immediately all the hardships of *tapas*. Trembling at the sight of Siva's celestial form, Parvati kept her face modestly turned down and replied respectfully to the lord, "If you are pleased with me and if you have compassion for me, then be my husband, O lord of the gods."

Thus addressed by Parvati, Siva took her hand according to the custom and went to Mount Kailash with her. Having won her husband, the mountain-born girl performed the divine offices for the gods.[5]

Legend says that their lovemaking was so intense, it shook the very foundations of the universe.

The hermaphroditic image of Siva and Parvati, joined into one being and known as the Ardhanarishvara, is a familiar symbol in India, with its right side representing Siva, complete with trident and serpent, and its left side Parvati, adorned with jewellery and flowers. Similarly, images of the *lingam* (male genitalia) and the *yoni* (female genitalia) are familiar objects in temples, as is the practice of dabbing a white dot on the forehead (*shweta bindu*) to represent semen and a red dot (*shona bindu*) to signify menstrual blood.

The union of two perfected lovers finds expression in much of Hindu literature, and none can be more beguiling and powerful than the *Ramayana*, composed around the second century BCE by the sage, Valmiki. The famous tale of Rama and Sita, who are the bodily incarnations of Vishnu and Lakshmi, it is an analogy of the human condition, with the deities representative of the ideal couple – Rama the strong discerning hero, Sita the beautiful loyal wife.

Rama is heir apparent to his father, the king of Ayodhya. He wins the hand of Sita, who is from a neighbouring kingdom, by stringing Siva's bow, in a similar test of strength to that undertaken by Odysseus proving his identity to Penelope at the end of Homer's *Odyssey*. Court intrigue and scandal force Rama and Sita into exile for 14 years, during which time they have many adventures, including the famous episode where Sita is kidnapped by the demon Ravana and taken to his kingdom in Lanka. Rama then enlists the help of Hanuman the monkey god to secure Sita's release.

When Rama and Sita return to the kingdom of Ayodhya, Sita's faithfulness during her year's captivity is brought into question. As a test of her purity, she is commanded to undergo an ordeal by fire. Accepting her fate, she steps into the inferno but Agni, the fire god, extinguishes the flames, angrily addressing Rama thus:

Here is [. . .] [Sita], O Rama, there is no sin in her! Neither by word, feeling or glance has thy lovely consort shown herself to be unworthy of thy noble qualities. Separated from thee, that unfortunate one was borne away against her will in the lonely forest by Ravana, who had grown proud on account of his power. Though imprisoned and closely guarded by titan women in the inner apartments, thou wast ever the focus of her thoughts and her supreme hope. Surrounded by hideous and sinister women, though tempted and threatened, [Sita] never gave place in her heart to a single thought for that titan and was solely absorbed in thee. She is pure and without taint [. . .]; it is my command that she should not suffer reproach in any way.[6]

Another literary masterpiece, the *Mahabharata*, written by an unknown poet sometime around the second century BCE, is the compelling Hindu epic that recounts the story of a great war between two rival households living in ancient India, similar again in its panoramic scope to Homer's *Odyssey*. Underpinning the many tales and adventures is the teaching of the Hindu sage Kapila and the philosophy of Samkhya – the knowledge that the drama of life is merely the play of *maya* (the creative spirit). Given that the direct experience of reality is so rare for most human beings, the medium of myth or *smriti* became the chosen means of the wise to communicate their esoteric message.

Many women feature in the *Mahabharata,* but it is Draupadi who is the most central female character – in fact, it is an argument over her virtue, similar to Sita's predicament, that precipitates the battle between the Pandava and Kaurava clans. In a game of dice, Yudhishthira, the eldest of the five Pandava brothers, gambles away himself, his brothers and Draupadi, their joint wife. The victor of the game, King Dhritarashtra's son, Duryodhana, who was the eldest of the Kaurava brothers, demands that defiant Draupadi be brought before him, dragged forward by the hair.

Being no ordinary wife, Draupadi displays a highly developed understanding of the Dharma. She reasons with Duryodhana that if Yudhishthira has gambled himself away, he is no longer a free man and, therefore, has no right to decide her fate and that of her other husbands.

In a fit of rage upon hearing the obvious truth of the situation, Duryodhana orders Draupadi and her spouses to be stripped of all their robes. As one of the king's sons pulls at Draupadi's sari, it miraculously continues to unravel unendingly, protecting her honour. As she is a devotee of the Lord Sri Krishna, an incarnation of Vishnu, her virtue is saved by her guru's intervention:

> Of all the women of mankind, famous for their beauty, of whom we have heard, no one have we heard accomplished such a deed! [. . .] Krishna Draupadi has become the salvation of the Pandavas! When they were sinking, boatless and drowning, in the plumbless ocean, [. . .] [Draupadi] became the Pandavas' boat, to set them ashore![7]

Draupadi and Lord Krishna share a very special relationship. Acknowledging her humiliation at King Dhritarashtra's court, Krishna tells Draupadi that, because of her steadfast belief in the Dharma, he promises to completely annihilate the house of the Kaurava brothers. The ensuing battle of Kurukshetra sees the destruction of the Kaurava Dynasty and forms one of the most famous passages in the *Mahabharata*, more commonly known as the Bhagavad Gita, meaning "The Song of God". Attributed to the sage Vyasa, and viewed essentially as a separate work, it is the most definitive treatise on Samkhya philosophy ever written.

The Bhagavad Gita opens with Arjuna, one of Draupadi's husbands, and Krishna, his chariot driver, on the eve of battle against the Kaurava household. Despite the enmity that exists between the families, Arjuna is overwhelmed and utterly despondent at the impending drama that is about to take place. Krishna, acting as a personification of the eternal Self, reminds Arjuna of his immortal being, going on to point out that the universe is merely the play of opposing forces. Through an understanding of the Dharma and knowing the phenomenal world to be ultimately an illusion, the individual can be set free from the bondage of ignorance and the chains of mortal life.

Krishna discriminates between Purusha and Prakriti, between the Absolute and *maya*, between the real and the unreal. He then reveals to Arjuna the four paths to liberation: devotion (*bhakti* yoga), action (*karma* yoga), knowledge (*jnana* yoga) and contemplation (*raja* yoga – the "royal road" and highest path). But whichever path we choose, all ultimately lead to the Self:

> He who realizes the divine truth concerning My birth and life, is not born again; and when he leaves his body, he becomes one with Me.
>
> Many have merged their existence in Mine, being freed from desire, fear and anger, filled always with Me, and purified by the illuminating flame of self-abnegation.
>
> Howsoever men try to worship Me, so do I welcome them. By whatever path they travel, it leads to Me at last.[8]

Moreover, the practice of meditation and the one-pointed focus on God will lead the devotee to everlasting freedom:

When the volatile and wavering mind would wander, let him restrain it, and bring it again to its allegiance to the Self.

Supreme Bliss is the lot of the sage, whose mind attains Peace, whose passions subside, who is without sin, and who becomes one with the Absolute.

Thus, free from sin, abiding always in the Eternal, the saint enjoys without effort the Bliss which flows from realization of the Infinite.[9]

The Bhagavad Gita is one of the most profound texts in existence on the nature of nonduality, in that it synthesizes living in the world and performing one's daily duty while simultaneously concentrating one's heart on the supreme Self:

.. the Great Souls, O Arjuna! filled with My Divine Spirit, they worship Me, they fix their minds on Me and on Me alone, for they know that I am the imperishable Source of being.

Always extolling Me, strenuous, firm in their vows, prostrating themselves before Me, they worship Me continually with concentrated devotion.

Others worship Me with full consciousness, as the One, the Manifold, the Omnipresent, the Universal.

I am the Oblation, the Sacrifice, and the Worship; I am the Fuel and the Chant, I am the Butter offered to the fire, I am the Fire itself; and I am the Act of Offering.

I am the Father of the universe and its Mother; I am its Nourisher and its Grandfather; I am the

Knowable and the Pure; I am Om; and I am the Sacred Scriptures.

I am the Goal, the Sustainer, the Lord, the Witness, the Home, the Shelter, the Lover and the Origin; I am Life and Death; I am the Fountain and the Seed Imperishable.

I am the Heat of the Sun. I release and hold back the Rains. I am Death and Immortality; I am Being and Not-Being.[10]

Vyasa's Bhagavad Gita very quickly became the standard bible of Hinduism, since it espouses the Advaita Vedanta doctrine in a practical way. Other great sages would also go on to reveal the mystical teachings in their own unique fashion – for example: Patanjali in the early centuries CE through his *Yoga Sutras*; Adi Shankara in the eighth century through his seminal work, *Vivekachudamani*, "The Crest Jewel of Wisdom"; and Dattatreya in the tenth century through his *Avadhuta Gita*, "Song of the Free Soul".

The Bhagavad Gita also engendered the cult of *bhakti* in the form of Krishna worship. As the eighth incarnation of Vishnu, Krishna is the male embodiment of the Self, and many sacred texts have been composed in his honour. Whereas the *Mahabharata* focuses on his wise counsel in the battle against the Kauravas, it is the *Bhagavata Purana*, also known as the *Srimad Bhagavatam*, that recounts his adventurous adolescence and his amorous exploits with the cowherdesses or *gopis* of Vrindavan.

Incredibly, it is said that Krishna was the lover of 16,000 *gopis*, who all leave their household cares behind to lose themselves in the *rasa lila*, the circular dance of the soul.

Through the beguiling tunes of his magic flute, Krishna lulls the women into a trance of erotic devotion and ecstasy:

> I know what is in your minds and I have accepted your devotion to me. Believe me, devotion to me has never gone unrewarded. You have given me your hearts and your minds and there is nothing in your minds except love for me. Listen to me. The love which is lodged in your hearts is so pure that it can never become lust of the type which lies in the ordinary human heart. The seed of a plant will give forth new shoots when planted in the earth. But if it is fried or baked, then it will not be able to sprout again. Even so, love of a human type which is for human beings will give birth to further involvements with this world. But love which is directed towards me will be an end in itself and it will never make you earth-bound. Go home with the assurance from me that your efforts will not go unrewarded.[11]

Despite treating all his *gopis* alike, one in particular was his supreme devotee and eternal consort. Named Radha and believed to be the embodiment of Lakshmi, she was a strikingly beautiful and discerning young woman. Similar to Rama and Sita before them, Radha and Krishna become the epitome of the divine couple, united in their mutual love.

The *bhakti* movement would continue to flourish throughout India, inspiring many sages and poets, including Narada, living sometime during the first centuries of the first millennium. Little is known of his life; however, his *Bhakti Sutras* are exquisite expositions on the nature of love:

> Now, in a spirit of auspiciousness, we shall commence to expound on *bhakti* – spiritual devotion.
>
> The nature of spiritual devotion is the supreme love.
>
> And its essence is the nectar of immortality.
>
> Obtaining spiritual devotion, a person becomes a siddha, a perfected one, beyond death and fully satisfied.
>
> Achieving spiritual devotion, one becomes completely desireless – grieving not, hating not, not rejoicing in fleeting happiness, without passion for personal concerns.
>
> With a realization of spiritual devotion, one becomes spiritually intoxicated; one becomes overwhelmed; one comes to rejoice in the Self.[12]

In the manner of Rumi, Narada attempts to define the indefinable:

> The essential nature of love is inexpressible.
>
> Like taste for one who is mute.
>
> Love is manifest where there is an able vessel.
>
> This love takes the form of an intimate experience of exquisite subtlety – devoid of the influence of the three modes of nature, devoid of desire – a boundless, perpetual expansion.
>
> Achieving that experience one sees only love, hears only love, speaks only of love, and thinks of love alone.[13]

For Narada, the highest bliss, the everlasting joy of eternal peace, is not through the attainment of wisdom but through the simple act of loving itself:

> Some assert that spiritual devotion can be developed solely by wisdom.
> Some assert that wisdom and devotion are both necessary.
> According to the son of Brahma, Narada, spiritual devotion is its own fruit.[14]

Indeed, the fruit of such intense devotion is union with the Absolute in its multifarious aspects:

> Spiritual devotion is singular, though it manifests as eleven forms: cherishing the glorious qualities of God, cherishing the spiritual forms, cherishing ritual worship, cherishing constant remembrance, cherishing service, cherishing God as a dear friend, cherishing God with parental affection, cherishing God like a loving wife, cherishing knowledge of the Self, cherishing oneness with God, cherishing the supreme separation.[15]

The cult of *bhakti* continued to dominate Hindu society throughout the centuries, with Krishna worship being the primary focus for the expression of devotees' love. Many poets have written of their devotion to Krishna, but one in particular stands above and beyond all others – Andal, the female Tamil saint from the middle of the 17th century.

According to legend, Andal was discovered as a baby under a holy basil plant (the herb sacred to Vishnu) in Srivilliputtur by the Brahmin priest, Periyalvar, who raised her as his own daughter. He initially called her Kodai, meaning "she who is born of Mother Earth".

As a child, she became so totally devoted to Krishna that she would wear garlands prepared by her father intended for the avatar's honour, with her only wish being that she would soon become his bride. Her father, catching Kodai admiring herself one day in the mirror covered in the garlands, reprimanded her, but Vishnu allegedly appeared to him later that night in a dream. He commanded her father that only the garlands that had been worn by Kodai could be used in offering, since they were drenched in the sweet fragrance of her pure self.

Periyalvar realized the holiness of his devoted daughter and renamed her Andal, meaning "she who dives deep into the ocean of divine love". Such were her longings for Krishna that Andal imagined herself to be one of the *gopi* girls, pining for the presence of her master. Inspired in this way despite being only a young girl, Andal composed the *Tiruppavai* ("Song Divine") as a record of her passionate yearning.

A poem of 30 stanzas, it recounts the ecstatic longing of the young Vrindavan women for their beloved Lord Krishna. The overall effect is an erotically charged exaltation of love:

Maidens bejewelled, keen on bathing, come out!
Darling girls of the cowherd clan
Whose hamlet brims over with beauty and wealth [. . .]
Narayana [Vishnu] himself has offered

His gracious drum all for us
To sing his praise and gain the world's.[16]

Krishna's affection is all the women require:

In morning's small hours we came to adore
Those golden lotuses, your feet: why?
Born are we in the cowherd caste
But you must take us in your own employ.
Not only for today do we seek your drum
But for ever and ever, seven times seven births!
Would be one with you, work only for you –
Change all our other wishes, Lord![17]

The *gopis'* love is total and similarly available to anyone who sincerely desires it:

These thirty stanzas in chaste Tamil
In honour of Him who churned the sea,
Were composed by Kodai the daughter
Of that Prince of Brahmin priests
With his garland fresh and cool,
Of the lovely village, Srivilliputtur.
Maids bejewelled, their face the moon
Seeking Kesava [Krishna] got his grace
As narrated in these lines.
Whoever will chant them without fail
Will be looked after by the Lord
His four shoulders high as hills,
Eyes red, face comely and benign:
Will gain his grace wherever they go
And be happy evermore![18]

To this day, her *Tiruppavai* poem is still sung in temples daily throughout southern India.

As her devotion ever deepened, so too Andal's literary talent continued to bloom. In her *Nachiyar Tirumozhi* ("Sacred Utterances"), she further explores her reverence for her beloved Krishna. In a sequence of 14 poems, similar in its eroticism to the biblical Song of Songs, Andal describes her yearning for her Beloved:

> *O famed and expert God of Love,*
> *   Take note of the penance I undergo –*
> *My body unwashed, my hair unbound,*
> *   My lips without colour, one meal a day.*
> *One thing I have to say, my Lord,*
> *   That my womanhood may not be a waste*
> *Grant me this, my life's aim,*
> *   That I become Kesava's [Krishna's] servant-maid.*[19]

So intense is her longing that Andal begs Krishna to reveal himself to her:

> *O lovely Koel [Krishna], through my greed to embrace*
> *   The one on the milky sea,*
> *My surging breasts in their ecstasy*
> *   Melt and distress my soul.*
> *What do you gain by hiding yourself?*
> *   If you will coo and bring to me*
> *The one with the discus, conch and mace*
> *   You will get a place in heaven.*[20]

In the poem "A Dream Wedding", Andal's hopes and imaginings are finally realized – she becomes the bride of Krishna:

My friend, I dreamt that numerous priests
  Brought water for holy sprinkling
From the four corners of the earth
  And raising Vedic chants,
Knotted the guardian string round my wrist
  That I may wed Kannan [Krishna] the pure.[21]

And later, Andal speaks of losing herself in her love:

Fair mothers, my sweet ambrosia
  Of Srirangam
With his lovely hair, his lovely mouth
  His lovely eyes
And the lovely lotus from his belly button –
  My husband –
Has my loose bangle
  Made me lose indeed!

My Lord of Srirangam,
  Rich and righteous,
Who owns this sea-swept earth entire
  And the sky
Has made his possessions
  Now complete
With the bangle which I wore
  On my hand![22]

Throughout her short life, Andal herself refused to marry any mortal man, declaring Krishna to be the sole object of her affection. Legend says that Vishnu, supremely pleased with her love, appeared to Periyalvar once more in a dream, instructing him to bring Andal to the holy shrine at Srirangam on the banks of the Kaveri in southern India. Upon the moment of entering the sanctum of the temple, she was allegedly surrounded by a blaze of light and absorbed into the image of Vishnu, the archetype of Krishna. She was only 15 years old.

Exactly when and where Andal composed her poetry is uncertain; however, she is keen to impart the understanding that it is she who is authoress of her immortal words and no one else. More specifically, throughout her verse, Andal teaches us that love can liberate us from pain and suffering, setting us free to live a life of everlasting peace and happiness:

Kodai [...]
Made these verses in her passion
For that jewelled lamp of the cowherd clan
Who wrought such mischief with his pranks.
Those who can recite them well
Shall never struggle in the sea of sorrows.[23]

CHAPTER TWELVE

CHRISTIANITY AND ABBESS HILDEGARD OF BINGEN

I blaze above the beauty of the fields,
I shine in the waters,
I burn in sun, moon, and stars.

In the West, Europe would have to wait until the early Middle Ages for a substantial body of mystical writings to blossom. Such was the associated expansion in human endeavour in all fields of artistic and intellectual expression that scholars have termed this period in history the early Renaissance. Despite the fact that many of the literary outpourings are steeped in Christian theology, making the nondualist vision all the more elusive, a handful of writers persevered in their expression of the oneness of God, peaking in the illuminated manuscripts of the German abbess, Hildegard of Bingen.

An important writer who lived many centuries earlier in Rome, and who was to have a profound effect upon metaphysical thought during this period, was the philosopher Boethius (480–524). A brilliant thinker in his own right, he translated the works of Plato from

Greek into Latin. Although he gained much respect in his lifetime, he fell out with the emperor Theodoric the Great, who sentenced him to a hideous death.

Boethius' famous *Consolation of Philosophy,* composed during his internment in prison in Pavia while awaiting his impending execution, is the account of a vision in which he is visited by a woman who reveals herself to be Sophia (also known as Sapientia):

While I was thus mutely pondering within myself, and recording my sorrowful complainings with my pen, it seemed to me that there appeared above my head a woman of a countenance exceedingly venerable. Her eyes were bright as fire, and of a more than human keenness; her complexion was lively, her vigour showed no trace of enfeeblement; and yet her years were right full, and she plainly seemed not of our age and time. Her stature was difficult to judge. At one moment it exceeded not the common height, at another her forehead seemed to strike the sky; and whenever she raised her head higher, she began to pierce within the very heavens, and to baffle the eyes of them that looked upon her. Her garments were of an imperishable fabric, wrought with the finest threads and of the most delicate workmanship; and these, as her own lips afterwards assured me, she had herself woven with her own hands. The beauty of this vesture had been somewhat tarnished by age and neglect, and wore that dingy look which marble contracts from exposure. On the lower-most edge was inwoven the Greek letter Π ["P", signifying the life of action], on the topmost the letter θ ["Th", signifying the life of thought], and between the two were to be seen steps, like a staircase, from the lower to the upper letter [. . .] Her right hand held a note-book; in her left she bore a staff.[1]

Over the course of several days, their discourse leads Boethius to a greater understanding of the world and its meaning. Sophia points out to him that it is everlasting joy that is truly sought by the wise:

> Why, then, ye children of mortality, seek ye from without that happiness whose seat is only within us? Error and ignorance bewilder you. I will show thee, in brief, the hinge on which perfect happiness turns. Is there anything more precious to thee than thyself? Nothing, thou wilt say. If, then, thou art master of thyself, thou wilt possess that which thou wilt never be willing to lose, and which Fortune cannot take from thee. And that thou mayst see that happiness cannot possibly consist in these things which are the sport of chance . . .[2]

Contentment only comes from within. Moreover, the entire world, in spite of its myriad configuration, is an expression of the Divine:

> This world could never have taken shape as a single system out of parts so diverse and opposite were it not that there is One who joins together these so diverse things. And when it had once come together, the very diversity of natures would have dissevered it and torn it asunder in universal discord were there

not One who keeps together what He has joined. Nor would the order of nature proceed so regularly, nor could its course exhibit motions so fixed in respect of position, time, range, efficacy, and character, unless there were One who, Himself abiding, disposed these various vicissitudes of change. This power, whatsoever it be, whereby they remain as they were created, and are kept in motion, I call by the name which all recognize – God.[3]

Such was the influence of Boethius' *Consolation of Philosophy* that it inspired the later 12th-century Italian writer Dante Alighieri (1265–1321) to compose his *La Vita Nuova* ("The New Life"). Composed of *canzoni* woven together with a prose commentary, it narrates Dante's love for Beatrice, a young woman whom he only saw by sight three times. After a premonition of her death in a dream and then her actual passing at the tender age of 20, he resolved to write a work that would be a worthy testament to her memory.

Seeing Beatrice for the first time, Dante knows that his fate is irrevocably sealed, as beautifully translated into English by the Pre-Raphaelite poet Dante Gabriel Rossetti:

At that moment, I say most truly that the spirit of life, which hath its dwelling in the secretest chamber of the heart, began to tremble so violently that the least pulses of my body shook therewith; and in trembling it said these words: "Here is a deity stronger than I; who, coming, shall rule over me." At that moment the animate spirit, which dwelleth in the lofty chamber whither all the senses carry their perceptions, was filled with wonder, and speaking more especially unto the spirits of the eyes, said these words: "Your beatitude hath now been made manifest unto you." At that moment the natural spirit, which dwelleth there where our nourishment is administered, began to weep, and in weeping said these words: "Woe is me! for that often I shall be disturbed from this time forth!"[4]

Beatrice continues to dominate Dante's work, including his famous *La Divina Commedia* ("The Divine Comedy"), in which she is the guiding image of grace, exalted as the symbol of divine wisdom. In similar vein, the Italian poet, Francesco Petrarch (1304–74), was also inspired by the unrequited love of a woman called Laura, with his *Canzoniere* ("Songbook") detailing the elevation of the human soul from earthly passion to union with God.

Dante and Petrarch's poetry belongs to the tradition of courtly love, the code of behaviour defining aristocratic romantic relationships. Deriving from the ideas set out by Ovid in his *Ars Amatoria* ("The Art of Love"), various rules were expounded through the songs and poems of wandering minstrels and troubadours. Courtly love, usually between a knight or nobleman and a lady of high ranking, was akin to a form of sanctioned adultery, since many status marriages of the period were merely contracts of business. Paradoxically, infidelity between lovers was considered more of an act of betrayal than an extra-marital affair.

The *Roman de la Rose*, the epic French dream allegory composed by Guillaume de Lorris and Jean de Meun, is an exquisite example of this type of literature, which tells of a poet's love for a young woman who is represented in his dreams as a rosebud blooming in a garden. The rose is the familiar symbol of love and mystical knowledge, with its picking representing the consummation of passion and union with the Divine. Such was the poem's impact that the 14th-century medieval writer Geoffrey Chaucer would go on to translate some of its verses into Middle English.

The legends of the Holy Grail also fall under the genre of courtly love poetry. Popularized through the works of the 12th-century French poet Chrétien de Troyes and the 15th-century English writer Sir Thomas Malory, the quest for the Holy Grail became synonymous with the Gnostic spiritual search. Moreover, Christ's chalice, from which he drank wine at the Last Supper, becomes an emblem of his unwavering love and salvation, with pursuit of this lost relic being the inspiration for the legendary knights of King Arthur's Court.

Worship of the sacred feminine, with emphasis on the Virgin Mary and Mary Magdalene, starts to re-emerge during this period, especially within specialist medieval religious cults, including the Knights Templar. A religious and military order formed to protect pilgrims en route to Palestine, their cause was championed by the French abbot Bernard of Clairvaux, who wielded great political influence. One woman in particular, a German Benedictine nun, sought his counsel in order to validate her spiritual experiences, believing the monk to be the only person in whom she could confide her innermost thoughts.

In 1146, Bernard received correspondence from Hildegard of Bingen in which she outlines how she has been blessed with a series of visions that she has recorded in a personal journal. Plagued with great doubt about the relative merits of her artistic output, she explains as much in her letter:

I am very concerned by this vision which has appeared to me in the spirit of mystery, for I have never seen it with the external eyes of the flesh. I, who am miserable and more than miserable in my womanly existence, have seen great wonders since I was a child. And my tongue could not express them, if God's Spirit did not teach me to believe.[5]

So impressed was Bernard by her letter that he discussed the matter with the incumbent pope, who gave his papal authority for the publication of her words. Within a few years, Hildegard became one of the most renowned female writers and spiritual advisors of Europe, being referred to as the "Sibyl of the Rhine".

Hildegard of Bingen (1098–1179) was born in Bermersheim, Germany, into a well-established noble household. The tenth and youngest child, at eight years old she was given as an "oblate" or offering to the Church, a not uncommon practice during that period. However, rather than being placed immediately into a convent, she was put under the care of a sister, Jutta of Sponheim. Several years later, she and Hildegard went on to establish the monastery of Disibodenberg, which housed both nuns and monks, and it is then that Hildegard took the veil, succeeding Jutta as abbess upon her death.

Hildegard experienced many visions throughout her lifetime. In her autobiographical notes, she recalls her childhood and how she was instructed to share her revelatory insights:

> Wisdom teaches in the light of love, and bids me tell how I was brought into this my gift of vision . . . "Hear these words, human creature, and tell them not according to yourself but according to me, and, taught by me, speak of yourself like this." In my first formation, when in my mother's womb, God raised me up with the breath of life, he fixed this vision in my soul [. . .] And in the third year of my life I saw so great a brightness that my soul trembled; yet because of my infant condition I could express nothing of it. But in my eighth year I was offered to God, given over to a spiritual way of life, and till my fifteenth year I saw many things, speaking of a number of them in a simple way, so that those who heard me wondered from where they might have come or from whom they might be.[6]

It was not until she was in her 40s, however, that Hildegard finally felt compelled to record her visions formally on paper, being keen to stress that they were nothing to do with trance or hallucination but viewed with the inner eye. Toward the end of her life, concerning the physiological symptoms that always accompanied such moments, she reflects:

> Since my infancy [. . .] when I was not yet strong in my bones and nerves and veins, I have always seen this vision in my soul, even till now, when I am more than seventy years old. And as God wills,

in this vision my spirit mounts upwards, into the height of the firmament and into changing air, and dilates itself among different nations, even though they are far-off regions and places remote from me. And because I see these things in such a manner, for this reason I also behold them in changing forms of clouds and other created things. But I hear them not with my physical ears, nor with my heart's thoughts, nor do I perceive them by bringing any of my five senses to bear – but only in my soul, my physical eyes open, so that I never suffer their failing in loss of consciousness (*extasis*); no, I see these wakefully, day and night. And I am constantly oppressed by illness, and so enmeshed in intense pains that they threaten to bring on my death; but so far God has stayed me.[7]

In 1150, inspired by yet another vision, Hildegard decided to leave Disibodenberg to establish her own independent nunnery at Rupertsberg on the Rhine, near the town of Bingen, where she was elected abbess. With a group of 20 or so nuns, physical life initially was intolerable, with few material comforts or supplies. Many nuns subsequently abandoned the newly formed monastery, including Hildegard's closest female confidante and protégée, Richardis of Stade, which caused immense feelings of loss and betrayal.

Nonetheless, as the years passed, Hildegard's inner life took on new fortitude. She undertook preaching tours and engaged in correspondence with all the major thinkers and theologians of the time. More importantly, she embarked on a writing project of encyclopedic proportions to systematize her mystical experiences, recording and arranging them into a sequence of three interconnected manuscripts written in Latin: *Scivias* ("Know the Way"), *Liber Vitae Meritorum* ("The Book of Life's Merits") and *Liber Divinorum Operum* ("The Book of Divine Works").

Within the framework of the books, Hildegard addresses subjects as diverse as the meaning of the Trinity and the nature of the cosmos, as well as various ethical and societal issues of the day. She also compiled non-mystical texts, in particular two prose works, titled *Causae et Curae* ("Causes and Cures") and *Physica* ("Health and Healing"), which focus on the natural world and medicine.

In *Scivias*, her major religious work comprising 26 visions and taking ten years to complete, an allegorical representation of the universe is presented in the third vision. In it, she describes a "cosmic egg", consisting of a series of concentric oval rings, exemplifying how human life and the cosmos are inextricably connected. She writes:

> I saw a huge form, rounded and shadowy, and shaped like an egg; it was pointed at the top, wide in the middle and narrower at the bottom. The large form [. . .] represents, on the level of faith, the omnipotent God, incomprehensible in its majesty, inconceivable in his mysteries, the hope of all the faithful.[8]

In her fourth vision, in a radical departure from her theological contemporaries, she places repeated emphasis on the sacred feminine by outlining the relationship between God and the mother of all beings:

> Then I saw a most great and serene splendour, flaming, as it were, with many eyes, with four corners

pointing towards the four parts of the world, which was manifest to me in the greatest mystery to show me the secret of the Supernal Creator; and in it appeared another splendour like the dawn, containing in itself a brightness of purple lightning. And behold! I saw on the earth people carrying milk in earthen vessels and making cheeses from it; and one part was thick, and from it strong cheeses were made; and one part was thin, and from it weak cheeses were curdled; and one part was mixed with corruption, and from it bitter cheeses were formed. And I saw the image of a woman who had a perfect human form in her womb. And behold! By the secret design of the Supernal Creator that form moved with vital motion, so that a fiery globe that had no human lineaments possessed the heart of that form and touched its brain and spread itself through all its members.

But then this human form, in this way vivified, came forth from the woman's womb and changed its colour according to the movement the globe made...[9]

The theme of the divine spirit pervading the created world as an eternal life-giving energy is a recurring metaphor in Hildegard's works, specifically through references to greenery and the moist pastures of paradise. In the same vision, she outlines the way the soul rules over the body by using an analogy taken directly from nature:

The soul in the body is like sap in a tree, and the soul's powers are like the form of the tree. How? The intellect in the soul is like the greenery of the tree's branches and leaves, the will like its flowers, the mind like its bursting first fruits, the reason like the perfected mature fruit, and the senses like its size and shape. And so a person's body is strengthened and sustained by the soul. Hence, O human, understand what you are in your soul . . .[10]

One of the most striking features of *Scivias* is how it was painstakingly illuminated by one of her monastic colleagues, each vision having an accompanying illustration bringing Hildegard's visionary message to life. One particularly captivating image shows her receiving divine inspiration, pen poised, with tendrils of red light connecting her to God above in heaven. Unfortunately, the original illuminated Rupertsberg manuscript vanished in the bombing of Dresden, where it was housed in a bank vault, and has not been seen since 1945. Thankfully, a hand-painted parchment facsimile made by the nuns of Eibingen Abbey between 1927 and 1933 provides an accurate copy.

Liber Vitae Meritorum, the second volume in Hildegard's epic trilogy, develops the sequence of her visions, concentrating this time on the ethical and moral position of humanity within the divinely ordered cosmos. However, it is her final text, *Liber Divinorum Operum*, that is the crowning glory of her creative achievement. Also taking a decade to write, it comprises ten visions and centres on the opening passage from the Gospel of St John, "In the beginning was the Word . . ."

More importantly, she employs yet again a female figure to convey her mystical message by opening the first vision with the image of a beautiful woman. Reminiscent of Sophia appearing to Boethius, Hildegard's literary powers are at their zenith:

> And I saw as amid the airs of the South in the mystery of God a beautiful and marvellous image of a human figure; her face was of such beauty and brightness that I could more easily have stared at the sun. On her head she had a broad band of gold. And in that golden band above her head there appeared a second face, like an old man, whose chin and beard touched the top of the first head. Wings protruded from behind the neck of the figure on either side and rising up clear of the golden band their tips met and joined overhead. On the right, above the sweep of the wing, was an image of an eagle's head, and I saw it had eyes of fire in which there appeared the brilliance of angels as in a mirror. On the left, above the sweep of the wing, was the image of a human face, which shone like the brightness of the stars. Their faces were turned towards the East.[11]

And in a remarkable passage, Hildegard pens one of the most exquisite nondualist pieces of prose ever written by any mystic, male or female. In the manner of a Gnostic Gospel or even an Upanishad, Hildegard describes the beatific vision:

> The figure spoke: I am the supreme fire and energy. I have kindled all the sparks of the living, and I have breathed out no mortal things, for I judge them as they are. I have properly ordained the cosmos, flying about the circling circle with my upper wings, that is

with wisdom. I am the fiery life of divine substance, I blaze above the beauty of the fields, I shine in the waters, I burn in sun, moon, and stars. And I awaken all to life with every wind of the air, as with invisible life that sustains everything. For the air lives in greenness and fecundity. The waters flow as though they were alive. The sun also lives in its own light, and when the moon has waned it is rekindled by the light of the sun and thus lives again; and the stars shine out of their own light as though they are alive [. . .]

Thus I am concealed in things as fiery energy. They are ablaze through me, like the breath that ceaselessly enlivens the human being, or like the wind-tossed flame in a fire. All these things live in their essence, and there is no death in them, for I am life. I also am rationality, who holds the breath of the resonant word by which the whole of creation was created; and I have breathed life into everything, so that nothing by its nature may be mortal, for I am life.

And I am life: not the life struck from stone, or blossoming from branches, or rooted in man's fertility, but life in its fullness, for all living things have their roots in me. Reason is the root, through which the resonant word flourishes.[12]

Everything in the creation is holy according to Hildegard. Even the sexual act, dismissed as "sinful" by so many of her contemporary theologians, is heralded as an ecstatic expression of the Absolute. In her medical notes, she writes:

When a woman is making love with a man, a sense of heat in her brain, which brings with it sensual delight, communicates the taste of that delight during the act and summons forth the emission of the man's seed.[13]

For a virgin (we assume), Hildegard displays a surprising and yet intuitive understanding of the sexual feelings between men and women:

The man's love, compared with the woman's, is a heat of ardour like a fire on blazing mountains, which can hardly be put out, whilst hers is a wood fire that is easily quenched; but the woman's love, compared with the man's, is like a sweet warmth proceeding from the sun, which brings forth fruits ...[14]

As well as being blessed with literary capabilities, Hildegard also possessed the gift of composing music. For her, the soul was "symphonic" and resonated with the rhythms and harmonies of the universe. Although she had no musical training, she often wrote choral music for the liturgy, presented as scores with neumes (medieval musical notation), which are collected in her *Symphonia Armonie Celestium Revelationum* ("Symphony of the Harmony of Celestial Revelations").

Again, Hildegard praises the sacred feminine, this time in a song titled "O Virtus Sapientie":

Power of Wisdom,
circling all things,
comprehending all things,
on one path, which has life.

Three wings:
one soars in the height,
one exudes from the earth,
one soars everywhere.
Praise to you, as befits you, Wisdom.[15]

Recent recordings of her songs reveal a haunting sophistication, often with melancholic undertones, more reminiscent of modern polyphony than medieval plainsong. Indeed, the contemporary ensemble Sequentia have performed an outstanding service in bringing Hildegard's exquisite music to life.

Hildegard of Bingen died aged 81, her lifelong creative output almost unsurpassed. Never before, or possibly even since, had there been a woman of such wilful determination and fortitude managing a thriving nunnery, as well as interpreting her spiritual visions into some of the profoundest artistic creations ever produced.

CHAPTER THIRTEEN

TAOISM AND IMMORTAL SISTER SUN BU-ER

Original energy is unified, yin and yang are one;
The spirit is the same as the universe.

Back in the East in China, at around the time that Hildegard of Bingen was having her extraordinary visions, yet another distinct philosophical system founded in the nondual teaching was flourishing, which came to be known as Taoism, one of the most illustrious exponents of which was the female spiritual adept and poet Sun Bu-er.

Prior to Taoism's systemization, the age-old beliefs of Chinese shamanism placed worship of the universal Mother Goddess at their very core. One of the most popular female deities was the Queen Mother of the West, who lived in the mythological Garden of Paradise. Reminiscent of Hildegard's visions of greenery, within the garden was an immense tree, laden with luscious peaches. It was said whoever ate the fruit of the tree would gain immortal life.

As her story became assimilated into the Taoist tradition, a legend also arose about the Queen Mother of the West meeting the King Father of the East, beautifully described in the *Quan Tangshi* ("Complete Tang Poetry"), an anthology of Taoist lyrical verse, commissioned at the behest of the Emperor of the Qing Dynasty in 1705:

That night, at the seventh division of the clock, there was not a cloud in the sky; it was dark, as if one might hear the sound of thunder, and stretching to the edge of the heavens there was a purple glow. By and by the Queen Mother arrived. She rode in a purple carriage, with the daughters of jade riding on each side; she wore the sevenfold crown upon her head; the sandals on her feet were black and glistening, embellished with the design of a phoenix; and the energies of new growth were like a cloud. There were two green birds, like crows, attending on either side of the Mother. When she alighted from her carriage the emperor greeted her and bowed down, and invited her to be seated. He asked for the drug of deathlessness, and the Queen said, "Of the drugs of long, long ago, there were those such as the Purple Honey of the Blossoms of the centre; the Scarlet Honey of the Mountains of the clouds; or the Golden Juice of the fluid of jade . . . But the emperor harbours his desires and will not let them go, and there are many things for which his heart still yearns; he may not yet attain the drug of deathlessness."

Then the Queen drew out seven peaches; two she ate herself and five she gave to the emperor . . . She stayed with him until the fifth watch, and although she discussed matters of this world, she was not willing to talk of ghosts or spirits; and with a rustle she disappeared . . .

Once she had gone the emperor was saddened for a long time.[1]

Other deities honoured by the Taoist tradition are collectively known as the Eight Immortals, mythological mentors celebrated for their holiness and wisdom. Comprising seven men and one woman, their biographies are told by the second-century BCE writer Huai Nan Tzu, grandson of Emperor Kao Tsu, founder of the Han Dynasty.

In his *History of the Great Light*, Huai Nan Tzu relates the tale of the only female Immortal, Ho Hsien Ku. In a story of tremendous courage and steadfastness, the young maiden is the servant of a bitter and miserly old crone. When Ho Hsien Ku feeds seven starving beggars, she is severely reprimanded afterwards by her mistress, who demands that she go and find the men so they may vomit up that which they have taken without the old crone's consent:

She pushed the tearful and frightened Ho Hsien Ku to the floor and the helpless girl was forced to put a handful of the vomited noodles in her mouth. As soon as the noodles touched her tongue she felt her body become lighter and lighter. She felt her legs rise from the ground and her body began to float away from the spiteful old woman, away from the home where she had suffered so miserably.

The old woman began to panic and turned round to demand an explanation from the beggars but they too had risen high above the house. She caught a last glimpse of the beggars before they disappeared into the clouds and her servant, Ho Hsien Ku, was in their midst.

The Seven Immortals had come to earth to test the young girl's character and she had proved herself worthy of immortality. Because she had endured suffering without complaint and given to the poor without thought for herself, she could work alongside the Immortals for eternity.[2]

Taoism has subsequently become one of the traditional religions of China, alongside Buddhism. Its mystical roots can be traced to sages living as far back as the fifth millennium BCE, as well as taking many precepts from the Chinese text the *I Ching* ("Book of Changes"). It was only in the sixth century BCE that the maxims of Taoism were transposed into a written format by the revered master Lao Tzu in his spiritual classic, the *Tao Te Ching* ("The Book of the Way of Integrity").

After a lifetime's service as the Curator of the Imperial Library at K'au, Lao Tzu was disillusioned with court life, and he decided to withdraw from the world and retire to the country. En route, he rested at the pass of Hsien-ku, where he stayed with its warden, Yin Hsi. A spiritual seeker, Yin Hsi persuaded Lao Tzu, whose wise reputation preceded him, to write down his philosophical insights. In 81 short chapters, the *Tao Te Ching*'s perennial wisdom is as profound today as it was when first recorded:

The Tao that can be told is not the eternal Tao.
The name that can be named is not the eternal name.
The nameless is the beginning of heaven and earth.
The named is the mother of ten thousand things.

Ever desireless, one can see the mystery.
Ever desiring, one sees the manifestations.
These two spring from the same source but differ in name;
*   this appears as darkness.*
Darkness within darkness.
The gate to all mystery.[3]

Interestingly, Lao Tzu was one of those rare sages who honoured the sacred feminine, appreciating that it is an intrinsic aspect of creation:

The valley spirit never dies;
It is the woman, primal mother.
Her gateway is the root of heaven and earth.
It is like a veil barely seen.
Use it; it will never fail.[4]

Perceiving the subtleties of the universe, he exquisitely recounts the understanding of the mystics:

Give up learning, and put an end to your troubles.

Is there a difference between yes and no?
Is there a difference between good and evil?
Must I fear what others fear? What nonsense!
Other people are contented, enjoying the sacrificial feast of
*   the ox.*
In spring some go to the park, and climb the terrace,
But I alone am drifting, not knowing where I am.
Like a newborn babe before it learns to smile,
I am alone, without a place to go.

Others have more than they need, but I alone have nothing.
I am a fool. Oh yes! I am confused.
Others are clear and bright,
But I alone am dim and weak.
Others are sharp and clever,
But I alone am dull and stupid.
Oh, I drift like the waves of the sea,
Without direction, like the restless wind.

Everyone else is busy,
But I alone am aimless and depressed.
I am different.
I am nourished by the great mother.[5]

Another great exponent of Taoism was the venerable Chuang Tzu, who, like Lao Tzu before him, had tasted the fruits of the Infinite. Living in the third century BCE, his written accounts of the Tao, collated in the *Book of Chuang Tzu,* are, by contrast, much longer, often allegorical, expositions. Legend has it that he lived in the kingdom of Wei and, because of his wise reputation, was offered employment by the king. Valuing his personal freedom above all else, he responded that he would rather work in a filthy ditch than be subject to the hypocrisy of a court palace. A man of supreme sagacity, Chuang Tzu says:

I guard my awareness of the One and rest in harmony with externals . . . My light is the light of the sun and the moon. My life is the life of heaven and earth. Before me is the Undifferentiated [Te] and behind me is the Unknowable [Tao]. Men may die but I will endure forever.

147

Keep correct your form, concentrate your vision, and the heavenly harmony will come to you. Control your mind, concentrate your attention, and the Spirit will reside in you. Te is your clothing, and Tao is your sanctuary.[6]

Both Lao Tzu and Chuang Tzu recognized that within the concept of Te is the dance of complementary forces – yang, the active principle and sometimes referred to as masculine; and yin, the passive principle and sometimes referred to as feminine. Given that creative energy is often deemed to be feminine in its entirety in other traditions, such as Shakti in Hinduism, a comparable example would be the Hindu *gunas* or qualities of *rajas* (activity) and *tamas* (passivity) respectively, the balancing of these forces yielding the *sattvic* (natural) state. As Chuang Tzu observes:

In the beginning, even nothing did not exist. There was only the Tao. Then something unnamed which did not yet have form came into existence from the Tao. This is Te, from which all the world came into being. Things had not received their forms, but the division of the yang (positive) and the yin (negative) Principles, which are intimately related, had already appeared. This vibratory motion constitutes all creation. When the yang and the yin become active, all things come into being. It is in this way that Te created all forms.[7]

The ritualization of Taoism throughout the centuries, as with all religious organizations, saw a patriarchal structure emerge in the officiating of duties and ceremonies, with women taking a subservient role. However, as female energy is an intrinsic element of the Tao, the sacred feminine itself remained highly esteemed in spiritual discipline.

Many alchemical practices were cultivated by Taoist adepts in order to harness the flow of yin, including the visualization of the Jade Woman, a celestial guardian, specifically during lovemaking:

> ... actualize a young woman as present within the sun or the moon. A purple cap is placed on her head, and she has a cloak and skirt of vermilion damask. She calls herself the Jade Woman of the Cinnabar Aurora of the Highest Mysteries of the Greatest Mystery [. . .] From her mouth she exhales a red pneuma which fills the space between the light-rays from sun or moon completely. It combines with them until rays and auroral glow are both used up, then gushes into one's own mouth. One masters it and gulps it down. Actualize the woman also as exhaling it in sequence; activate it nine times ten. After these have been gulped down, actualize a conscious command to the phosphor of sun or moon to press intimately close upon one's face, and command the Jade Woman's mouth to press a kiss upon your own mouth [. . .] This done, actualize the salival liquid from the mouth of the Jade Woman, commanding it to gush into one's own mouth. Then, having rinsed it with the liquor, proceed to swallow it [. . .] Perform these things for five years and the Jade Woman of Greatest Mystery will come down to you, and lie down to take her ease with you [. . .] This is the ultimate in accumulating resonance, in knotting germinal essences together, in transmuting life ...[8]

Not only were abstract manifestations of the sacred feminine like the Jade Woman revered, but there was also one mortal woman who was held in the highest esteem, honoured in the anonymous 16th-century text *Seven Taoist Masters*.

Like Yeshe Tsogyal before her, Sun Bu-er's story is a scintillating blend of fact and fiction, but her biography gives an insight into a woman possessing mystical knowledge. Meaning "peerless", Sun Bu-er (1119–82) was born in the Shantung province of China. She had three children and her husband, Ma Tan-yang, was a devotee of the respected Taoist teacher Wang Ch'ung-yang, from whom she also wanted to receive spiritual instruction.

Unfortunately, Wang Ch'ung-yang was not entirely satisfied that Sun Bu-er was committed enough to undertake the Taoist training. To receive the proper instruction, he informed her, she would need to travel to the city of Loyang, over 1,000 miles away – the journey would be long and, because of her physical beauty, she would be risking molestation along the way. Needless to say, Sun Bu-er was undeterred.

Immediately, she went to the kitchen and heated a wok full of oil; then, after pouring in cold water to make the oil sizzle, she leaned over the wok and let the burning liquid splatter her face. Returning to Wang Ch'ung-yang, pockmarked with painful blisters, she asked again if she could receive his spiritual blessing. This time, impressed by her sacrificial actions, he agreed.

After teaching her the methods of internal alchemy, Wang Ch'ung-yang showed Sun Bu-er how to unite yin and yang. When he was satisfied that she had progressed enough, he told her:

Remember, hide your knowledge. Do not let people know you are a seeker of the Tao. After you have finished the Great Alchemical Work, then you may reveal yourself and teach others. In the meantime, let your face heal. Do not even let your servants know of your plans. Leave as soon as you are ready. You need not come to say farewell to me. We shall meet again soon at the celebration of the ripening of the immortal peach.[9]

Feigning madness, she ran away from her husband at the age of 51 and set off for Loyang, begging for alms from local townsfolk and living in caves. After a decade of seclusion and spiritual practice, she finally achieved union with Universal Mind.

Legend says that when she wanted to teach others her newly found insight, she transmuted two branches of a tree, one into a man and the other into a woman, bidding them to cavort shamelessly through the city streets. This caused a public outcry and the community gathered to burn the infamous couple. A fire was lit but then, suddenly, Sun Bu-er allegedly appeared seated on a cloud:

I have finally attained the Tao and today I shall be carried into the heavens by fire and smoke. I transformed two branches into a man and a woman so that circumstances would lead you here to witness the mystery and the powers of the Tao. In return for your kindness and hospitality to me through the years I shall give you this couple. They will be your guardians, and I shall see to it that your harvests will be plentiful and your city protected from plagues and natural disasters.[10]

151

In view of her supreme knowledge of the Tao, Sun Bu-er was given the honorary title of Immortal Sister, collecting many devotees over the years. She also recorded her nondual understanding in three secret "treasure texts" (scripture hidden in a sacred site to be discovered by later generations, similar to that of Yeshe Tsogyal), which were revealed to her through the words of contemporary Taoist adepts, channelling beings from higher levels of existence.

In one particular text, *Unexcelled True Scripture of Inner Experiences of Jadelike Purity*, she points to the way human beings can rekindle their inner vitality and gain a deeper level of awareness:

> *One mind produces right concentration,*
> *Myriad forms are spontaneously arrayed,*
> *Five energies are distributed through the quarters.*
> *The five energies are pregnant with one spirit,*
> *The one spirit pervades transformations,*
> *Crystallizing and refining the original reality.*
> *The original reality is not something with form:*
> *It is neither existent nor nonexistent.*
> *If people can penetrate this principle,*
> *Then they'll understand the pearl that unifies sense experience.*[11]

As well as treasure texts, Sun Bu-er composed poetry, her *Fourteen Verses* forming a sequence of aphorisms upon which the earnest seeker may meditate, the opening poem titled "Gathering the Mind":

> *Before our body existed,*
> *One energy was already there.*
> *Like jade, more lustrous as it's polished,*

Like gold, brighter as it's refined.
Sweep clear the ocean of birth and death,
Stay firm by the door of total mastery.
A particle at the point of open awareness,
The gentle firing is warm.[12]

Addressed to both men and women, Sun Bu-er's invocation urges us to remain vigilant. Only through controlling the breath and reining in thought can the spiritual seeker be restored to the sweet taste of the Tao and the secret of immortality, as outlined in her poem, "The Womb Breath":

If you want the elixir to form quickly,
First get rid of illusory states.
Attentively guard the spiritual medicine;
With every breath return to the beginning of the creative.
The energy returns, coursing through the three islands;
The spirit, forgetting, unites with the ultimate.
Coming this way and going this way,
No place is not truly so.[13]

In Taoist iconography, the enduring symbol of the Tao is ubiquitously represented by the *taijitu* ("a diagram of the supreme ultimate"), which comprises two swirling "teardrops" (one black, representing yin; one white, representing yang), fitting within each other to form a perfect circle. Each shape contains a part of the other, with a black dot in the white segment of the circle and a white dot in the black.

Symbolic of sacred harmony, these seemingly opposing yet complementary halves embody the mysteries of Taoism. As Sun Bu-er says of the cosmic unity in "Facing a Wall":

All things finished,
You sit still in a little niche.
The light body rides on violet energy,
The tranquil nature washes in a pure pond.
Original energy is unified, yin and yang are one;
The spirit is the same as the universe.
When the work is done, you pay court to the Jade Palace;
A long whistle gusts a misty gale.[14]

Sun Bu-er not only understood the nature of the sacred feminine but knew it to be an intrinsic aspect of the One, a vital partner in the dance of the Tao. Indeed, interest in modern times in the teachings of Taoism is testament to the need still felt for harmony between yin and yang and the appreciation of how they complement each other, both in the universe and our daily lives.

Having predicted the time of her departure, just before she died, Sun Bu-er prepared herself by bathing and dressing in ceremonial robes before presenting herself to her disciples. After reciting a poem, she realized her destiny by returning to the realm of the Immortals, precisely as her poem "Flying" foretells:

At the right time, just out of the valley,
You rise lightly into the spiritual firmament.
The jade girl rides a blue phoenix,
The gold boy offers a scarlet peach.
One strums a brocade lute amidst the flowers,
One plays jewel pipes under the moon.
One day immortal and mortal are separated,
And you coolly cross the ocean.[15]

CHAPTER FOURTEEN
CHRISTIANITY AND BEGUINE MARGUERITE PORETE

You send your rays, says Truth,
through divine knowledge;
We know it through true Wisdom:
Her splendour makes us completely luminous.

Meanwhile, back in the West, Thomas Aquinas, who was one of the most influential thinkers of medieval Europe, was born in 1225. With strong links to Aristotle, his greatest work *Summa Theologica* is a survey of Catholic theology, whose legacy can be felt even to this day. Despite his impressive reasoning acumen, drawing on biblical and classical sources, Aquinas held again the widespread belief that women were inferior to men, a view staunchly challenged by a group of women known as "beguines", specifically Marguerite Porete, who would place emphasis on the unitive power of love.

Although Aquinas conceded that the female form was necessary for procreation, he was adamant about a woman's position in the cosmos:

When all things were first formed, it was more suitable for the woman to be made from the man than (for the female to be from the male) in other animals. First, in order thus to give the first man a certain dignity consisting in this, that as God is the principle of the whole universe, so the first man, in likeness to God, was the principle of the whole human race [. . .] in which each has his or her particular duty, and in which the man is the head of the woman. Wherefore it was suitable for the woman to be made out of man, as out of his principle.[1]

Interestingly, in the year before his death, Aquinas had a complete realization of the unity of God. On 6 December 1273, after a lifetime's research into the nature of reality, he was sitting in Mass when he had a sudden revelation. Describing the timeless wisdom of the mystics he had experienced, he declared that all that he had ever written seemed to him like straw compared to what had been revealed to him on that day. He died four months later without writing another single word.

A near contemporary of Aquinas living in Germany was also writing about the nature of God – the scholar Johannes Eckhart (1260–1328). After joining the Dominican priory in Erfurt at the age of 15, he quickly excelled in his religious studies, eventually earning a place at the University of Paris. There he was made Master of Sacred Theology and subsequently became known as Meister Eckhart. As well as writing innumerable sermons in both Latin and German, his major works include *Talks of Instruction*, *The Book of Divine Consolation* and *On the Noble Man*.

In a synthesis of Greek and Christian thinking, Meister Eckhart's writings are essentially grounded in the concept of oneness, from which all of creation emanates and to which it ultimately returns:

God is infinite in his simplicity and simple in his infinity. Therefore he is everywhere and is everywhere complete. He is everywhere on account of his infinity, and is everywhere complete on account of his simplicity. Only God flows into all things, their very essences. Nothing else flows into something else. God is in the innermost part of each and every thing, only in its innermost part, and he alone is *One*.[2]

Reminiscent of the teachings in the Upanishads, Eckhart heralds the ultimate understanding:

One with One, one from One, one in One and one in One in all eternity.[3]

Although he makes no issue over gender and regards men and women as equal elements, Eckhart is keen to demonstrate how oneness differentiates itself in relation to the created world as a whole. In similar ways to the transcendent and immanent concepts of Purusha and Prakriti, Tao and Te, Eckhart distinguishes between the Godhead (*Gottheit*) and God (*Gott*):

God and the Godhead are as different from each other as heaven and earth . . . Creatures speak of God – but why do they not mention the Godhead?

Because there is only unity in the Godhead and there is nothing to talk about. God acts. The Godhead does not ... The difference between God and the Godhead is the difference between action and non-action.[4]

Sadly, as with so many other sages of the past, Eckhart's mystical message did not sit well in the orthodox Catholic Church. He was officially charged with heresy and, in 1327, was summoned to the Papal Court in Cologne, where he skilfully answered all accusations against him, successfully managing to escape the penalty of death. Despite being a thorn in the side of the religious authorities, his writings have survived as proof of the eternal teachings, his nondualist philosophy influencing many recent German thinkers, including the philosopher Arthur Schopenhauer (1788–1860).

One other important theme that Eckhart expounds in his work is the concept of nothingness, the total annihilation of the ego in the Self. In one of his most famous sermons, the *Beati Pauperes Spiritu* ("Blessed in Spirit are the Poor"), he points to the place beyond time, space and causation, to the place even beyond God:

In that breaking-through, when I come to be free of my own will and of God's will and of all His works and of God Himself, then I am above all created things, and I am neither God nor creature, but I am what I was and what I shall remain, now and eternally [. . .]

When I stood in my first cause, I then had no "God", and then I was my own cause. I wanted nothing, I longed for nothing, for I was empty

Being and the only truth in which I rejoiced was in the knowledge of my Self. Then it was my Self that I wanted and nothing else. What I wanted I was, and what I was I wanted and so I stood empty of God and every thing.[5]

It is this theme of nothingness and abandonment in the face of the Eternal that permeates the writings of a group of women mystics living between the 12th and 14th centuries around the Low Countries of north-west Europe, collectively known as the beguines.

Although they lived an essentially communal life, often attached to nearby Franciscan, Cistercian or Dominican communities, they were different from more conventional nuns in that they did not take permanent vows, promising instead to care for the sick and engage in shared manual labour as long as they lived in the beguinage. As well as offering spiritual sustenance, beguine communities were also refuges for widowed or unmarried women affected by the large numbers of men either killed or absent in the Crusades. Whatever their reasons for existing in such a way, they strove to live an unworldly life while similarly living in the world – the middle way between the ascetic and the householder.

The first communities of beguines (men living in the same manner were called beghards) seem to have been organized around 1170 by the revivalist priest Lambert le Bègue. As their lives were simple and devoid of more orthodox doctrine and supervision, they naturally gained a purer appreciation of the Gospels and a desire to penetrate the very heart of Jesus' teachings. What set them apart from their contemporaries was the belief that the imitation of Christ – the practice of following his example – was not just a means of joining together with him in mystical marriage (*unio spiritus*) but a way to actually become one with him (*unio indistinctionis*). Inevitably, then, as the centuries passed, the beguines became subject to increasing suspicion from an imperious Catholic Church and charges of heresy inevitably followed.

One such beguine was Marguerite Porete. Believed to have been born in Hainault in north-east France (formerly in the Flanders region), her exact date of birth is lost, and nothing is known of her early life. However, sometime around 1300, she composed *The Mirror of Simple Souls*, one of the most important documents detailing the mystical life. Such was its profound effect that the Church authorities felt threatened by its powerful insight, offering a path to the Divine that circumvented traditional worship. As a consequence, they ordered Marguerite to be burned at the stake. Unlike Meister Eckhart, she did not argue an effective defence but chose instead to remain silent throughout the proceedings. She died on 1 June 1310 in the Place de Grève in Paris, becoming one of the first "heretics" to be torched to death at the hands of the French Inquisition.

Although all copies of the text were banned by the Church, a number of facsimile editions – translated into Latin, Italian and Middle English – were distributed to various theologians and scholars across Europe, ensuring its survival. One such scholar, upon whom *The Mirror* had a considerable influence, was none other than Meister Eckhart. In fact, there is ample evidence to suggest that while Eckhart was on a trip to Paris, he saw an unauthorized copy.

Written in Old French and addressed to a female audience, the manuscript extends to over 60,000 words and is a dialogue in the manner of troubadour love poetry between Dame Amour (Lady Love) and Raison (Reason), concerning the conduct of Ame (the Soul). Unlike Hildegard of Bingen (see Chapter 12), Marguerite makes no apology for writing such a work. Her words are imbued with a dazzling self-confidence unique for the period, with the opening of *The Mirror* immediately setting the tone:

You who would read this book,
If you indeed wish to grasp it,
Think about what you say,
For it is very difficult to comprehend;
Humility, who is keeper of the treasury of
Knowledge
And the mother of the other Virtues,
Must overtake you.

Theologians and other clerks,
You will not have the intellect for it,
No matter how brilliant your abilities,
If you do not proceed humbly.
And may Love and Faith, together,
Cause you to rise above Reason,
[Since] they are ladies of the house [. . .]

Humble, then, your wisdom
Which is based on Reason,
And place all your fidelity
In those things which are given
By Love, illuminated through Faith.

And thus you will understand this book
Which makes the Soul live by love. [6]

Written as a spiritual handbook, the work outlines the "seven states of grace" leading to absorption in the Absolute. With an intimate understanding of human psychology, she describes the soul's ascent toward a oneness of being between lover and Beloved, merging into love itself.

After the lower three stages, including all outward signs of moral virtue and religious practice, the soul must experience two deaths, namely of "sin" and "nature", to move on to the next stage. The fourth stage is where the soul is drenched in love from repeated ecstasies of prayer and contemplation and, according to Marguerite, is where most spiritual aspirants falter because their individual soul still exerts its independent will.

It is the fifth stage where the soul must undergo yet another death – that of the individual ego – so that the fullness of divine love can flood unimpeded through the aspirant, reducing the soul to naught:

> Now such a Soul is nothing, for she sees her nothingness by means of the abundance of divine Understanding, which makes her nothing and places her in nothingness [. . .] Therefore she wills only one thing: the Spouse of her youth, who is only One [. . .] Now she is All, and so she is Nothing, for her Beloved makes her One.[7]

Here, the liberated soul is no longer subject to the more conventional sacraments of the Holy Church and its ideological restraints. And yet there are still two more stages of grace she must navigate through. At the sixth stage, the soul no longer has a separate identity and is merged into everything that is God:

> . . . the Soul does not see herself on account of such an abyss of humility which she has within her. Nor does she see God on account of the highest goodness which He has. But God sees Himself in her by His divine majesty, who clarifies this Soul with Himself, so that she sees only that there is nothing except God Himself who is, from whom all things are. And He who is, is God Himself.[8]

This echoes the Old Testament psalm "Be still and know that I am God." Likewise, willing nothing, being nothing, extinguishing oneself in the Absolute is the kindred message of Meister Eckhart, the parallels between the two being strikingly similar in nature. Marguerite continues:

> Ah, Love, says this Soul, the meaning of what is said makes me nothing, and the nothingness of this alone has placed me in an abyss below less than nothingness without measure. And the understanding of my nothingness, says this Soul, has given me the All, and the nothingness of this All, says the Soul, has taken from me prayer, and I pray nothing.[9]

All and nothing – two diametrically opposed states and yet simultaneously coexisting in God. This is the paradox of mysticism. Marguerite then goes on to describe how, through renunciation of the individual ego, the universal soul is attained:

I repose completely in peace, says this Soul, alone and nothing [. . .] It is the goal of my work, says this Soul, always to will nothing. For as long as I will nothing, says this Soul, I am alone in Him without myself, completely unencumbered. And if I should will something, she says, I am with myself, and therefore I have lost freeness. But when I will nothing I have lost everything beyond my will, therefore nothing is lacking to me. To be unencumbered is my conduct. I would will nothing at all.[10]

Akin to the nondualist message of the Upanishads, all that remains is silent awe and wonderment. (The seventh and final stage, Marguerite declares, is only knowable when the soul has left the body.)

Toward the end of *The Mirror of Simple Souls*, the character of Truth makes an appearance and praises the soul, who has reached the penultimate stage:

O emerald and precious gem,
True diamond, queen and empress,
You give everything from your fine nobility,
Without asking from Love her riches,
Except the willing of her divine pleasure.
Thus is this right by righteousness,
For it is the true path
Of Fine Love, whoever wishes to remain on it.
O deepest spring and fountain sealed,
Where the sun is subtly hidden,
You send your rays, says Truth, through divine knowledge;
We know it through true Wisdom:
Her splendour makes us completely luminous.[11]

The soul answers with a song in praise of herself and the fruits of her spiritual journey. First, she acknowledges her former encumbered state of being:

I used to be enclosed
   in the servitude of captivity,
When desire imprisoned me
   in the will of affection.
There the light of ardour
   from divine love found me,
Who quickly killed my desire,
   my will and affection,
Which impeded in me the enterprise
   of the fullness of divine love.[12]

Once all attachments have fallen away, the face of the Beloved is then revealed:

And Divine Love tells me
   that she has entered within me,
And so she can do,
   whatever she wills,
Such strength she has given me,
From One Lover whom I possess in love,
To whom I am betrothed,
Who wills what He loves,
And for this I will love Him.

I have said that I will love Him.
I lie, for I am not.
It is He alone who loves me:
He is, and I am not;

And nothing more is necessary to me
Than what He wills,
And that He is worthy.
He is fullness,
And by this am I impregnated.
This is the divine seed and Loyal Love.[13]

Marguerite offers a book that acts as a looking glass revealing God's luminosity and fullness, a vision which is ultimately known to be a reflection of oneself. Sadly, it was also a revelation that came at the expense of her own life.

Another important beguine, about whom we know very little, is Mechthild of Magdeburg (1210–97), born into an aristocratic household in Saxony. At the age of 23, she decided to leave the comforts of her noble upbringing and become a beguine in the nearby town of Magdeburg. At 40, she confided in her confessor, the Dominican Heinrich of Halle, that she had been experiencing mystical phenomena. Urging her to write them all down, he later helped her to collate the subsequent manuscript.

Over the following 20 years, Mechthild composed the first six books of her spiritual masterpiece, written in Middle Low German but given the Latin title *Lux Divinitatis* ("The Flowing Light of the Godhead"). Then, after moving to the Cistercian community at Helfta, where she became gravely ill and almost blind, she dictated the seventh and final book before her death.

The Flowing Light is an intensely powerful treatise on the nature of divine love. Employing many literary genres in its composition – visions, sermons, poetry, allegorical dialogues between Lady Love and Lady Knowledge –

Mechthild's work is an attempt to convey the immediacy of her mystical experience. Her first encounter with the Divine, which occurred in her early 20s, is described in raw intimacy as she recounts the journey of her soul toward the Creator:

> God's true greeting, coming from the heavenly flood out of the spring of the flowing Trinity, has such force that it takes away all the body's strength and reveals the soul to herself, so that she sees herself resembling the saints, and she takes on a divine radiance. Then the soul leaves the body, taking all her power, wisdom, love and longing. Just the tiniest bit of her life force remains with the body as in a sweet sleep. Then she sees one complete God in three Persons and knows the three Persons in one God undivided.[14]

In the same manner as Hildegard, Mechthild immediately sanctions her writing with God's authority:

> *"Ah, Lord God, who made this book?"*
> *"I made it in my powerlessness, for I cannot restrain myself as to my gifts."*
> *"Well then, Lord, what shall the title of the book be, which is to your glory alone?"*
> *"It shall be called a flowing light of my Godhead into all hearts that live free of hypocrisy."*[15]

It is the relationship between the hearts of the individual and the Absolute that consumes Mechthild's spiritual journey – the ecstasy and agony of two souls involved in the erotic dance of courtship, ultimately merging and dissolving in their mutual love:

"Stay, Lady Soul."
"What do you bid me, Lord?"
"Take off your clothes."
"Lord, what will happen to me then?"
"Lady Soul, you are so utterly formed to my nature
That not the slightest thing can be between you and me.
Never was an angel so glorious
That to him was granted for one hour
What is given to you for eternity.
And so you must cast off from you
Both fear and shame and all external virtues.
Rather, those alone that you carry within yourself
Shall you foster forever.
These are your noble longing
And your boundless desire.
These I shall fulfil forever
With my limitless lavishness."

"Lord, now I am a naked soul
And you in yourself are a well-adorned God.
Our shared lot is eternal life
Without death."

Then a blessed stillness
That both desire comes over them.
He surrenders himself to her,
And she surrenders herself to him.
What happens to her then – she knows –
And that is fine with me.

But this cannot last long.
When two lovers meet secretly,
They must often part from one another inseparably.[16]

In poetry reminiscent of the Song of Songs, Mechthild is lost in rapture for her Lord, who speaks to her through his "loving mouth":

"You are the feelings of love in my desire.
You are a sweet cooling for my breast.
You are a passionate kiss for my mouth.
You are a blissful joy of my discovery.
I am in you
And you are in me.
We could not be closer,
For we two have flowed into one
And have been poured into one mould.
Thus shall we remain forever content."[17]

Like Marguerite, she renounces all earthly ties and surrenders herself to love:

Thus you become full of the fire of love.
This makes you here utterly happy.
You can no longer teach me anything.
I cannot turn away from love.
I must be its captive.
Otherwise, I cannot go on living.
Where it dwells, there I must remain,
Both in death and in life.
This is the folly of fools
Who live free of anguish.[18]

And in a similar way to the Zen masters of the East, Mechthild understands the paradoxical nature of liberation:

> *Under this immense force she loses herself.*
> *In this most dazzling light she becomes blind in herself.*
> *And in this utter blindness she sees most clearly.*
> *In this pure clarity she is both dead and living.*
>
> *The longer she is dead, the more blissfully she lives.*
> *The more blissfully she lives, the more she experiences.*
> *The less she becomes, the more flows to her.*[19]

So radical was Mechthild's vision that many of her conservative contemporaries tried to eradicate its message. Asking for help, God rouses her thus:

> *"My dear One, do not be overly troubled.*
> *No one can burn the truth.*
> *For someone to take this book out of my hand,*
> *He must be mightier than I [. . .]*
> *The words symbolize my marvellous Godhead.*
> *It flows continuously*
> *Into your soul from my divine mouth.*
> *The sound of the words is a sign of my living spirit*
> *And through it achieves genuine truth."*[20]

Mechthild inspired many other female contemplatives to impart their unique mystical experiences, including Mechthild of Hackeborn in *The Book of Special Grace* and Gertrude the Great in *The Herald of Divine Love*.

In spite of its moving message, *The Flowing Light of the Godhead* fell into oblivion after Mechthild's death – it was only in the 19th century that any serious interest in her book materialized, and an English translation had to wait until 1953.

Another great female mystic of the 13th century was the Flemish woman Hadewijch of Brabant (near Antwerp), though nothing much is known about who she was and precisely when she lived. However, we do know that Hadewijch was a beguine just like Marguerite and Mechthild. Hadewijch also wrote poetry and a series of letters, as well as compiling a sequence of 14 visions, which were all recorded in a Brabantine dialect. At the beginning of the seventh vision, "Oneness in the Eucharist", she states:

> On a certain Pentecost Sunday I had a vision at dawn. Matins were being sung in the church and I was present. My heart and my veins and all my limbs trembled and quivered with eager desire and, as often occurred with me, such madness and fear beset my mind that it seemed to me that if I did not content my Beloved, and my Beloved did not fulfil my desire, so that dying I must go mad, and going mad I must die. On that day my mind was beset so fearfully and so painfully by desirous love that all my separate limbs threatened to break, and all my separate veins were in travail.[21]

Hadewijch also conveys the same nondualist vision as her beguinal counterparts. In her letter, "He in Me and I in Him", she speaks of the soul immersed in the One:

> May God make known to you, dear child, who he is and how he deals with his servants and especially

171

with his handmaids – and may he submerge you in him!

Where the abyss of his wisdom is, he will teach you what he is, and with what wondrous sweetness the loved one and the Beloved dwell one in the other, and how they penetrate each other in such a way that neither of the two distinguishes himself from the other. But they abide in one another in fruition, mouth in mouth, heart in heart, body in body, and soul in soul, while one sweet *divine Nature* flows through them both, and they are both one thing through each other, but at the same time remain two different selves – yes, remain so forever.[22]

Hadewijch also employs the language of courtly love to describe her feelings of spiritual desire for the Beloved, not least its bittersweet flavour, a theme that continued to fascinate her and which finds beautiful expression in the poem "The Paradoxes of Love":

The storming of love is what is sweetest within her,
Her deepest abyss is her most beautiful form,
To lose our way in her is to arrive,
To hunger for her is to feed and to taste,
Her despairing is sureness of faith,
Her worst wounding is to become whole again,
To waste away for her is to endure,
Her hiding is to find her at all times,
To be tormented for her is to be in good health,
In her concealment she is revealed.
What she withholds, she gives,
Her finest speech is without words,

Her imprisonment is freedom,
Her most painful blow is her sweetest consolation,
Her giving is her taking away,
Her going away is her coming near,
Her deepest silence is her highest song,
Her greatest wrath is her warmest thanks,
Her greatest threatening is remaining true,
Her sadness is the healing of all sorrow.[23]

Despite having a profound effect on the famed Flemish mystic Jan van Ruysbroeck, Hadewijch's work fell into obscurity, not unlike the work of other beguines. Again, it was not until the 19th century that her manuscripts were uncovered in the Royal Library of Brussels and the light of her wisdom was revealed for all to behold.

In 1312, the Council of Vienne, the ecumenical legislature of the Roman Catholic Church, decreed that the way of life of the beguines and beghards was strictly forbidden. Sadly, even worse was yet to come. In the middle of the 15th century Heinrich Kramer and James Sprenger, two Dominican Inquisitor priests, composed a handbook outlining the evil nature of women, as well as practices they classified as witchcraft. Known as the *Malleus Maleficarum* ("The Hammer of Witches"), it became the authoritative text used to flush out perceived female dissenters throughout Europe for the following 300 years.

Continuing in the same vein as Augustine, women were seen as inferior beings to men. According to the *Malleus Maleficarum*:

. . . it should be noted that there was a defect in the formation of the first woman, since she was formed from a bent rib, that is, a rib of the breast, which is bent as it were in a contrary direction to a man. And since through this defect she is an imperfect animal, she always deceives [. . .] And all this is indicated by the etymology of the word; for *Femina* comes from *Fe* and *Minus*. . .[24]

More alarmingly, Kramer and Sprenger believed women to be sex-obsessed consorts of the devil:

All witchcraft comes from carnal lust, which is in women insatiable. There are three things that are never satisfied [infidelity, ambition, lust], yea a fourth thing which says not "It is enough"; that is, the mouth of the womb. Wherefore for the sake of fulfilling their lusts they consort even with devils [. . .]

Now there are, as it is said in the Papal Bull, seven methods by which they infect with witchcraft the venereal act and the conception of the womb: First, by inclining the minds of men to inordinate passion; second, by obstructing their generative force; third, by removing the members accommodated to that act; fourth, by changing men into beasts by their magic art; fifth, by destroying the generative force in women; sixth, by procuring abortion; seventh, by offering children to devils, besides other animals and fruits of the earth with which they work much harm.[25]

Unfortunately, the specific references to children and childbirth put the lives of many midwives in jeopardy, as well as women who were well versed in the use of medicinal herbs. And so, the burning of "witches" became pandemic throughout medieval Europe, with its practice continuing well into the 18th century. Estimates of the number of women who died at the hands of the Catholic Church place the figure as high as 50,000.

The most illustrious victim of such heinous victimization was the French peasant girl Joan of Arc. Inspired by voices and visions of God, she helped the French drive out British forces from France during a bloody international war. Captured by the enemy, she was tried as a witch and heretic, being accused of three specific crimes – first, that the voices she heard were in fact those of evil spirits; second, that she had refused to submit to the authority of the Church, claiming she only obeyed a higher power; and third, that as a woman, she should never dress in men's clothes. Guilty as charged, Joan was burned at the stake in Rouen, Normandy, on 30 May 1431.

It truly beggars belief that such a horrific holocaust of the female sex should ever have happened, let alone been endured for so long. More appallingly, such acts of barbarity and violence against so many women were committed by corrupt Catholic clerics peddling fallacious theories, who failed irrevocably in their duty as guardians of Jesus' teachings, which were rooted solely in compassion and love.

CHAPTER FIFTEEN
CHRISTIANITY AND ANCHORITE JULIAN OF NORWICH

All shall be well,
and all shall be well,
and all manner of things shall be well.

As the Catholic Church continued to debate the minutiae of Christian theology (and commit its heinous misogynistic acts), many ordinary men and women were turning their attention to a more profound and personal experience of the oneness of God. Indeed, Meister Eckhart's legacy set the tone for the next wave of mystical writings that would flourish throughout mainland Europe, as well as British shores through the pen of one of the most celebrated women writers of the period, Julian of Norwich.

One such European work was *The Imitation of Christ*, composed by the German monk Thomas à Kempis (1380–1471) – in one of the most moving and exuberant expressions of an individual's love for the Absolute, he pays particular attention to the mystical relationship between lover and Beloved:

He who is thus a spiritual lover knows well what his voice means which says: "Thou, Lord God, art my whole love and my desire! Thou art all mine and I all Thine! Spread my heart into Thy love that I may know how sweet it is to serve Thee, and to be as though I were entirely melted into Thy love. O I am immersed in love and go far above myself for the great fervour that I feel of Thy unspeakable goodness! I shall sing to Thee the song of love; and my soul shall never be weary to praise Thee with the joyful song of love that I shall sing to Thee. I shall love Thee more than myself, and not myself but for Thee."[1]

England also witnessed its own period of spiritual testament. In the 1380s, the first-ever hand-written English manuscripts of the Bible were translated into vernacular Middle English by John Wycliffe, an Oxford theologian and scholar, enabling so-called common folk to receive the Christian teachings directly.

More importantly, an anonymous 14th-century text, *The Cloud of Unknowing*, would also provide one of the most beautiful expositions on the nature of mystical experience. Veiled from God by a "cloud", the individual can penetrate the misty layers of separation through use of a single-word prayer, rather like a mantra and the technique of transcendental meditation more prevalent in the East:

. . . take thee but a little word of one syllable: for so it is better than of two, for ever the shorter it is the better it accordeth with the work of the Spirit. And such a word is this word GOD or this word LOVE

[. . .] And fasten this word to thine heart, so that it never go thence for thing that befalleth.

This word shall be thy shield and thy spear, whether thou ridest on peace or on war. With this word, thou shalt beat on this cloud and this darkness above thee. With this word, thou shalt smite down all manner of thought under the cloud of forgetting.[2]

Other writers of the period include the hermit Richard Rolle of Hampole, in Yorkshire (1300–49). As spiritual counsellor, he composed many of his later works specifically for women, despite starting life as a staunch misogynist. In his *The Form of Living*, written specifically for the anchoress Margaret Kirkby, a member of the Cistercian community at Hampole, Rolle asks the question "What is love?" and replies:

Love is an ardent yearning for God, with a wonderful delight and security . . . Love is one life, coupling together the one loving and the one beloved . . . Love is the beauty of all virtues . . . a device through which God loves us and we God and each of us one another. Love is the desire of the heart . . . a yearning between two people . . . a stirring of the soul to love God for himself and all other things for God . . . Truth may exist without love, but it cannot be of any use without it. Love is the perfection of scholarship, the strength of prophecy, the fruit of truth, the spiritual strength of the sacraments, the confirming of intellect and knowledge, the wealth of the poor, the life of the dying.[3]

Life for women in medieval Britain was particularly harsh. Like their European counterparts, they were in the main restricted to the household, with patriarchal Church establishments preventing them from participating in any form of public life. With a population that also had a surplus of unmarried women, many sought the seclusion of religious orders as an escape from the wretchedness of the material world in preparation for a glorious existence in the afterlife.

One specific text, composed toward the end of the 12th century by an anonymous male author, was a guide for nuns titled the *Ancrene Wisse* ("The Anchorite's Rule"). Written in eight parts in a West Midlands dialect, it outlines specific behaviour to be adopted by the nun in her quest for spiritual perfection. Once again, the notion of the female gender being the weaker sex, carrying the sinful legacy of Eve, forms the subtext of the *Rule*. As she is believed to be morally defective, it is for her own good that she must succumb to religious instruction – and it is only through the redemptive power of her love for God that the nun can gain salvation. Her relationship with Christ, as God's conduit, must become the focus of her existence:

> Therefore, my dear sisters, over everything else, be energetic about having a pure heart. What is a pure heart? I have said it before: that is, that you wish for nothing, and love nothing, and love nothing except God alone – and those things, for God's sake, which help you towards him.[4]

It was only a matter of time before the voice of a woman writer would eventually emerge, defending her feminine right to express her mystical experiences completely on her own terms.

In spite of being well known in her day, Julian of Norwich (c.1342–c.1416) has proved elusive historically, as very few facts about her life have survived. Even her true name is unknown, as she has simply been named after the church where she once lived. (The original church was destroyed by the Germans in 1942; however, it has subsequently been rebuilt.)

Born into a wealthy household in Norwich and educated at a boarding school attached to Carrow Abbey convent, she took her vows as a nun, though it is not clear exactly when. However, we do know that she chose to live her life as an anchoress (deriving from the Greek word meaning "to retire"), which meant she was literally entombed in a sealed cell attached to the priory. Although her daily needs, such as food and firewood, would have been attended to by a servant, she effectively chose to cut herself off completely from the outside world and focus her attention exclusively on the interior life.

In her early 30s, Julian was struck down by an acute illness, which lasted for nearly a week and brought her to the brink of death. During this harrowing period, she received a total of 16 "showings" of Christ and his Passion. After a miraculous recovery, she then set about recording her visions as the *Revelations of Divine Love*. Two decades later, she rewrote the entire manuscript, expanding the narrative and adding commentary and theological reflection. And so the Short Text was composed in 1373 and the Long Text in roughly 1393:

And when I was thirty and a half years old, God sent me a bodily sickness in which I lay for three days and three nights; and on the fourth night I received all the rites of Holy Church and did not believe that I would live until morning. And after this I lingered on for two days and two nights. And on the third night I often thought that I was dying, and so did those who were with me. But at this time I was very sorry and reluctant to die, not because there was anything on earth that I wanted to live for, nor because I feared anything, for I trusted in God, but because I wanted to live so as to love God better and for longer, so that through the grace of longer life I might know and love God better in the bliss of heaven.[5]

However, all is well and Julian makes a full recovery:

Then I truly believed that I was at the point of death. And at this moment all my suffering suddenly left me, and I was as completely well, especially in the upper part of my body, as ever I was before or after. I marvelled at this change, for it seemed to me a mysterious work of God, not a natural one.[6]

Julian would have been acutely aware of the patriarchal message of her male clerical colleagues, as well as the legacy of St Paul, and so, despite proclaiming how uneducated and humble she is, she defiantly defends her right to speak:

. . . God forbid that you should say or assume that I am a teacher, for that is not what I mean, nor did

I ever mean it; for I am a woman, ignorant, weak and frail [. . .] Just because I am a woman, must I therefore believe that I must not tell you about the goodness of God, when I saw at the same time both his goodness and his wish that it should be known?[7]

Similar to other female mystics of the period, Julian employs the familiar metaphor of divine lovers to convey her feelings of awe and devotion. As the embodiment of love, Christ is Julian's beloved – through their divine marriage, the two become One:

And in this binding and union he is a real and true bridegroom, and me his loved bride and his fair maiden, a bride with whom he is never displeased; for he says, "I love you and you love me, and our love shall never be divided."[8]

Julian also introduces into her writing a different form of relationship, one that is arguably more profound – that between mother and child. Only appearing in the Long Text, when she presumably had had more time to reflect upon the idea, she cleverly juxtaposes the portrayal of God the Father, more associated with fear and punishment, with the figure of Christ the Mother, nurturing and all-forgiving:

And so our Mother, in whom our parts are kept unparted, works in us in various ways; for in our Mother, Christ, we profit and grow, and in mercy he reforms and restores us, and through the power of his Passion and his death and rising again, he unites us to our essential being. This is how our Mother mercifully acts to all his children who are submissive and obedient to him.[9]

As Christ's children, we return to his "motherhood" for our spiritual support and sustenance. Julian is also reinforcing the medieval idea that milk was reprocessed blood. Christ's bleeding on the Cross is, therefore, seen as the nourishing flow of love from the Mother's breast.

Like Hildegard, Julian is also blessed with a vision of the universe in which she is made to understand everything that exists as a manifestation of the Absolute:

And in this vision he showed me a little thing, the size of a hazelnut, lying in the palm of my hand, and to my mind's eye it was as round as any ball. I looked at it and thought, "What can this be?" And the answer came to me, "It is all that is made." I wondered how it could last, for it was so small I thought it might suddenly disappear. And the answer in my mind was, "It lasts and will last for ever because God loves it; and in the same way everything exists through the love of God." In this little thing I saw three attributes: the first is that God made it, the second is that he loves it, the third is that God cares for it. But what does that mean to me? Truly, the maker, the lover, the carer; for until I become one substance with him, I can never have love, rest or true bliss; that is to say, until I am so bound to him that there may be no created thing between my God and me.[10]

In spite of her nondual explanation, something still deeply perplexes Julian. Regarding the nature of sin, she asks her

Lord how it can possibly exist when he is responsible for all that is made in the universe. Contemplating this paradox, she writes:

> And after this I saw God in an instant, that is in my understanding, and in seeing this I saw that he is in everything. I looked attentively, knowing and recognizing in this vision that he does all that is done. I marvelled at this sight with quiet awe, and I thought, "What is sin?" For I saw that God does everything, no matter how small. And nothing happens by accident or luck, but by the eternal providence of God's wisdom. Therefore I was obliged to accept that everything which is done is well done, and I was sure that God never sins. Therefore it seemed to me that sin is nothing, for in all this vision no sin appeared.[11]

What is striking about Julian's prose is her capacity to rationalize her visions into a comprehensive philosophical argument. She explains further that the logical reason why God compels us to suffer is to test our love and make us humble. Moreover, as her Lord reiterates, everything is as it should be and in one of her most immortal lines, quoted centuries later by T S Eliot in his beautiful poem *Four Quartets*, she states:

> . . . all shall be well, and all shall be well, and all manner of things shall be well.[12]

The theme of oneness also permeates Julian's writings. She boldly asserts her nondualist message in a way reminiscent of Vedic scripture:

God is our mother as truly as he is our father; and he showed this in everything, and especially in the sweet words where he says, "It is I," that is to say, "It is I: the power and goodness of fatherhood. It is I: the wisdom of motherhood. It is I: the light and the grace which is all blessed love. It is I: the Trinity. It is I: the unity. I am the sovereign goodness of all manner of things. It is I that make you love. It is I that make you long. It is I: the eternal fulfilment of all true desires."[13]

This is the final truth that she reiterates in both the Short and Long Texts – God is omniscient, omnipresent, omnipotent, and knowledge of this fact is paramount:

. . . all men and women who wish to lead the contemplative life need to have knowledge of it; they should choose to set at nothing everything that is made so as to have the love of God who is unmade. This is why those who choose to occupy themselves with earthly business and are always pursuing worldly success have nothing here of God in their hearts and souls: because they love and seek their rest in this little thing where there is no rest, and know nothing of God, who is almighty, all wise and all good, for he is true rest. God wishes to be known, and is pleased that we should rest in him; for all that is below him does nothing to satisfy us. And this is why, until all that is made seems as nothing, no soul can be at rest. When a soul sets all at nothing for love, to have him who is everything that is good, then it is able to receive spiritual rest.[14]

It is highly unlikely that Julian would have been familiar with the writings of the beguines, but once again we hear the common theme of reducing oneself to nothing in order to become everything and all with the Divine:

> For if I look solely at myself, I am really nothing; but as one of mankind in general, I am in oneness of love with all my fellow Christians; for upon this oneness of love depends the life of all who shall be saved; for God is all that is good, and God has made all that is made, and God loves all that he has made.[15]

Everything that God wills for us is owing to His love. And this is what Julian finally comes to understand in one final revelation some 15 years after the initial sequence of showings and a few years prior to her composing the Long Text:

> "Do you want to know what your Lord meant? Know well that love was what he meant. Who showed you this? Love. What did he show? Love. Why did he show it to you? For Love. Hold fast to this and you will know and understand more of the same; but you will never understand or know from it anything else for all eternity." This is how I was taught that our Lord's meaning was love.[16]

Without doubt, her showings are one of the most discerning pieces of confessional literature written by any woman. Through her intellectual rigour and impassioned revelation, Julian of Norwich's work joins the great canon of sacred female testimony, stretching as far back as

Enheduanna, Sappho and Mary Magdalene. Julian lived until her mid-70s, although the exact date of her death is still a mystery and her burial place remains similarly unknown. However, David Holgate's impressive stone statue, flanking the west door of Norwich Cathedral and completed in 2000, is a fitting tribute to Julian, depicting her as a steadfast figure clutching her book *Revelations of Divine Love* firmly under her left arm and pressed against her heart.

As well as her English contemporary Margery Kempe, other venerable European nuns of the period were also writing of the mystical life, including Clare of Assisi, Angela of Foligno, Margaret Ebner, Bridget of Sweden and the Catherines of Siena, Bologna and Genoa. Each was blessed with a unique style of composition, making the Middle Ages an era unmatched in its exploration of feminine experience within the context of the Christian teachings – a literary movement arising perhaps in defiance of the wicked crimes perpetrated against women by the Catholic Church.

CHAPTER SIXTEEN
HINDUISM AND BHAKTA MIRABAI

To take this path is to walk the edge of the sword;
Then the noose of birth and death is suddenly cut.

As the sacred feminine struggled against political and ecclesiastic prejudice in Europe, her worship continued unimpeded throughout the Indian continent specifically through the devotional verse of several female *bhakti* poets, in particular the Rajasthani princess, Mirabai.

Many male sages also continued to revere the feminine aspect of the mystical nondual doctrines, one of the most prevalent being Jnaneshvar (1271–96). Born in northern India, the poet had an understanding at a very young age of the perennial wisdom. Although he is best known for his *Jnaneshvari*, a commentary on the Bhagavad Gita, it is his *Amrutanubhav* ("The Nectar of Mystical Experience") that details the passionate relationship between Siva and Shakti – the divine lovers inseparably bound:

I offer obeisance to the God and Goddess,
The limitless primal parents of the universe.

The lover, out of boundless love,
Has become the Beloved.

Both are made of the same substance
And share the same food.

Out of love for each other, they merge;
And again they separate for the pleasure of being two [...]

Two lutes: one note.
Two flowers: one fragrance.
Two lamps: one light.

Two lips: one word.
Two eyes: one sight.
These two: one universe [...]

In the same way, the duality of Siva and Shakti
Vanishes, when their essential unity is seen.[1]

One particular scripture that was to emerge during this period and further eulogized Shakti was the *Devi Gita* ("Song of the Goddess"). Similar in overall structure and theme to the Bhagavad Gita, it forms part of the *Devi Bhagavata Purana*, the chief Puranic text of Shakti worshippers.

Composed in Sanskrit *shlokas* (a special type of Vedic verse) sometime around the 15th century, the Goddess offers wise counsel to her special devotee, the Mountain King Himalaya, in front of an assembly of gods. Expounding an esoteric blend of Advaitic and Tantric philosophy, the Goddess proclaims that all phenomenal existence is supported in the eternal Self – the only difference here is that the eternal oneness of Being is personified as the feminine principle.

Manifesting as a blinding flash of light, the three-eyed, four-armed Goddess, Mother of the World, emerges before the Mountain King:

She was exceedingly beautiful of limb, a maiden in the freshness of youth.
Her full, upraised breasts put to shame the swelling buds of the lotus.
Her girdle and anklets jingled with clusters of tinkling bells.
She was adorned with necklace, armlets and bracelets of gold [...]

The Mother's kindly face, so gracious, displayed a tender smile on the lotus mouth.
This embodiment of unfeigned compassion the gods beheld in their presence.
Seeing her, the embodiment of compassion, the entire host of gods bowed low,
Unable to speak, choking on tears in silence.
Struggling to regain their composure, their necks bending in devotion,
Their eyes brimming with tears of loving joy, they glorified the World Mother with hymns.[2]

The Goddess then reveals her mystical knowledge:

May all the gods attend to what I have to say.
By merely hearing these words of mine, one attains my essential nature.
I alone existed in the beginning; there was nothing else at all, O Mountain King.

My true Self is known as pure consciousness, the highest
intelligence, the one supreme Brahman.
It is beyond reason, indescribable, incomparable,
incorruptible.
From out of itself evolves a certain power renowned as Maya.

Neither real nor unreal is this Maya, nor is it both, for that
would be incongruous.
Lacking such characteristics, this indefinite entity has always
subsisted.
As heat inheres in fire, as brilliance in the sun,
As cool light in the moon, just so this Maya inheres firmly in
me.
Into that Maya the actions of souls, the souls themselves, and
the ages eventually
Dissolve without distinctions, as worldly concerns disappear
in deep sleep.
By uniting with this inherent power of mine, I become the
cosmic seed.[3]

Echoing the wisdom of the Gnostic Gospels, as well as
Hildegard's vision of the cosmos, the Goddess knows that,
ultimately, she pervades everything:

I am the sun and the stars, and I am the Lord of the stars.
I am the various species of beasts and birds; I am also the
outcaste and thief.
I am the evildoer and the wicked deed; I am the righteous
person and the virtuous deed.
I am certainly female and male, and asexual as well.
And whatever thing, anywhere, you see or hear,
That entire thing I pervade, ever abiding inside it and outside.

There is nothing at all, moving or unmoving, that is devoid of me...[4]

Worship of the goddess and cultivation of ecstatic yearning for the Absolute continued to flourish within the *bhakti* movements that proliferated throughout India, similar in style to the poems of Andal (see Chapter 11).

Another greatly loved writer, who also composed devotional verse, was the Kashmiri poet Lalla, also known as Lal Ded (c.1355–c.1391). Although we know she was born in the village of Pandrenthan, very little is known of her actual life. Married at the age of 12, she was mistreated by her cruel husband and jealous mother-in-law. Abandoning her home at 24, she became a student of both a Shaivite teacher and a Sufi master and, as a consequence, she is revered by Hindus and Muslims alike to this very day.

As Lalla fell more and more in love with God, she lost all concern for her worldly existence and lived a life allegedly dancing naked through the streets in a state of trancelike ecstasy. One such legend tells of the time when she was ridiculed for her state of undress. Obtaining cloth from a merchant, she ripped it equally into two strips, placing one strip upon each shoulder. Throughout the day, when she received praise, she would tie a knot in one strip; when she received criticism, she would tie a knot in the other. At the end of the day, Lalla asked the cloth merchant to weigh both pieces to prove they were of identical weight, concluding that praise and criticism should be greeted with equanimity, for they are complementary elements of the fabric of life.

Written in an old Kashmiri dialect, Lalla's poetry is structurally sparse and yet suffused with metaphor and emotion. Comparing living in the world with taking the mystical path, she says:

Loosen the load of sweetness I'm carrying.
The sling-knot is biting into my shoulder.

This day has been so meaningless.
I feel I can't go on.

When I was with my teacher, I heard a truth
that hurt my heart like a blister,

the tender pain of seeing
something I loved as an illusion.

The flocks I tended are gone.
I am a shepherd without even a memory

of what that means, climbing this mountain.
I feel so lost.

This is my inward way, until I came
into the presence of a Moon, this new knowledge

of how likenesses unite. Good Friend,
everything is You, I see only God.

Now the delightful forms and motions
are transparent. I look through them

and see myself as the Absolute. And here's
the answer to the riddle of this dream:

You leave, so that we two
can do One Dance.[5]

As a devotee of Siva, her verse also explores the passionate and erotic infatuation she has for her Lord, where lover and Beloved are united:

I, Lalla, entered the jasmine garden,
where Siva and Shakti were making love.

I dissolved into them,
and what is this
to me, now?

I seem to be here,
but really I'm walking
in the jasmine garden.[6]

Her beliefs being a philosophical blend of Sufism and Kashmiri Shaivism (a Tantric path wherein Siva represents universal consciousness), Lalla's words are steeped in the knowledge that the purpose of life is to merge with the universal Self, reiterating *tat tvam asi* ("thou art That"), the maxim from the Upanishads:

Everything is new now for me.
My mind is new, the moon, the sun.
The whole world looks rinsed with water,
washed in the rain of I am That.

Lalla leaps and dances inside the energy
that creates and sustains the universe.[7]

As she cavorts and sings through the streets, she has the realization that her ego must die if she is to attain immortal life:

Self inside self, You are nothing but me.
Self inside self, I am only You.

What we are together
will never die.

The why and how of this?
What does it matter?[8]

Many other beautiful poems and songs were written during this period, including the celebrated *Gita Govinda*, the erotic love song of Radha and Krishna. Written by the wandering mendicant and poet Jayadeva in the 12th century, its popularity spread throughout the subcontinent and is still sung in temples today. Recalling the intense passion of the biblical Song of Songs, the explicit eroticism of the *Gita Govinda* weaves its way through the psychology of courtship, with the delight and delirium of two young lovers ultimately merging in their love for one another and their devotion to God.

Up until Jayadeva's classic work, Radha had little place in Indian literature, being only referred to in selected texts, specifically the poetry of Andal. Now, she takes centre stage. As the proud and passionate woman who absorbs

Krishna's full attention, the Lord of the Gopis pleads with Radha to win her as his principal consort:

You are my ornament, my life,
My jewel in the sea of existence.
Be yielding to me forever,
My heart fervently pleads!
    Radha, cherished love,
    Abandon your baseless pride!
    Love's fire burns my heart –
    Bring wine in your lotus mouth![9]

Testing and teasing Krishna, Radha ultimately yields to her lover in an act of ecstatic lovemaking:

Displaying her passion
In loveplay as the battle began,
She launched a bold offensive
Above him
And triumphed over her lover.
Her hips were still,
Her vine-like arm was slack,
Her chest was heaving,
Her eyes were closed.
Why does a mood of manly force
Succeed for women in love?

Then, as he idled after passionate love,
Radha, wanting him to ornament her,
Freely told her lover,
Secure in her power over him.[10]

Many women were inspired by Radha's example, each wanting to be Krishna's exclusive lover. The Rajasthani poet Mirabai (1498–1565) was no exception, and her verse has made her one of the most commemorated female saints in northern India. Born in the village of Chaukari in the Merta District of Rajasthan, she lived during a time of intense political unrest under the ruling Afghan Empire. Legend recounts how the young and beautiful princess answered the palace gate to give food to a *sadhu*, who in return thrust into her palm a tiny statue of Krishna, which she treasured for the rest of her life, resolving to marry him and addressing him by the name, Shyam, the Dark One.

Unfortunately, as was the custom, she was forced into an arranged marriage with Prince Bhoj Raj, the son of a great warrior from a neighbouring household. Knowing herself to be already betrothed to her beloved Shyam, she refused to consummate the marriage, causing great animosity between herself, her husband and her interfering mother-in-law. Chance played a role when her husband lost his life soon after on the battlefield, leaving Mirabai to devote herself exclusively to her true beloved.

However, fuelled by grief and anger, her husband's family allegedly attempted to have her murdered, so she quickly left town, spending the rest of her days visiting temples and wandering through forests. She ended up in the holy city of Vrindavan in Uttar Pradesh, Shyam's childhood home.

Composed in Marwari, a dialect of Hindi, Mirabai's exquisite poetry joins the distinguished canon of *bhakti* literature. Although similar in theme to Lalla's spiritual eroticism, Mirabai's style is much more visceral in its use of metaphor. Speaking of the price she has paid regarding her mystical life, she writes:

My friend, I went to the market and bought the Dark One.
You claim by night, I claim by day.
Actually, I was beating a drum all the time I was buying him.
You say I gave too much; I say too little.
Actually, I put him on a scale before I bought him.
What I paid was my social body, my town body, my family
    body, and all my inherited jewels.
Mirabai says: The Dark One is my husband now.
Be with me when I lie down; you promised me this in an
    earlier life.[11]

Krishna is presented as a bewitching and beguiling lover, just out of reach and always in the arms of another. And yet, just when all hope is fading, a glimpse is enough to restore her faith:

Another night
sleepless;
tossing in bed,
reaching for someone not there.
Tossed darkness
life wasted
a tossed mind convulsing all night.
Another night sleepless and then,
the bright dawn.[12]

After the dark night of the soul, liberation finally comes with the morning sunlight, her very being transcending life and death itself:

What do I care for the words of the world?
The name of the Dark One has entered my heart.
Those who praise, those who blame,
Those who say I am crazy, wicked, an uncontrollable fire –
All ignorant fools, caught in their senses.
It is true, Mira has no sense: she is lost in the sweetness.
To take this path is to walk the edge of the sword;
Then the noose of birth and death is suddenly cut.
Mira lives now beyond Mira.
She swims, deep mind and deep body, in Shyam's ocean.[13]

Mirabai was acutely conscious of her female status in the world – on the one hand it meant subjugation to the rules of patriarchs and the men in her life; on the other, it gave her licence for a lover's relationship with Shyam. However, ultimately it is all spume on the sea of samsara:

Why life,
why again,
and what reason birth as a woman?
Good deeds in former lives they say.
But –
growth, cut, cut, decline –
life disappears second by second
and never comes back,
a leaf torn from its branch
twists away.
Look at this raging ocean of life forms,
swift, unappeasable,
everything caught in its tide.
O beloved, take this raft quickly
and lead it to shore.[14]

When Mirabai died, she was the distinguished author of some 1,400 verses, comprising poems, *ragas* (melodic frameworks for improvisation in Indian classical music) and *bhajans* (religious songs). Such is her literary legacy that her image has been immortalized in many of the delicate paintings produced by the 18th-century Kangra artists from Himachal Pradesh in northern India, who were similarly inspired by the love stories of the *Devi Bhagavata Purana*.

Of course, the most famous treatise to come out of India celebrating the nature of love between a man and a woman is the *Kama Sutra* ("Aphorisms of Love"), commonly viewed as a manual on the art of lovemaking but originally conceived as a Tantric aid to spiritual development. Composed by Vatsyayana, sometime during the opening half of the first millennium, it contains over a thousand *shlokas* guiding the spiritual aspirant in their perfection of sexual intimacy:

> Kama is the enjoyment of appropriate objects by the five senses of hearing, feeling, seeing, tasting and smelling, assisted by mind together with the soul. The ingredient in this is a peculiar contact between the organ of sense and its object, and the consciousness of pleasure which arises from that contact is called Kama.[15]

Later texts such as the *Ananga Ranga* ("The Art of Love"), written by the Indian poet, Kalyanamalla, and *The Perfumed Garden* by the Muslim poet, Shaykh Umar Ibn Muhammed al-Nefzawi, both in the 15th century, also give advice for choosing the best lover, sexual positions and the most auspicious times of the month for having the most satisfying intercourse.

What a liberating contrast to the West's dismissal of the body, perceived merely as a lump of stinking flesh, fit only for self-inflicted pain and flagellation. No wonder the sacred texts of India, specifically those associated with sexual pleasure, have found an enthusiastic audience in modern-day homes in the West.

CHAPTER SEVENTEEN

NEOPLATONISM AND CARMELITE TERESA OF AVILA

When the soul is, in this prayer,
truly dead to the world,
a little white butterfly comes forth . . .

After the scholasticism of the Middle Ages in the West, the next notable period in history would see a rebirth of the classical values associated with ancient Greece and Rome. The Renaissance, starting in 14th-century Italy and continuing throughout Europe for the following three centuries, saw yet another profound shift in the level of human consciousness. Drawing much on the metaphysical ideas of Plato, Renaissance Humanism advocated that human beings were at the centre of the universe, untainted by original sin and controlling their very own destiny. This independent attitude would particularly inspire one of the most respected Spanish female mystics of the period, Teresa of Avila.

One such body of writing that had considerable influence on Renaissance thinking was the *Corpus Hermeticum*, believed to be written by the legendary figure Hermes Trismegistus (a contemporary of the biblical Moses) and brought to Florence by a monk from Macedonia. Belonging to a non-Christian lineage of Hellenistic Gnosticism, it was translated from the Greek by Marsilio Ficino (1433–99) at the behest of Cosimo de Medici, a wealthy patron of the Arts.

The books of the *Corpus Hermeticum* deal with subject matter concerning the individual's relationship with the Divine and, more specifically, the way the universe is a manifestation of masculine and feminine principles, yet cradled in the All:

> Look upon things through me and contemplate the Kosmos as it lies before your eyes, that body which no harm can touch, the most ancient of all things, yet ever in its prime and ever new. See too the seven subject worlds, marshalled in everlasting order, and filling up the measure of everlasting time as they run their diverse courses. And all things are filled with light . . . and the Sun is the begetter of all good, the ruler of all ordered movement, and the governor of the seven worlds. Look at the Moon, who outstrips all the other planets in her course, the instrument by which birth and growth are wrought, the worker of change in matter here below. Look at the earth, firm-seated at the centre, the foundation of this goodly universe, the feeder and nurse of all terrestrial creatures . . . And all are filled with soul, and all are in movement, immortals in heaven and mortals upon earth [. . .]
>
> God is the All; and there is nothing that is not included in the All . . . and the All permeates all things, and has to do with all things.[1]

Neoplatonism reached many shores, including England and the court of Queen Elizabeth I (1533–1603), a keen champion of artistic endeavour and philosophical enquiry. The radical ideas from the continent blossomed under her reign and, in a time when women had little say in public life, she was able to utilize her femininity to full advantage.

One particular poet who attended the palace circle of the Virgin Queen was Edmund Spenser (1552–99). In honour of his sovereign, he composed the epic lyrical poem *The Faerie Queene*, an allegory of the human soul. Set in the court of Gloriana, it is also a celebration of Elizabeth, one of the greatest monarchs England has ever known:

> ... *O Goddess heavenly bright,*
> *Mirror of grace and majesty divine,*
> *Great Lady of the greatest isle, whose light*
> *Like Phoebus' lamp throughout the world doth shine,*
> *Shed thy fair beams into my feeble eye,*
> *And raise my thoughts too humble and too vile,*
> *To think of that true glorious type of thine ...*[2]

Interestingly, in an age that saw the triumph of reason over religious superstition, Elizabeth becomes the personification of the Mother Goddess. Portraits commissioned by her make use of the traditional symbols always associated with a female deity – the Tudor rose and the fleur-de-lis, the serpent and the sword, the branches of the olive tree.

However, the most important writer of Elizabeth's royal household was William Shakespeare (1564–1616), probably the greatest poet and dramatist who has ever written in the English language. Deeply passionate about contemporary Neoplatonist philosophy, he embodied his beliefs in his masterpiece *The Tempest*, an allegory of the human psyche and its yearning for love and self-knowledge.

Speaking of the fragile nature of human existence, Prospero (based on the Renaissance magus Doctor John Dee) declares:

> *Our revels now are ended. These our actors,*
> *As I foretold you, were all spirits and*
> *Are melted into air, into thin air:*
> *And, like the baseless fabric of this vision,*
> *The cloud-capp'd towers, the gorgeous palaces,*
> *The solemn temples, the great globe itself,*
> *Ye all which it inherit, shall dissolve*
> *And, like this insubstantial pageant faded,*
> *Leave not a rack behind. We are such stuff*
> *As dreams are made on, and our little life*
> *Is rounded with a sleep.*[3]

Time and transience, love and loss, were common themes within much of the literary output of this period, in particular a group of writers known as the Metaphysical Poets, which included John Donne, George Herbert, Andrew Marvell, Henry Vaughan and Thomas Traherne.

In many ways, the nondual vision of the medieval Christian mystics was distilled within the literary conceits of writers of the Renaissance. For example, in Andrew Marvell's "The Garden", which extols a paradise in nature, the poet recalls a moment of transcendental ecstasy:

> *What wondrous life is this I lead!*
> *Ripe apples drop about my head;*
> *The luscious clusters of the vine*

Upon my mouth do crush their wine;
The nectarene, and curious peach,
Into my hands themselves do reach;
Stumbling on melons, as I pass,
Ensnared with flowers, I fall on grass.

Meanwhile the mind, from pleasures less,
Withdraws into its happiness:
The mind, that ocean where each kind
Does straight its own resemblance find,
Yet it creates, transcending these,
Far other worlds, and other seas,
Annihilating all that's made
To a green thought in a green shade.[4]

Indeed, the idea of sacred greenness is also reminiscent of Hildegard's own mystical vision of the natural world and the immanence of the Absolute.

Back in mainland Europe, scholars and monks were describing the nondual message in more conventional terms, specifically through the format of autobiographical prose and dialogue. One such exponent was Nicholas of Cusa (1401–64), who was born in the Rhineland and grew up with an insatiable appetite for the mystical writings of philosophers such as Plato and Meister Eckhart.

At 28, he experienced the complete realization of God and, thereafter, spent the rest of his life writing about the spiritual path. In his book, *De Sapientia* ("On Wisdom"), Nicholas outlines the difference between knowledge attainable through intellectual learning and that from direct experience. Written as a dialogue between teacher and pupil, he states that true wisdom is only achieved through love and grace:

Wisdom is not to be found in the art of oratory, or in great books, but in a withdrawal from these sensible things and in turning to the most simple and infinite forms. You will learn how to receive it into a temple purged from all vice, and by fervent love to cling to it until you may taste it and see how sweet That is which is all sweetness. Once this has been tasted, all things which you now consider as important will appear as vile and you will be so humbled that no arrogance or other vice will remain in you. Once having tasted this wisdom, you will inseparably adhere to it with a chaste and pure heart. You will choose rather to forsake this world and all else that is not of this wisdom, and living with unspeakable happiness you will die. After death, you will rest eternally in that fond embrace which the eternally blessed wisdom of God Himself vouchsafed to grant both to you and to me.[5]

Despite Nicholas trying to make the case for direct experience as the goal, various schisms and political upheavals focusing on the minutiae of interpretation of Christ's teachings were rocking the Western religious establishment. The Renaissance may have freed men and women's minds but, as in any break with tradition, its repercussions had both positive and negative effects.

In an attempt to expose the corrupt practices within the Roman Catholic Church, the German theologian Martin Luther (1483–1546) published his infamous *Ninety-Five*

Theses, which in turn precipitated the Protestant Reformation. And yet, despite his desire for change, Luther still clung on to his misogynistic ideas regarding the value of women. In a series of lectures given on Genesis, he repeatedly emphasizes the inferiority of the female gender because of Eve's transgression:

> Hence it follows that if the woman had not been deceived by the serpent and had not sinned, she would have been the equal of Adam in all respects. For the punishment, that she is now subjected to the man, was imposed on her after sin and because of sin, just as the other hardships and dangers were: travail, pain, and countless other vexations.[6]

On the contentious issue of sex, Luther takes the extraordinary position of condemning women for being wanton temptresses on the one hand yet exonerating men's lustful desire for them on the other:

> And so, in the case of the woman, we must think not only of the managing of the household which she does, but also of the medicine which she is. In this respect, Paul says (I Corinthians 7:2): "Because of fornication let each one have his own wife." And the Master of the *Sentences* declares learnedly that matrimony was established in Paradise as a duty, but after sin also as an antidote. Therefore we are compelled to make use of this sex in order to avoid sin. It is almost shameful to say this, but nevertheless it is true. For there are very few who marry solely as a matter of duty.[7]

Luther's "cake-and-eat-it" philosophy truly beggars belief. Furthermore, his French contemporary, John Calvin (1509–64) in his *Institutes of the Christian Religion* was also an advocate of the importance of marriage for men as a means of avoiding the "sin" of lust and fornication.

Luther and Calvin's philosophical stance produced a retaliatory revolution within the Catholic Church itself, known as the Counter Reformation, in an attempt to oppose the rising effects of Protestantism. Central to the enforcement of this movement were the Roman Inquisitors, originally established by the papacy in the Middle Ages, who were now responsible for flushing out perceived Protestant traitors throughout Renaissance Europe.

In Spain, the Inquisition effortlessly shifted its focus from recent ethnic cleansing of Muslims and Jews onto more general dissenters, who were perceived to be against the Catholic teachings. In fact, Tomas de Torquemada, the infamous Inquisitor General, would torture and murder tens of thousands of heretics – particularly women – all in the name of upholding the accepted orthodoxy of the Catholic Church.

Into such a heated climate was born one of the most famous mystics of all time – Juan de la Cruz (1542–91). More commonly known as John of the Cross, he was born Juan de Yepes y Alvarez in Fontiveros, a small village just outside Avila in Old Castile. At a young age he was sent to a church orphanage, where he quickly showed a calling for the priesthood, and, at the age of 25, he was ordained.

It was around this time that John met the nun Teresa of Avila, who had already founded a Reformed Order of Carmelite nuns called the Discalced (barefoot) Carmelites. She had been searching for a suitable monk to serve as confessor to the sisters in a convent in Medina, and John readily agreed, as her more ascetic approach to the contemplative life greatly appealed to him. He proved to be a great inspiration and guide to both the sisters and all those he graced with his presence.

However, the ecclesiastical authorities were less impressed, and mounting jealousies and suspicions culminated in John's imprisonment by the Inquisition. Entombed in a small stone privy-closet for nine months, he eventually managed to escape and, despite the physical ordeal, was inspired to compose his seminal *Dark Night of the Soul*, a beautiful allegory describing the anguish of the inner being for its Beloved:

In a dark night,
With anxious love inflamed,
O, happy lot!
Forth unobserved I went,
My house being now at rest.

In darkness and in safety,
By the secret ladder, disguised,
O, happy lot!
In darkness and concealment,
My house being now at rest.

In that happy night,
In secret, seen of none,
Seeing nought myself,
Without other light or guide
Save that which in my heart was burning.

That light guided me
More surely than the noonday sun
To the place where He was waiting for me,
Whom I knew well,
And where none appeared.

O, guiding night;
O, night more lovely than the dawn;
O, night that hast united
The lover with His beloved,
And changed her into her love.

On my flowery bosom,
Kept whole for Him alone,
There He reposed and slept;
And I cherished Him, and the waving
Of the cedars fanned Him.

As His hair floated in the breeze
That from the turret blew,
He struck me on the neck
With His gentle hand,
And all sensation left me.

I continued in oblivion lost,
My head was resting on my love;
Lost to all things and myself,
And, amid the lilies forgotten,
Threw all my cares away.[8]

In the same manner as the beguines, John implores seekers
to renounce all worldly attachments to denude the soul of

its desires and cravings, a theme he reiterates in another of his profound works, *Ascent of Mount Carmel*:

> To reach satisfaction in all, desire its possession in nothing. To come to possess all, desire the possession of nothing. To arrive at being all, desire to be nothing. To come to the knowledge of all, desire the knowledge of nothing. To come to the pleasure you have not, you must go by a way of no pleasure. To come to the knowledge you have not, you must go by a way of unknowing. To come to the possession you have not, you must go by way of poverty. To come to be what you are not, you must go by a way of non-existence.[9]

John remained a close friend and confidant of Teresa until her death, and yet they outwardly led very different lives. Born in Avila of mixed Jewish and Christian heritage, Teresa Sanchez de Cepeda y Ahumada (1515–82) was one of ten children, and when she was only 12 years old her mother died. At 16, she was placed in a girls' boarding school run by Augustinian nuns where she decided to take the veil herself, entering the Carmelite Monastery of the Incarnation in Avila at the age of 21 as a novice.

Two years later, Teresa was struck down by an illness so severe that it put her in a coma for four days, leaving her almost paralysed for the following three years. Her acute suffering lasted well into her late 30s, and she also struggled inwardly between a life devoted toward God and a life in thrall to the world.

Then, in 1554, an experience reconfirmed her allegiance to the cloistered life. While reading the *Confessions* of St

Augustine, in which he hears the voice of God calling him homeward, she too felt a similar presence beckoning her from within. She would later write that such was the overwhelming intensity from this time onward that she began a newly committed life.

Teresa's conversion precipitated a sequence of mystical visions and intellectual insights. In an attempt to make sense of them, she set about writing them all down. Her autobiography, *Life*, published in 1562, immediately attracted praise for its depth of spiritual understanding, executed with breathtaking candour. Like her Christian sisters before her, she was also at pains to excuse her "wretched" female status, indicating that she only wrote about her experiences at her confessor's instruction.

Writing in basic Spanish in peculiar syntax with little punctuation, she repeatedly describes her abject condition:

> For I am not learned nor have I led a good life, and I have neither a scholar nor anyone else to guide me. Only those who have commanded me to write this know that I am doing so, and they are not here at present. I have almost to steal the time for writing, and that with difficulty, because it hinders me from spinning, and I am living in a poor house where there is a great deal to do. If the Lord had given me greater skill and a better memory, I might have profited by what I have heard and read. But I have very little of either. So if anything I have said is right, it is because the Lord has willed it for some good purpose of His own . . .[10]

This may not be as self-deprecatory as it first appears – the Spanish Inquisition would have been hot on the heels of anyone offering anything other than an orthodox interpretation of Christ's message. So, by renouncing all responsibility for authorship, Teresa was effectively protecting herself and her fellow sisters from potentially lethal repercussions.

Shortly after, Teresa founded the monastery of St Joseph in Avila. In contrast to the 200 or so nuns living in the Carmelite Monastery of the Incarnation in Avila, only 12 sisters shared the new convent. In spite of the physical hardships, the project was a great success – life was focused predominantly on contemplative prayer, which suited Teresa's thoughtful temperament. By 1567 and inspired by her initiative, she had already had her fateful meeting with John of the Cross, who helped her go on to establish further Carmelite monasteries throughout Spain.

Teresa spent the rest of her life travelling, meeting both the learned and the unlettered in an attempt to popularize her unique way of devotion. In the face of ecclesiastical resistance and many hardships, particularly as a woman in her later years, her fortitude was testament to her courage and piety. By the time of her death in Alba, she was still out on the road dispensing her godly advice and had established 14 Carmelite monasteries, as well as amassing a voluminous correspondence with some of the most famous people of the day, including King Philip II of Spain.

Throughout her busy life, Teresa still managed to produce some of the most beautiful and profound mystical writings, combining theoretical teaching with personal experience. Never pausing to reflect upon what she had just written, she once stated that she wished she could write with both hands so she could get her thoughts onto paper more quickly.

In *Life*, Teresa speaks of her bodily afflictions and spiritual struggles. A keen user of metaphor, she outlines the stages along the mystical path in terms of irrigating a plot of land, in her analogy of the "four waters". The soul, Teresa explains, is a garden, growing on barren soil and full of weeds. "His Majesty" pulls out the weeds and then plants good seeds in the freshly ploughed soil. It is then the individual's responsibility to water the garden, with four methods of irrigation described, representing the stages of prayer through which the soul must pass to obtain salvation.

The first stage is extremely hard because of the individual's inexperience, and to demonstrate this, Teresa uses the image of drawing water from a well. The second stage is similarly challenging, illustrated by turning the crank of a waterwheel and using a system of aqueducts. The third stage is where God intervenes in the process, with Teresa describing using water that comes straight from a spring or a river. The fourth and final stage is where the metaphorical garden is simply watered by the celestial rains from above:

I am now speaking of that rain that comes down abundantly from heaven to soak and saturate the whole garden. If the Lord never ceased to send it whenever it was needed, the gardener would certainly have leisure; and if there were no winter but always a temperate climate, there would never be a shortage of fruit and flowers, and the gardener would clearly be delighted. But this is impossible while we live, for we must always be looking out for one water when another fails. The heavenly rain very often comes down when the gardener least expects it. Yet it is true that at the beginning it almost comes after long mental prayer.[11]

The Lord then speaks to Teresa about the nature of the individual soul upon the blossoming of the garden:

"It dissolves utterly, my daughter, to rest more and more in Me. It is no longer itself that lives: it is I. As it cannot comprehend what it understands, it understands by not understanding."[12]

Her next major text, written for her fellow sisters in the convent and completed in 1565, is *The Way of Perfection*, a treatise on the power of prayer in which she insists that being dispassionate toward worldly things is a prerequisite for peace of the soul:

Once we have detached ourselves from the world, and from our kinsfolk, and are cloistered here, in the conditions already described, it must look as if we have done everything and there is nothing left with which we have to contend. But, oh my sisters, do not feel secure and fall asleep, or you will be like a man who goes to bed quite peacefully, after bolting all his doors for fear of thieves, when the thieves are already in the house. And you know there is no worse thief *than one who lives in the house*. We ourselves are always the same; unless we take great care and each of us looks well to it that she renounces her self-will, which is the most important business of all, there will be many things to deprive us of the holy freedom of spirit *which our souls seek* in order to soar to their Master unburdened by the leaden weight of the earth.[13]

However, this does not mean that one should cultivate a sterile heart. Just like the replenishing rain, every sister's soul needs constant love and reassurance:

The soul is like an infant still at its mother's breast: such is the mother's care for it that she gives it its milk without its having to ask for it so much as by moving its lips. That is what happens here. The will simply loves, and no effort needs to be made by the understanding, for it is the Lord's pleasure that, without exercising its thought, the soul should realize that it is in His company, and should merely drink the milk which His Majesty puts into its mouth and enjoy its sweetness.[14]

Without doubt, Teresa's masterpiece is *The Interior Castle*, written a decade later, when she was in her early 60s. The most extraordinary fact concerning its composition is that it fell under the shadow of the Inquisition and, in particular, the encroaching presence of Tomas de Torquemada. Rumours abounded that he was on his way to Avila to quash Teresa's work and the Carmelite Order. Thankfully, a Spanish papal ambassador who favoured her efforts was able to divert the Inquisitor's attention elsewhere.

Incredibly, in the midst of such deadly political machinations, she was able to write what is arguably one of the most sublime allegories on the human soul ever produced. Setting the scene of her work, Teresa writes:

> . . . there came to my mind what I shall now speak about, that which will provide us with a basis to begin with. It is that we consider our soul to be like a castle made entirely out of a diamond or of very clear crystal, in which there are many rooms, just as in heaven there are many dwelling places.[15]

In her dazzling analogy, there are seven dwelling places in total – the first three representing the stages of human effort, principally through prayer and divine intervention, and the remaining four dealing with mystical aspects of the spiritual path. However, Teresa is quick to point out the underlying paradox of her explanation:

> It seems I'm saying something foolish. For if this castle is the soul, clearly one doesn't have to enter it since it is in oneself. How foolish it would seem were we to tell someone to enter a room he is already in. But you must understand that there is a great difference in the ways one may be inside the castle. For there are many souls who are in the outer courtyard – which is where the guards stay – and don't care at all about entering the castle, nor do they know what lies within that most precious place, nor who is within, nor even how many rooms it has. You have already heard in some books on prayer that the soul is advised to enter within itself; well, that's the very thing I'm advising.[16]

In the fifth dwelling place, Teresa uses the metaphor of a silkworm to describe the soul's metamorphosis, spinning itself a cocoon:

> Therefore, courage, my daughters! Let's be quick to do this work and weave this little cocoon by taking away our self-love and self-will, our attachment to any earthly thing [. . .] Let it die; let this silkworm die, as it does in completing what it was created to do! And you will see how we see God, as well as ourselves placed inside His grandeur, as is this little silkworm within its cocoon [. . .]
>
> When the soul is, in this prayer, truly dead to the world, a little white butterfly comes forth [. . .] Truly, I tell you that the soul doesn't recognize itself. Look at the difference there is between an ugly worm and a little white butterfly.[17]

This is not quite the end of the journey. In spite of its newly found freedom, the butterfly cannot find rest, flitting from one place to another. It is only in the sixth dwelling place that union with God may take place, where Teresa switches to the allegory of the esoteric relationship between lover and Beloved. Yet there is still one final stage, the seventh dwelling place, where there is total absorption in God and the two lovers are joined in mystical marriage:

> The spiritual betrothal is different, for the two often separate. And the union is also different because, even though it is the joining of two things into one, in the end the two can be separated and each remains by itself [. . .] Let us say that the union is like the

joining of two wax candles to such an extent that the flame coming from them is but one, or that the wick, the flame, and the wax are all one. But afterward one candle can be easily separated from the other and there are two candles; the same holds for the wick. In the spiritual marriage the union is like what we have when rain falls from the sky into a river or fount; all is water, for the rain that fell from heaven cannot be divided or separated from the water of the river. Or it is like what we have when a little stream enters the sea, there is no means of separating the two. Or, like the bright light entering a room through two different windows; although the streams of light are separate when entering the room, they become one.[18]

Teresa composed many other short tracts and testimonies, drawing on her wealth of self-examination and insight. Her lesser-known work, *Meditations on the Song of Songs*, is one of the pinnacles of her devotional prose, composed in roughly 1566. Only seven chapters long, it focuses on the image of Christ personified as the Divine Mother, a similar motif to that found in the writings of Julian of Norwich (see Chapter 15).

When Teresa was on her deathbed and ready to be received into the bosom of Christ, she recited verses from the original Song of Songs. How befitting it is that her statue, the *Ecstasy of St Teresa*, sculpted by Gian Lorenzo Bernini and housed in the Cornaro Chapel of the Church of Santa Maria della Vittoria in Rome, depicts a woman swathed in flowing robes, lost in the rapture of love.

CHAPTER EIGHTEEN
JUDAISM AND MYSTIC GRACE AGUILAR

This – this is peace! Disturb it not,
To heav'n that dream has won me,
Oh let me lie, the world forgot –
God's eye alone upon me!

There is no doubt that the Spanish Inquisition perpetrated some of the most heinous crimes against humanity the modern world has ever seen, in an attempt to crush unorthodox teachings. But Spain had also been the centre of a great mystical tradition. Conquered by Arabs in the eighth century, it was home to a handful of eminent Muslim sages who were versed in the Platonist philosophy of the Greeks as well as the esoteric message of Islam.

In the 11th century, Spain also became refuge to a large Jewish population, who brought with them their own wisdom traditions of the Apocrypha and books of the Old Testament. A similar community would flourish centuries later in England, with one woman, Grace Aguilar, taking it upon herself to document the entire history of Jewish women right back to the time of Eve.

Into this metaphysical mix was born Solomon Ibn Gabirol (1021–58) in Malaga, southern Spain, whose most famous prose work, *Fons Vitae* ("Fountain of Life"), is a description of the nature of reality and the creation of the universe. However, it is within his poetry where Gabirol's mystical insight is the most beautifully crafted. Like many enlightened sages before him, he also employs a feminine soul to be the embodiment of life:

> *At Thy word, "Be, O soul," she took on existence,*
> *And from Thy Emptiness Thou didst draw her forth as light*
> *   from the eye.*
> *It was Thee who didst breathe in her life; I shall proclaim and*
> *   affirm this with uplifted hands.*
> *And therefore she shall pour out her thanks and give witness*
> *   that she was bidden to do by Thee.*
> *While yet in the body, she serves Thee as a handmaid;*
> *And on that day when she returns to the land from whence*
> *   she came,*
> *In Thee will she dwell, for in Thee is her being.*
> *Whether she sits or rises, Thou art with her the same.*
> *She was Thine before she was born and breathing;*
> *She was nourished by Thee with wisdom and knowledge,*
> *And it is to Thee she looks for her guidance and sustenance [...]*
> *Let her pour out her tears as the wine on the altar,*
> *And let the breath of her sighs rise as fragrance to Thee.*
> *At her gate and her doorway, she watches in prayer;*
> *She is burning like flame with her passion for Thee.*[1]

The idea of the sacred feminine would be developed further in a related but separate phenomenon known as the Kabbalah (meaning "the tradition"), which flourished during 12th-century Spain and southern France. The Kabbalistic teaching was later systematized by Moses de Leon (1240–1305) in his book *Zohar* ("Splendour"), a mystical interpretation of the first five books of the Torah, the Hebrew Bible. To accelerate its popularity, he cunningly claimed that the text was an ancient tract written by Shimeon ben Yohai, a second-century CE Palestinian monk, and it was only in the 19th century that scholars learned of the fraud.

The *Zohar* starts by describing the birth of the created world out of the Infinite:

In the beginning, when the Will of the King began to take effect, He impressed His signs into the heavenly sphere. Within the Most Hidden, the Infinite, a dark flame issued forth, like a fog forming in the Unformed.

Forming the concentric ring of that [first] sphere, [this flame was] neither white nor black, neither red nor green, of no colour whatever. Only after this flame began to assume size and dimension, did it produce radiant colours. From the innermost centre of the flame gushed forth a host of colours which spread on everything beneath. Concealed within all was the hidden mystery of the Infinite.[2]

In the Kabbalah tradition, the Infinite or Yahweh is perceived as masculine, while the soul, known as the Shekhinah, is regarded as feminine and is separated from Yahweh by a veil of ignorance. The purpose of every individual's life is to lift the veil to merge with Yahweh – in other words, reconciling masculine and feminine into one.

Sadly, yet again, veneration of the sacred feminine effectively became outlawed in the Judaic tradition, with women being exiled from scholastic and mystical practice. The irony of such a misogynistic interpretation is that at the very heart of the Kabbalah is the equal status of men and women alike. In the *Zohar* itself, Moses de Leon stresses their role as embodiments of divine consciousness. Commenting on the first two verses of Genesis 5, he emphasizes the simultaneous creation of both sexes, equal before God:

High mysteries are revealed in these two verses.
"Male and female He created them"
to make known the Glory on high,
the mystery of faith […]

From here we learn:
Any image that does not embrace male and female
is not a high and true image.
We have established this in the mystery of our Mishnah [Bible
commentary].

Come and see:
The Blessed Holy One does not place His abode
in any place where male and female are not found together.
Blessings are found only in a place where male and female
are found,
as it is written:
"He blessed them and called their name Adam
on the day they were created."
It is not written:
"He blessed him and called his name Adam."
A human being is only called Adam
when male and female are as one.[3]

To all intents and purposes, by the 18th century the Kabbalah was the province of male scholarship alone in Europe. It was during this time that some women decided to redress the balance by creating a body of literature specifically for their own daily purposes. Called *tkhines*, these Yiddish supplicatory prayers were written by women for women. One specific *tkhine* redefines the symbolism of the candle-lighting ceremony on the Sabbath. Rather than accepting the traditional meaning that the burning of the wick is an act of atonement for Eve's "sinfulness" of bringing darkness into the world, it is reinterpreted as the celebration of the sacred Shekhinah.

It would not be until the following century that the voice of an individual woman would emerge to further champion the cause of Jewish women. Grace Aguilar (1816–47) was born in Hackney, London, to Portuguese parents. As a child, she contracted a mysterious disease that left her physically weak for the rest of her short life. Indeed, serious illness appears to be a recurring motif in many of the lives of female mystics.

Being of a Sephardic family, her father was keen to teach Grace about her Portuguese Jewish inheritance. This culminated in her first attempt at writing – a historical romance set during the Spanish Inquisition, titled *The Vale of Cedars*, which she completed while still a teenager and was published after her death.

After living on the south coast of Devon for several years during Grace's teens, the family finally settled in Brighton, where both parents became increasingly infirm. With two younger brothers to take care of, Grace took on the responsibility of providing financially for the family by earning an income through her writing. Initially, her output was predominantly mainstream – she produced a book of flower poems as well as regularly contributing short sketches on domestic life to journals and magazines. She also composed a series of novels – *Home Influence: A Tale for Mothers and Daughters*, *A Mother's Recompense* and *Woman's Friendship* – in which she offers portraits of female role models and the necessity for giving children a religious education.

Although Grace never married, she was a keen advocate of the domestic life as a place for spiritual growth, which in turn would provide a firm foundation for an enlightened society. In the manner of Plato and his analogy of children being like soft wax, Grace stresses the importance of shaping young minds with a moral hand. In *The Spirit of Judaism*, a reworking of the Jewish teaching into a female-centred theology, she emphasizes the responsibility of Jewish mothers toward their offspring:

There is a peculiar sweetness in the remembrance of a mother. When a young man has raised himself by his own virtues and talents in the world, when he feels himself esteemed and beloved by his fellow-men: he will still think of his mother, if it have been from her lips, the first lesson of virtue were imbibed; and if religion were as zealously and carefully implanted, would not her memory have equal influence in guarding him from temptation, strengthening him to walk on the paths she loved? It may be that continued occupation, perhaps arduous labour, or severe thought and study have withdrawn his attention awhile from his God; or that the paths of pleasure, encircling him with their delusive rays, conceal from his eyes the light of eternity. Some sudden association recalls his mother to his mind [. . .] He hears again the sweet and gentle voice which first spoke to him of God; he sees again those happy hours when, seated at her feet, he rested his little hands upon her lap, and repeated with her the words of prayer or listened with tearful eyes, and swelling heart, to the tales of sacred love . . .[4]

Understandably, Grace abhorred the way that the male and female genders were separated in the synagogue, making it quite clear that she believed women should receive the same religious instruction as men. After all, as the biological nurturers of their children's lives and moral guardians of their developing minds and spirits, did it not make rational sense to honour their feminine role?

In 1845, Grace published what is believed to be her literary masterpiece, the three-volume *Women of Israel*, in which she further advocates the female cause by chronicling biographical accounts of significant Jewish women from Eve up to her own time. In it, she reaffirms women's religious experience and offers her own theological commentary. With passion and vigour, she takes the root of misogyny to task:

How or whence originated the charge that the law of Moses sank the Hebrew female to the lowest state of degradation, placed her on a level with slaves or heathens, and denied her all mental and spiritual enjoyment, we know not: yet certain it is that this most extraordinary and unfounded idea obtains credence even in this enlightened age. The word of

God at once proves its falsity; for it is impossible to read the Mosaic law without the true and touching conviction that the female Hebrew was even more an object of the tender and soothing care of the Eternal than the male [. . .]

The Eternal's provision for her temporal and spiritual happiness is proved in His unalterable word; and therefore no Hebrew can believe that He would issue another law for her degradation and abasement [. . .]

The women of the Bible are but mirrors of ourselves. And if the Eternal, in His infinite mercy, extended love, compassion, forbearance, and forgiveness unto them, we may believe He extends them equally unto us . . .[5]

In a reassessment of her Hebrew heritage, Grace also composed the prose short story *Spirit of Night*, a Jewish fable founded on Rabbi Morris Jacob Raphall's *The Sun and the Moon*, itself a creation story based on Genesis. In Raphall's version, the female Moon only receives the reflected light of the male Sun, whereas in Grace's version, the Moon's jealousy of the Sun prompts the Eternal to take pity on her and honour her with equal status:

Queen of the lovely night will thine orb be hailed; the tears of thy repentance shall be a reviving balm to all that languish; imparting consolation to the mourner, rest to the weary, soothing to the care-worn, strength to the exhausted. Peace shall be thy whisper, and in thy kingdom of stillness and repose, breathe thrillingly the promise of Heaven and its rest. Go forth, then, on thy mild and vivifying career. The Orb of Day will do his work, and be hailed with rejoicing mirth; but many a one shall turn to thee from him, and in the radiance of thy tears find consolation.[6]

Also renowned for her poetry, Grace was in fact one of the first Anglo-Jewish women ever to publish verse. Romantic in theme, her poems are infused with the mystical presence of the Eternal. In the opening stanzas of "An Hour of Peace", she speaks of her wish to die and find union with God:

Oh, wake me not from this sweet dream
*   Now o'er my spirit stealing,*
Of heaven's deep calm, a shadowy gleam,
*   This care-worn heart is feeling.*

This is not suff'ring, though my frame,
*   Be weak and pain-struck lying;*
While life's sad cares no thought can claim,
*   There is no need for sighing.*

This – this is peace! Disturb it not,
*   To heav'n that dream has won me,*
Oh let me lie, the world forgot –
*   God's eye alone upon me!...[7]*

And in one of her most beautiful verses, "The Address to the Ocean", which obliquely refers to Lord Byron's "Childe Harold's Pilgrimage" (a poem charting the hero's melancholic reflections), Grace loses her soul in the crash and hiss of the waves:

229

Sound on, thou mighty Deep, sound on, thou Sea,
  Lash thy blue waves to snowy crested foam,
Wake into music, glorious and free,
  Proclaim thee bulwark of our island home.

Sound on! Thou hast a voice of freedom, Sound!
  My soul hath thrilling echoes to thy voice,
And throbs and bounds, as if on thee were found,
  A home where life all chainless, might rejoice! [...]

Let thy rich voice sound on! Roll on thy waves
  'Mid storm and sunshine, still the blue, the free!
Life is upspringing from my soul's deep caves,
  To hail, to bless thee, oh, thou glorious sea![8]

Evoking the ocean iconography of ancient civilizations, the sea is a metaphor for the universal Source, leaving Grace in no doubt about the mystical oneness of the Creator.

To improve her failing health, Grace travelled to Frankfurt and visited her brother, who recommended that she consult an eminent German physician. Her diary entries from this period reveal a woman in great physical pain and emotional turmoil. As she deteriorated further, her new doctor advised her to stop writing, something she had done almost every day from her earliest childhood. And so her journal entry ends abruptly, mid-sentence, on 29 July 1847, just weeks before her death. She was just 31 years old.

Having only had modest success during her lifetime, Grace's literary output subsequently grew in popularity, owing primarily to the efforts of her mother, Sarah

Aguilar, who helped edit and publish all her daughter's books after her death. Similarly, the Aguilar Free Library Society, which is now a branch of the New York Public Library, was established in 1896 in Grace's honour to encourage a love of reading in local Jewish communities. A picture of her engraved portrait, also held at the library, depicts a demure woman with penetrating eyes that hint at the encyclopedic mind behind them, which would go on to enlighten so many generations of women through her revelatory body of work.

CHAPTER NINETEEN

TRANSCENDENTALISM AND POET EMILY DICKINSON

Behind Me – dips Eternity –
Before Me – Immortality –
Myself – the Term between –

By the time we reach the 17th and 18th centuries in Europe, a radical shift in human thinking was yet again taking place. Whereas prior to this, dogma and tradition had been breaking down to allow for more inclusive attitudes toward universal consciousness, philosophers and scientists were now sidelining the spiritual realm in favour of a better understanding of the material world. With its emphasis on reason and empirical evidence, the somewhat ironically titled "Age of Enlightenment" had finally dawned. Although God was still given credence for being the Creator of the world, it was now man and woman who were responsible for understanding Him, unaided by any act of divine intervention, with almost all Christian theology rejected, and, in particular, the concept of original sin. In America, the poet Emily Dickinson would even align herself with a personalized form of paganism.

Out of the array of great European thinkers of the period, it would be René Descartes (1596–1650) who was responsible for inexorably changing the way in which the universe was perceived. Using his "method of doubt", he was able to deconstruct both the physical and mental world around him right down to his very own self. It was only this fact – his own existence – of which he was in absolutely no doubt, leading in turn to his famous axiom, *Je pense, donc je suis* ("I think therefore I am").

Immanuel Kant (1724–1804) would develop Descartes' ideas by labelling the universe according to its component pieces – the physical world, which he called phenomenon; and the spiritual world, which he called noumenon. And yet, in spite of Kant and Descartes' belief in the existence of a divine power, it was now reduced to a philosophical abstraction. Humankind's attention had subsequently shifted from the metaphysical to the physical, from intuition to logic, from sensation to science. In short, reason had triumphed over faith.

However, the pendulum was about to swing back the other way. The following century saw one of the greatest philosophers ever to live, who would synthesize Western philosophy with Eastern mysticism – the German scholar, Arthur Schopenhauer (1788–1860). In his immortal tract, *The World as Will and Representation*, he outlines his unique vision of the cosmos:

> Past and future (apart from the consequences of their content) are as empty and unreal as any dream; but present is only the boundary between the two, having neither extension nor duration. In just the same way, we shall also recognize the same emptiness in all

the other forms of the principle of sufficient reason, and shall see that, like time, space also, and like this, everything exists simultaneously in space and time, and hence everything that proceeds from causes or motives, has only a relative existence, is only through and for another like itself, i.e., only just as enduring. In essence this view is old; in it Heraclitus lamented the eternal flux of things; Plato spoke with contempt of its object as that which for ever becomes, but never is; Spinoza called it mere accidents of the sole substance that alone is and endures; Kant opposed to the thing-in-itself that which is known as mere phenomenon; finally, the ancient wisdom of the Indians declares that "it is Maya, the veil of deception, which covers the eyes of mortals and causes them to see a world of which one cannot say either that it is or that it is not; for it is like a dream, like the sunshine on the sand which the traveller from a distance takes to be water or like the piece of rope on the ground which he regards as a snake."[1]

Allegedly Schopenhauer came to his nondualist vision *before* reading the ancient texts of India, which merely confirmed his understanding and point of view.

He also held that appreciation of the Arts could lead the individual to a momentary release from the independent ego. Painting, sculpture, poetry and, above all, music, lifted the soul above normal concerns and responsibilities, liberating and nourishing it on a wave of artistic bliss:

. . . aesthetic pleasure in the beautiful consists, to a large extent, in the fact that, when we enter the state of pure contemplation, we are raised for the moment above all willing, above all desires and cares; we are, so to speak, rid of ourselves. We are no longer the individual that knows in the interest of its constant willing, the correlative of the particular thing to which objects become motives, but the eternal subject of knowing purified of the will, the correlative of the Idea. And we know that these moments, when, delivered from the fierce pressure of the will, we emerge, as it were, from the heavy atmosphere of the earth, are the most blissful that we experience. From this we can infer how blessed must be the life of a man whose will is silenced not for a few moments, as in the enjoyment of the beautiful, but for ever, indeed completely extinguished, except for the last glimmering spark that maintains the body and is extinguished with it.[2]

Artists directly influenced by his ideas on aesthetics include the writers Leo Tolstoy, Thomas Hardy and Thomas Mann, as well as the composers Richard Wagner and Gustav Mahler, all considered paragons in their respective fields of creative endeavour.

Schopenhauer's metaphysical ideas regarding the Arts were also indirectly reflected in the more general movement of Romanticism, starting in Europe in approximately 1750 and lasting roughly until 1870, and emerging as a backlash against the Age of Enlightenment. Propelled by the belief in the power of the subjective imagination, freedom of individual expression and the inherent sacredness of nature, its raison d'être was in contradistinction to Descartes' infamous declaration.

In fact, the French philosopher Jean-Jacques Rousseau (1712–78) famously retorted in defence of emotion *Je sentis avant de penser* ("I felt before I thought").

Above all, Romantic artists founded their interpretation of the world within the context of an immanent, all-pervading consciousness. This was nowhere more beautifully articulated than by a group of English poets, namely Samuel Taylor Coleridge, Lord Byron, Percy Bysshe Shelley, John Keats and William Wordsworth, whose own "Intimations of Immortality from Recollections of Early Childhood" not only encapsulates the Romantic imagination but is also an exquisite example of the plight of the human soul searching for its source:

> *Our birth is but a sleep and a forgetting:*
> *The Soul that rises with us, our life's Star,*
>   *Hath had elsewhere its setting,*
>   *And cometh from afar:*
>   *Not in entire forgetfulness,*
>   *And not in utter nakedness,*
> *But trailing clouds of glory do we come*
>   *From God, who is our home:*
> *Heaven lies about us in our infancy!*
> *Shades of the prison-house begin to close*
>   *Upon the growing Boy*
>   *But he*
> *Beholds the light, and whence it flows,*
>   *He sees it in his joy;*
> *The Youth, who daily farther from the east*
>   *Must travel, still is Nature's Priest,*
>   *And by the vision splendid*
>   *Is on his way attended;*

At length the Man perceives it die away,
And fade into the light of common day.[3]

The ability to express oneself freely beyond the confines of societal and religious convention enabled more and more women to publish their own writings, with the realm of emotional sensitivity and appreciation of nature being aptly suited for the female pen. One such woman, Christina Rossetti (1830–94), sister of the Pre-Raphaelite painter Dante Gabriel Rossetti, wrote many poems focusing on sacred devotion and romantic love.

Despite living as a recluse in the last 15 years of her life, Christina was still popular and accomplished enough to be considered for the honorific position of Poet Laureate. In the opening stanzas of "Confluents", it is easy to see why:

As rivers seek the sea,
Much more deep than they,
So my soul seeks thee
Far away:
As running rivers moan
On their course alone,
So I moan
Left alone.

As the delicate rose
To the sun's sweet strength
Doth herself unclose,
Breadth and length;
So spreads my heart to thee
Unveiled utterly,

I to thee
Utterly…[4]

Another eminent female writer who lived during this period was Elizabeth Barrett Browning (1806–61). Married to the poet Robert Browning, she too was considered by Wordsworth to be a worthy contender for the illustrious Laureate role. A lover of classical poetry and aesthetic theory, she lived with her husband in Italy, where she wrote *Aurora Leigh*, her major work. A controversial, nine-book novel in blank verse, its epic scope deals with a range of contemporary issues, such as the limited education available to women at that time. The first-person narrator of the poem becomes a writer but, notably, her artistic vocation seems to be incompatible with a woman's domestic role as wife and mother.

Despite the poem's critical social commentary, Elizabeth is enchanted by the natural world around her, as well as being consciously aware of the way it is also the manifestation of something much greater than herself:

Truth, so far, in my book – the truth which draws
Through all things upwards – that a twofold world
Must go to a perfect cosmos. Natural things
And spiritual – who separates those two
In art, in morals or the social drift
Tears up the bond of nature and brings death,
Paints futile pictures, writes unreal verse,
Leads vulgar days, deals ignorantly with men,
Is wrong, in short, at all points. We divide
This apple of life, and cut it through the pips –
The perfect round which fitted Venus' hand

Has perished as utterly as if we ate
Both halves. Without the spiritual, observe,
The natural's impossible – no form,
No motion: without sensuous, spiritual
Is inappreciable – no beauty or power:
And in this twofold sphere the twofold man
(For still the artist is intensely a man)
Holds firmly by the natural, to reach
The spiritual beyond it –...[5]

However, not all women believed that an emotional sensibility was the best means through which a woman could express herself. The rising voice of feminism was growing in Europe, fostered by the enormous political, economic and sociological changes of the time. The most notable female voice was Mary Wollstonecraft (1759–97), whose *A Vindication of the Rights of Women* was essentially the first great feminist treatise. For her, the intellect was the key to individual freedom and, in a stunning piece of wit and intellectual integrity, she states her cause:

My own sex, I hope, will excuse me, if I treat them like rational creatures, instead of flattering their FASCINATING graces, and viewing them as if they were in a state of perpetual childhood, unable to stand alone. I earnestly wish to point out in what true dignity and human happiness consists – I wish to persuade women to endeavour to acquire strength, both of mind and body, and to convince them, that the soft phrases, susceptibility of heart, delicacy of sentiment, and refinement of taste, are almost synonymous with epithets of weakness, and that those beings who are only the objects of pity and that kind of love, which has been termed its sister, will soon become objects of contempt.

Dismissing then those pretty feminine phrases, which the men condescendingly use to soften our slavish dependence, and despising that weak elegancy of mind, exquisite sensibility, and sweet docility of manners, supposed to be the sexual characteristics of the weaker vessel, I wish to show that elegance is inferior to virtue, that the first object of laudable ambition is to obtain a character as a human being, regardless of the distinction of sex; and that secondary views should be brought to this simple touchstone.[6]

Interestingly, her daughter Mary would become the wife of Percy Bysshe Shelley and a writer in her own right.

Not only were feminism and Romanticism infiltrating British and European civilization, but their spirit was also kindling in the United States. A group of predominantly male writers and thinkers emerged, who also placed emphasis on transcendental knowledge and the belief that the soul was immanent throughout the created world. Collectively known as the American Transcendentalists, the movement was a reaction to the intellectual rationalism of the 18th century and the strict Puritan attitudes brought over by Protestant Pilgrim Fathers a century before. Indeed, the Transcendentalists' chief exponent Ralph Waldo Emerson actively campaigned alongside female suffrage movements, championing the equal rights of all women.

Born into this extraordinary transitional period of American history was the female poet Emily Dickinson

(1830–86). Raised in the Massachusetts village of Amherst along with an older brother and a younger sister, this was the time of the Second Great Awakening, a Protestant revival that was sweeping through New England. Refusing to participate in this wave of religious fervour, she decided simply to call herself a "pagan".

Emily started writing poetry in her late 20s, her words revealing the full extent of her unhappiness and sense of isolation as a child. Brought up under strict parentage and religious discipline, she desperately searches for some form of joy beyond her mortal existence:

A loss of something ever felt I –
The first that I could recollect
Bereft I was – of what I knew not
Too young that any should suspect

A Mourner walked among the children
I notwithstanding went about
As one bemoaning a Dominion
Itself the only Prince cast out –

Elder, Today, a session wiser
And fainter, too, as Wiseness is –
I find myself still softly searching
For my Delinquent Palaces –

And a Suspicion, like a Finger
Touches my Forehead now and then
That I am looking oppositely
For the site of the Kingdom of Heaven –[7]

In 1862, Emily submitted four poems to the journal *Atlantic Monthly*, whose editor Colonel Thomas Wentworth Higginson was less than enthusiastic about her verse, finding her poetry unruly and lacking any meaningful structure. However, despite initially advising Emily to delay publication of the poems, he went on to have a 20-year correspondence with her, encouraging her to explore her poetic self.

Emily wrote about many themes: death, nature, romantic love. And yet despite the feeling of mutability and loss of the created world in her work, there is always hope of eternal life. Like the Romanticists before her, the mystical vision of transcendental knowledge beyond all human comprehension suffuses her words:

I felt a Funeral, in my Brain,
And Mourners to and fro
Kept treading – treading – till it seemed
That Sense was breaking through –

And when they all were seated,
A Service, like a Drum –
Kept beating – beating – till I thought
My Mind was going numb –

And then I heard them lift a Box
And creak across my Soul
With those same Boots of Lead, again,
Then Space – began to toll,

As all the Heavens were a Bell,
And Being, but an Ear,

And I, and Silence, some strange Race
Wrecked, solitary, here –

And then a Plank in Reason, broke,
And I dropped down, and down –
And hit a World, at every plunge,
And finished knowing – then –[8]

And then? The poet is poignantly silent. Nonetheless, the death of self is a theme she returns to time and again:

Me from Myself – to banish –
Had I Art –
Impregnable my Fortress
Unto All Heart –

But since Myself – assault Me –
How have I peace
Except by subjugating
Consciousness?

And since We're mutual Monarch
How this be
Except by Abdication –
Me – of Me?[9]

Emily employs an array of visual imagery to represent her metaphysical ideas. Coupled with her eccentric use of pauses, punctuation and irregular rhyming schemes, her verse is a reflection of the unpredictability and transience of both her interior world and the universe itself. She has often been compared to the Metaphysical

Poets, owing to her unique expression and brevity of wit.

One particularly stunning poem employs a landscape analogous to the shapeshifting states of the soul:

I cross till I am weary
A Mountain – in my mind –
More Mountains – then a Sea –
More Seas – And then
A Desert – find –

And My Horizon blocks
With steady – drifting – Grains
Of unconjectured quantity –
As Asiatic Rains –

Not this – defeat my Pace –
It hinder from the West
But as an Enemy's Salute
One hurrying to Rest –

What merit had the Goal –
Except there intervene
Faint Doubt – and far Competitor –
To jeopardize the Gain?

At last – the Grace in sight –
I shout unto my feet –
I offer them the Whole of Heaven
The instant that we meet –

They strive – and yet delay –
They perish – Do we die –
Or is this Death's Experiment –
Reversed – in Victory?[10]

Despite the literary freedom Emily enjoyed in her poems, she was still subjugated to prevailing 19th-century ideology and, in particular, concepts regarding whether or not a female poet should appear in print. Emily was inconsistent on the matter, on the one hand believing equal rights should exist for both male and female artists, and on the other shying away from fame – merely ten of her poems were actually published in her own lifetime.

It was only after her death from Bright's disease (an inflammation of the kidneys) that Emily's vast body of work – nearly 1,800 short lyrics – was discovered, stitched into packets known as fascicles, accumulated in a wooden chest. It was Thomas Wentworth Higginson, her loyal friend and publisher, who was left with the main responsibility of editing and publishing all her poems, bringing her artistic genius finally into the world.

One poet who had a profound effect on Emily was Elizabeth Barrett Browning, her verse novel *Aurora Leigh* having been given to her by Emily's brother's wife, Susan Dickinson. Emily outlines her debt of inspiration to her female muse in one of her most startling poems:

I think I was enchanted
When first a sombre Girl –
I read that Foreign Lady –
The Dark – felt beautiful –

And whether it was noon at night –
Or only Heaven – at Noon –
For very Lunacy of Light
I had not power to tell – [...]

I could not have defined the change –
Conversion of the Mind
Like Sanctifying in the Soul –
Is witnessed – not explained –

'Twas a Divine Insanity
The Danger to be Sane
Should I again experience –
'Tis Antidote to turn –

To Tomes of solid Witchcraft –
Magicians be asleep –
But Magic – hath an Element
Like Deity – to keep –[11]

As Emily grew older, she shunned the outside world more and more. Her reclusive behaviour even saw her closest friends refused entry into the family home. Various myths have arisen to describe such seclusion: agoraphobia, a literary "pose" that enabled her to write, unrequited love. Moreover, her only known black-and-white portrait shows a thin, gaunt-faced young woman, with serious dark eyes betraying no hint of emotion – perhaps a façade concealing the maelstrom of feeling beneath.

Tantalizingly, although Emily was seen as being ambivalent toward marriage and resenting the restraint it placed on a woman's freedom, three draft epistles were discovered after her death suggesting otherwise. Collectively known as the Master Letters, they are directed at an unidentified correspondent, and are intimate declarations of her love. Some commentators have suggested possible candidates including her editor Higginson, as well as her sister-in-law Susan, as some feminist critics have identified a thread of homoeroticism in her verse.

Whoever the intended recipient was, they reveal a side to Emily not prevalent in her poetry. In the first letter, she cordially wishes her Master well after an illness. However, it is the second letter that is unashamedly urgent and direct in its confession of romantic attachment:

MASTER.

If you saw a bullet hit a Bird – and he told you he wasn't shot – you might weep at his courtesy but you would certainly doubt his word.

One drop more from the gash that stains your Daisy's bosom – then would you *believe*? [. . .] God made me – [Sir] Master – I didn't be – myself [. . .]

I am older – tonight, Master – but the love is the same – so are the moon and the crescent. If it had been God's will that I might breathe where you breathed – and find the place – myself – at night – if I (can) never forget that I am not with you – and that sorrow and frost are nearer than I – if I wish with a might I cannot repress – that mine were the Queen's place – the love of the Plantagenet is my only apology [. . .]

Have you the Heart in your breast – Sir – is it set like mine – a little to the left – has it the misgiving –

if it wake in the night – perchance – itself to it – a
timbrel is it – itself to it a tune? . . .[12]

Emily fantasizes about the possibility of a relationship
with the Master but there is an undertone of doom,
with all hope fading into the unrequited reality of her
affection. The letter can also be read as a microcosm of
Emily's life and her friendships with others. Not only
did she remain forever single, but she did not have even
one sustaining relationship, either platonic, intimate or
otherwise. It is said that such was the intensity of her
personality, both intellectually and emotionally, that any
potential friends or suitors simply shied away and always
kept their distance.

The third letter is much more subdued and sombre
in its acknowledgement of the utter hopelessness of her
devotion:

You send the water over the Dam in my brown eyes – [. . .]
Oh how the sailor strains, when his boat is
filling – Oh how the dying tug, till the angel comes.
Master – open your life wide, and take me in forever,
I will never be tired – I will never be noisy when you
want to be still. I will be [glad] [as] your best little
girl – nobody else will see me, but you – but that is
enough – I shall not want any more – and all that
Heaven only will disappoint me – will be because it's
not so dear.[13]

Some years later, after the letters were believed to have
been written, Susan Dickinson gave Emily *The Imitation
of Christ* – the mystical tract infused with the passionate

intensity of an individual's love for God. Although it is highly unlikely that the Master of Emily's three letters is the Saviour, Thomas à Kempis' text had a subsequently profound effect on her verse:

Given in Marriage unto Thee
Oh thou Celestial Host –
Bride of the Father and the Son
Bride of the Holy Ghost.

Other Betrothal shall dissolve –
Wedlock of Will, decay –
Only the Keeper of this Ring
Conquer Mortality –[14]

As is the case with so many women who composed verse and prose in a radical style with elusive meaning, she only became appreciated long after her death, in modern times. And yet, like her male contemporary Walt Whitman, the Transcendentalist poet whose celebrated poem *Song of Myself* inspired generations of mystical poets, so too do the haunting lines of Emily Dickinson:

Behind Me – dips Eternity –
Before Me – Immortality –
Myself – the Term between –

Death but the Drift of Eastern Gray,
Dissolving into Dawn away,
Before the West begin –

'Tis Kingdoms – afterward – they say –
In perfect – pauseless Monarchy –
Whose Prince – is Son of None –
Himself – His Dateless Dynasty –
Himself – Himself diversify –
In Duplicate divine –

'Tis Miracle before Me – then –
'Tis Miracle behind – between –
A Crescent in the Sea –
With Midnight to the North of Her –
And Midnight to the South of Her –
And Maelstrom – in the Sky –[15]

CHAPTER TWENTY
HINDUISM AND HOLY MOTHER SARADA DEVI

Learn to make the world your own,
no one is a stranger, my child;
the whole world is your own.

Changes in human consciousness similar to those happening in the West were filtering into the Asian continent, but the effect was far less pronounced. Essentially, attitudes toward women in the East were still bound by their respective religious traditions and misogynistic perspectives. After the formidable likes of Adi Shankara, countries such as India would have to wait until the 19th century for another great teacher to emerge – one who almost eclipsed all those before him in terms of his wisdom and humility, as well as venerating women as the sacred feminine. One whose wife, Sarada Devi, would continue his legacy as the perfect embodiment of his spiritual values and beliefs.

Gadadhar Chattopadhyaya was born in Kamarpukur, West Bengal, though he is more commonly known as the sage Ramakrishna (1836–86). Interested in religion at a very early age, he would often listen to the tales from the Puranas as well as sit with *sannyasin* (wandering holy men) passing through the village. At the age of six, Ramakrishna had his first taste of the Absolute. Walking through paddy fields on a hot summer's afternoon carrying a basket of puffed rice, he looked up and saw a dark thundercloud. Suddenly, a flock of snow-white cranes flew across the sky – the contrasting beauty of white on black was so overwhelming that he fell down in a swoon, immersed in a state of ecstasy.

At 16 his older brother, who lived in Kolkata, sent for Ramakrishna and took him to the local temple devoted to Mother Kali where he was the incumbent priest, just outside Dakshineswar on the eastern bank of the Ganges. Ramakrishna was assigned to help him run the temple, a job which at first held little interest. However, over time he began to love the temple and its beautiful surroundings – so much so that he would spend the rest of his life there in meditation and service.

The most remarkable aspect of Ramakrishna's spiritual practice was his overwhelming desire to have an inner experience of the Divine Mother. For many nights, sitting alone in the nearby forest, he would implore her to reveal herself to him. Eventually, after much petitioning, his prayers were finally answered:

I felt as if my heart were being squeezed like a wet towel. I was overpowered with a great restlessness and a fear that it might not be my lot to realize Her in this life. I could not bear the separation from Her any longer. Life seemed to be not worth living. Suddenly my glance fell on the sword that was kept in the Mother's temple. I determined to put an end to my life. When I jumped up like a madman and seized it, suddenly the blessed Mother revealed Herself. The buildings with their different parts, the temple, and everything else vanished from my sight, leaving no trace whatsoever, and in their stead I saw a limitless, infinite, effulgent Ocean of Consciousness. As far as the eye could see, the shining billows were madly rushing at me from all sides with a terrific noise, to swallow me up! I was panting for breath. I was caught in the rush and collapsed, unconscious. What was happening in the outside world I did not know; but within me there was a steady flow of undiluted bliss, altogether new, and I felt the presence of the Divine Mother.[1]

Ramakrishna's behaviour became more and more eccentric as his perception of the sacred feminine grew and he saw everything as an expression of the Mother. One story even recounts how, during one of these states of divine madness, rather than offering rice to Kali in holy ritual, he fed it to the temple cat. A complaint was made but it had little effect:

The Divine Mother revealed to me in the Kali temple that it was She who had become everything. She showed me that everything was full of Consciousness. The image was Consciousness, the altar was Consciousness, the water-vessels were Consciousness, the door-sill was Consciousness, the marble floor was Consciousness – all was Consciousness. I found everything inside the room soaked, as it were, in Bliss, the Bliss of God. I saw a wicked man in front of the Kali temple; but in him also I saw the power of the Divine Mother vibrating. That was why I fed the cat with the food that was to be offered to the Divine Mother.

I clearly perceived that all this was the Divine Mother –
even the cat. The manager of the temple garden wrote
to Mathur Babu [manager of the temple] saying that
I was feeding the cat with the offering intended for
the Divine Mother. But Mathur Babu had insight into
the state of my mind. He wrote back to the [temple
garden] manager: "Let him do whatever he likes. You
must not say anything to him."[2]

This was only the beginning. Ramakrishna then came
under the wing of a wandering female renunciate known
as Brahmani, who initiated him into Tantra. She explained
to Ramakrishna the nature of his ecstatic experiences
in terms of the kundalini energy within the body. After
becoming a Tantric adept, he then met Totapuri, another
teacher who was a strict Advaitin in the manner of Adi
Shankara, whose approach to reality was completely
different to Brahmani's. Totapuri urged Ramakrishna to
go beyond all created phenomena instead of dwelling on
mystical visions, such as the Divine Mother:

In spite of all my attempts, I could not altogether
cross the realm of name and form and bring my
mind to the unconditioned state. I had no difficulty
in taking the mind from all the objects of the world.
But the radiant and too familiar figure of the Blissful
Mother, the Embodiment of the essence of Pure
Consciousness, appeared before me as a living reality.
Her bewitching smile prevented me from passing into
the Great Beyond. Again and again I tried, but She
stood in my way every time. In despair I said to Nangta
(Totapuri): "It is hopeless. I cannot raise my mind to

the unconditioned state and come face to face with Atman." He grew excited and sharply said, "What? You can't do it? But you have to!" He cast his eyes around. Finding a piece of glass, he took it up and stuck it between my eyebrows. "Concentrate the mind on this point!" he thundered. Then with stern determination I again sat to meditate. As soon as the gracious form of the Divine Mother appeared before me, I used my discrimination as a sword and with it clove Her in two. The last barrier fell. My spirit at once soared beyond the relative plane and I lost myself in samadhi."[3]

Ramakrishna remained in this state for the following three days, after which he declared that he had now seen the Self in both its phenomenal and noumenal (intrinsically real) aspects, both as expressions of the One:

When I think of the Supreme Being as inactive – neither creating nor preserving nor destroying – I call Him Brahman or Purusha, the Impersonal God. When I think of Him as active – creating, preserving, destroying – I call Him Shakti or Maya or Prakriti, the Personal God. But the distinction between them does not mean a difference. The Personal and the Impersonal are the same thing, like milk and its whiteness, the diamond and its lustre, the snake and its wriggling motion. It is impossible to conceive of the one without the other. The Divine Mother and Brahman are one.[4]

This is considered by many to be the highest teaching of all – everything is ultimately perceived as God, whether existent or non-existent, created or uncreated, personal or impersonal. Expounding further, Ramakrishna says:

> After the creation, the Primal Power dwells in the universe itself. She brings forth this phenomenal world and then pervades it. In the Vedas, creation is likened to the spider and its web. The spider brings the web out of itself and then remains in it. God is the container of the universe and also what is contained in it.[5]

He then embarked on a spiritual journey through all the world's major religions in an attempt to validate further his experience of unity. He studied Islam and Christianity, Buddhism, Jainism and Sikhism, acknowledging yet again that all faiths are paths to the Divine. The more Ramakrishna became absorbed in his practice and research, the more devout the followers he attracted around him, eager to benefit from his wisdom and luminous presence. One such devotee was Swami Vivekananda (1863–1902), who would go on to take his Master's message to America, most notably to the World Parliament of Religions in Chicago in 1893.

Ramakrishna's principal disciple was Sarada Devi (1853–1920), known as the Holy Mother, who was also his devoted wife. Born of Brahmin parents in Jayrambati, a small neighbouring village of Kamarpukur, Sarada was considered a serious child who took little interest in playing with her childhood friends, finding pleasure instead in making clay models of Kali and Lakshmi, which she decorated with garlands of flowers.

At the instigation of his mother, Ramakrishna married Sarada when she was only five years old, a practice not uncommon for Hindu women at the time. Sarada remained with her family and only met her new husband occasionally until she was 18, after which she remained with him on a permanent basis.

As the archetypal divine couple, akin to the ideal of Rama and Sita, both would support and honour the other. Speaking of their time together, Sarada observed:

During my days at Dakshineswar, I used to get up at three o'clock in the morning and sit in meditation. Often I used to be totally absorbed in it. Once, on a moonlit night, doing *japa,* I was sitting on the steps of the *nahabat* [music tower]. Everything was quiet. I did not even know when the Master passed that way. On other days I would hear the sound of his slippers but on this, I did not. I was totally absorbed in meditation ... On this day the cloth had slipped off from my back owing to the breeze but I was unconscious of it [...]

Ah! The ecstasy of those days. On moonlit nights I would look at the moon and pray with folded hands, "May my heart be as pure as the rays of yonder moon!" If one is steady in meditation, one can clearly see the Lord in one's heart and hear His voice. The moment an idea flashes in the mind of such a one, it will be fulfilled then and there. One will be bathed in peace. Ah! What a mind I had at that time [...]

In the fullness of one's spiritual realization, one will find that He who resides in one's heart resides in the hearts of others as well – the oppressed, the persecuted, the Untouchable and the outcast. This realization makes one truly humble.[6]

Ramakrishna taught Sarada many spiritual practices in the knowledge she would one day carry on his legacy of helping humanity understand the immanence of the sacred feminine. Meanwhile, she continued to serve her husband dutifully, especially during his final years while suffering from cancer of the throat.

Ramakrishna's body was cremated on the eastern bank of the Ganges. Distraught with grief, Sarada began to discard her jewellery, in keeping with the Hindu custom. As she was about to remove her bracelets, a vision of Ramakrishna allegedly appeared before her, asking her why she was behaving as a widow, when he had merely moved from one room into another. From that day forth, she never took off her bracelets for as long as she lived.

The handful of disciples who had collected around Ramakrishna during his lifetime decided to renounce their worldly activities and form a monastery in a small, dilapidated house in Baranagar, a northern suburb of Kolkata on the Ganges' western bank. Known as the Belur Math, it became the permanent headquarters of the Ramakrishna Order, also housing Ramakrishna's ashes.

Sarada herself embarked on a pilgrimage, visiting Vrindavan in Uttar Pradesh, the birthplace of Krishna, where she identified with the grief of his principal *gopi* Radha at the loss of her own beloved teacher. Once again, Sarada was visited by an image of Ramakrishna – this time on three consecutive evenings – instructing her to initiate her devotees with a sacred mantra, which he revealed to her in the dream. From that moment, she resolved to carry on her Master's teaching until the day she died.

Despite this, her soul yearned to free itself from the shackles of the physical body. Relating an out-of-body experience, she declared:

> I found in that state that I had travelled into a distant country. Everybody there was very affectionate to me. My beauty was beyond description. Sri Ramakrishna was also there. With great tenderness they made me sit by his side. I cannot describe to you the nature of that ecstatic joy. When my mind came down from that exalted mood, I found my body lying there. I thought, "How can I possibly enter into this ugly body?" I could not at all persuade my mind to do so. After a long while, it did, and the body became conscious again.[7]

Throughout her final years, dressed in a white sari and still wearing her marriage bangles, Sarada was surrounded by hordes of devotees, eager for her maternal love. Fittingly, Ramakrishna had often told his disciples to be like children before the Holy Mother.

Through her nondual teaching, with particular emphasis on meditation and detachment, Sarada helped hundreds of men and women find liberation from suffering. Despite never writing a single word herself, her utterances were recorded by her devoted disciple, Swami Nikhilananda (1895–1973), who preserved her wisdom for generations to come:

> The aim of life is to realize God and remain immersed in contemplation of Him. God alone is real and everything else is false. God is one's very own, and this is the eternal relationship between God and creatures.

One realizes God in proportion to the intensity of one's feelings for Him. He who is really eager to cross the ocean of the world will somehow break his bonds.[8]

In another beautifully recorded lunar analogy, Sarada explains the veils of the mind:

The moon is in the sky, but it is hidden by a cloud. The cloud must be slowly blown away by the wind, and then you will see the moon. Can anything happen abruptly? The vision of God is also like that. Slowly one gets rid of one's past karma [. . .] That is nature's law. Haven't you noticed the new moon and full moon? The mind, likewise, sometimes feels pure and sometimes impure.[9]

It is often said that the guru takes on the suffering of their devotees, and Sarada was no exception. Throughout her life, she was afflicted with acute physical pain, eventually falling ill with black fever, becoming confined to bed. A devotee, distressed by Sarada's dying body, pressed her about what would happen to all her followers without her:

Why should you be afraid? You have seen the Master. What should frighten you? [. . .] Let me tell you something. My child, if you want peace, then do not look into anybody's faults. Look into your own faults. Learn to make the world your own, no one is a stranger, my child; the whole world is your own.[10]

In the early hours of 21 July 1920 she took her final breath, entered into samadhi and passed away. Later her body was taken across the Ganges to the Belur Math, where it was bathed and dressed in a ceremonial sari. A funeral pyre of sandalwood was constructed, and later that afternoon Sarada was cremated at the *ghat* (steps leading down to the river). Her ashes were placed in the Ramakrishna temple, close to those of her husband.

Throughout her life, Sarada was accompanied by a small circle of female disciples, most notably the Irish woman Sister Nivedita. Speaking of Sarada, she said:

> In her one sees realized that wisdom and sweetness to which the simplest of women may attain. And yet to myself the stateliness of her courtesy and her great open mind are almost as wonderful as her sainthood. I have never known her hesitate in giving utterance to large and generous judgement, however new and complex might be the question put before her. Her life is one long stillness of prayer.[11]

What Sarada Devi showed the world through her modesty and piety was that even the humblest of women is an embodiment of the Absolute. What Ramakrishna showed the world was the way his wife should be honoured as such. In effect, the treatment of Sarada as a manifestation of the Divine Mother not only gave her the holy status she was entitled to but also served as an example for all Hindu women throughout India.

Paradoxically, in spite of the rising tide of Western feminism that was empowering women with self-respect and the desire to be treated more equally, for some it appeared to come at a hefty price. According to Swami Vivekananda after his trip to America, the image of softness and grace normally associated with the female embodiment was being undermined through her weary struggle for independence, leading him to remark:

> In the West the women did not very often seem to be women at all, they appeared to be replicas of men [...] In India alone the sight of feminine modesty and reserve soothes the eye [...] Still on this sacred soil of India, this land of Sita and Savitri, among women may be found such character, such spirit of service, such affection, such compassion, contentment and reverence, as I could not find anywhere else in the world.[12]

And in a letter written while still in the United States regarding Sarada Devi and sent to one of his fellow monks back at the Belur Math, he observed:

> You have not understood the wonderful significance of the Mother's life. But gradually you will know. Without Shakti there is no regeneration for the world ... Mother has been born to revive that wonderful Shakti in India; and making her the nucleus, once more will Gargis [learned women] and Maitreyas [avatars] be born into the world.[13]

The millennia-long debate about women's appearance and place in society still continues to provoke a multitude of attitudes and prejudices. Perhaps taking a moment to gaze upon Sarada's black and white portrait, which depicts a serene woman with flowing hair and eyes fixed upon the distance, may temporarily put aside such discussion, silencing our minds and filling our hearts with peace.

CHAPTER TWENTY-ONE
INTEGRAL YOGA AND SWEET MOTHER MIRRA ALFASSA

There is something that is worth waking to,
worth living for,
and it is love!

While Vivekananda's observations about women in the West were shockingly blunt, they were made through the eyes of an Indian male, who was accustomed to clearly defined female roles and a religion that honoured the sacred feminine principle. Women in America and Europe had had to live through political, economic and sociological changes not yet witnessed in the East, significantly altering their societal and psychological status in the eyes of both men and themselves, a stance that would be directly addressed by the formidable artist and occultist Mirra Alfassa.

Indeed, the Women's Movement in Europe at the turn of the 20th century was vigorously campaigning for control of personal property, equality of opportunity in education and employment, sexual emancipation and women's suffrage. In Britain, the feminist Emmeline

Pankhurst (1858–1928) founded the Women's Social and Political Union and was one of the first to be instrumental in pushing through political reform and women's right to vote. Is it any wonder it all took its toll?

Over in France, the existential writer Simone de Beauvoir (1908–86), companion and lover of Jean-Paul Sartre, was outlining her feminist theories in her classic text *The Second Sex*, the inspiration point for "second wave" feminism. Famously, she asks what it means to be a woman, a discussion never so pertinent as in the current modern age, and summarized that, up until the last century, she was merely regarded as "Other" and defined always in relation to a man.

Speaking about the feminine sensibility in the context of religious activity, Simone offers an examination of the female mystic:

> Love has been assigned to woman as her supreme vocation, and when she directs it towards a man, she is seeking God in him; but if human love is denied her by circumstances, if she is disappointed or over-particular, she may choose to adore divinity in the person of God Himself. To be sure, there have been men who burned with that flame, but they are rare, and their fervour is of a highly refined intellectual cast; whereas the women who abandon themselves to the joys of the heavenly nuptials are legion, and their experience is of a peculiarly emotional nature.[1]

Her great work is a breathtaking re-examination of the plight of women throughout human history. While acknowledging their feminine qualities, Simone argues for equality of the sexes so that there can be a form of meaningful connection between them, concluding:

> To gain the supreme victory, it is necessary, for one thing, that by and through their natural differentiation men and women unequivocally affirm their brotherhood.[2]

Other powerful women were also making their voices heard, particularly in the fields of spiritualism, occultism and theosophy. One such woman was Mirra Alfassa (1878–1973), who would go on to establish her own organization in the pursuit of esoteric knowledge, together with her life companion, the Indian sage Sri Aurobindo. Responsible for one of the most important metaphysical renaissances the modern world has ever known, they continue to attract a significant following of disciples from all around the world.

Born in Paris to an Egyptian mother and a Turkish father, Mirra was already aware of her life's mission at a very young age:

> I started contemplating or doing my Yoga from the age of four. There was a small chair for me on which I used to sit still, engrossed in my meditation. A very brilliant light would then descend over my head and produce some turmoil inside my brain. Of course, I understood nothing, it was not the age for understanding. But gradually I began to feel, "I shall have to do some tremendously great work that nobody yet knows."[3]

Throughout her teens, Mirra continued to immerse herself in mystical phenomena:

When I was a child of about thirteen, for nearly a year every night as soon as I had gone to bed it seemed to me that I went out of my body and rose straight up above the house, then above the city, very high above. Then I used to see myself clad in a magnificent golden robe, much longer than myself; as I rose higher, the robe would stretch, spreading out in a circle around me to form a kind of immense roof over the city. Then I would see men, women, children, old men, the sick, the unfortunate coming out from every side; they would gather under the outspread robe, begging for help, telling of their miseries, their suffering, their hardships. In reply, the robe, supple and alive, would extend towards each one of them individually, and as soon as they had touched it, they were comforted or healed, and went back into their bodies happier and stronger than they had come out of them.[4]

During these ecstatic trances, Mirra would encounter teachers and holy beings, one of whom she called Krishna, knowing that one day she would meet him incarnated here on earth.

Growing up with the avant-garde in Paris during the great Impressionistic era, Mirra studied painting at the École des Beaux-Arts and even exhibited at the famous Salon. A black-and-white photograph taken later in India shows a woman with smiling kohl-lined eyes wearing an elaborate brocaded headscarf, testament to her innate sense of French style.

At 19, she married Henri Morisset, a student of the painter Gustave Moreau, and together they had a son,

André. Despite her blossoming family life and love of the cultural arts, personal fulfilment lay far beyond the material realm, something which she had striven hard for on her own terms:

> Between the age of eighteen and twenty I had attained a conscious and constant union with the divine Presence and . . . I had done it *all alone*, with *absolutely nobody* to help me, not even books, you understand!⁵

In 1905, Mirra met the occultist Max Théon, a Polish Jew who had been the Grand Master of a philosophy group in Egypt, known as the Hermetic Brotherhood of Luxor. Théon had a house in Tlemcen, northern Algeria, and invited Mirra to stay with him and his wife. She thus spent the following three years with them learning about the occult and the Kabbalah tradition, practising her new-found mystical powers.

Her marriage to Henri Morisset now over, she returned to Paris and took a new husband, Paul Richard, a man deeply interested in philosophy and Vedantic yoga. She also started Cosmique, a study group in which she taught the perennial wisdom of the Upanishads, the Bhagavad Gita and Patanjali's *Yoga Sutras*.

Richard had political ambitions and journeyed to Puducherry in India to further his career as part of an election campaign. While staying there, he sought the advice of a holy man and in 1910 had his first encounter with Aurobindo. Greatly impressed by his presence, Richard could not wait to tell his wife about the enigmatic guru when he returned to Paris. Inspired by all she heard, Mirra immediately started to correspond with Aurobindo, and, four years later, she and her husband set sail for India to meet the illustrious guru in person.

Born in Kolkata, Aurobindo Ghose (1872–1950) was taken at a young age with his two elder brothers to England for his education, where he lived with an English family in Manchester. He attended St Paul's public school in London from the age of 12 and then King's College, University of Cambridge. Returning to India in 1893, he became involved with Indian nationalism and campaigned for total independence from British rule, editing the *Bande Mataram* ("Long Live the Motherland"), a Nationalist newspaper. He also became deeply passionate about *raja* yoga, often experiencing states of transcendental awareness:

> An absolute stillness and blotting out, as it were, of all mental, emotional and other inner activities – the body continued indeed to see, walk, speak, and do its other business but as an empty automatic machine and nothing more. I did not become aware of any pure "I" nor even of any self, impersonal or other – there was only an awareness of That as the sole Reality, all else being quite insubstantial, void, non-real. As to what realized that Reality, it was a nameless consciousness which was other than That ... Neither was I aware of any lower soul or outer self called by such and such a personal name that was performing this feat of arriving at the consciousness of Nirvana ...[6]

A year later, Aurobindo was remanded in custody, suspected of terrorist acts against the British. In prison, he experienced the taste of nirvana again and he resolved to devote his entire life to the spiritual path. Upon his release, he moved to Puducherry, then under French rule, where he developed his theories of "Integral Yoga".

For Aurobindo, enlightenment came about through realizing the Supermind, the Truth-Consciousness of the Divine within oneself. By means of a series of three distinct steps, the complex *sadhana* (dedicated practice) of Integral Yoga proceeds through psychic, spiritual and supramental (transcending the limitations of the mind) transformation, leading to identification with God. Furthermore, this process is helped by universal Shakti, the Divine Mother, who acts as an intermediary between all human beings and the Supermind:

> The supramental change [this evolutionary change that Aurobindo came to pioneer in his own body, mind and work] is a thing decreed and inevitable in the evolution of the earth-consciousness, for its upward ascent is not ended and mind is not its last summit. But that the change may arise, take form, and endure, there is needed the call from below with a will to recognize and not deny the light when it comes. There is needed the sanction of the Supreme from above. The power that mediates between the sanction and the call is the presence and power of the Divine Mother.[7]

After four years of practising silently on his own, Aurobindo began publishing his ideas in *Arya*, a monthly philosophical journal, where he initially serialized most of his important works, including *The Divine Life*, *The*

Synthesis of Yoga, *Essays on the Gita* and *The Isha Upanishad*. The journal ceased publication after several years, but by then a community of devotees had already formed around Aurobindo, becoming what is now known as the Sri Aurobindo Ashram.

It is not surprising that Mirra was so inexorably drawn to meet the great Indian teacher. In a diary note describing the sea journey from France to India and the boat she and her husband were travelling in, she said:

> ... [it is] a marvellous abode of peace, a temple sailing in Thy honour over the waves of the subconscient passivity which we have to conquer and awaken to the consciousness of Thy divine Presence.[8]

The very next day after their arrival in Puducherry, Mirra Alfassa met Aurobindo and immediately recognized in him the special being she had once called Krishna in the visions of her childhood. In fact, she believed that her whole life had merely been a preparation for this moment, stating that she had finally arrived at the threshold she had long sought. The Richards subsequently spent every afternoon conversing with Aurobindo and, during their year-long stay, helped collaborate on the *Arya* journal, contributing several philosophical pieces and poems of their own.

The Richards returned to Paris during the middle of World War I, during which Mirra and Aurobindo resumed their correspondence. In 1917, the Richards set sail again, this time for Japan, where they remained until 1920. However, Mirra's yearning to be with Aurobindo was so intense that she decided to return to Puducherry to be by his side forever, her marriage to Paul Richard effectively at an end.

For the first six or so years, Mirra blended in with the other disciples in the ashram, content just to receive Aurobindo's *darshan* (spiritual audience) and help with domestic chores. But it was not long before her powerful personality was taking charge by conducting meditation groups in the manner of her Cosmique days in Paris. As Aurobindo was withdrawing more and more from public engagements, appearing only for special occasions, he inevitably would leave Mirra to orchestrate activities within the ashram.

Then, on 24 November 1926, a remarkable event occurred. Aurobindo declared that Krishna had descended into the physical realm, enabling humanity to work toward realizing its divine potential to become one with the Supermind. Various "miracles" allegedly took place but, most significantly, Aurobindo started calling Mirra "Sweet Mother".

For Aurobindo, the Mother's grace was the nourishing and life-sustaining force of the created universe. Out of all his prolific writings, it is in a small book titled *The Mother* that he extols his unique theories on the quadruple aspects of the sacred feminine:

Four great Aspects of the Mother, four of her leading Powers and Personalities have stood in front in her guidance of this Universe and in her dealings with the terrestrial play. One is her personality of calm wideness and comprehending wisdom and tranquil benignity and inexhaustible compassion and sovereign and surpassing majesty and all-ruling greatness. Another embodies her power of splendid strength and irresistible passion, her warrior mood, her overwhelming will, her impetuous swiftness and world-shaking force. A third is vivid and sweet and wonderful with her deep secret of beauty and harmony and fine rhythm, her intricate and subtle opulence, her compelling attraction and captivating grace. The fourth is equipped with her close and profound capacity of intimate knowledge and careful flawless work and quiet and exact perfection in all things. Wisdom, Strength, Harmony, Perfection are their several attributes and it is these powers that they bring with them into the world . . . To the four we give the four great names, Maheshwari, Mahakali, Mahalakshmi, Mahasaraswati . . .[9]

When asked whether Mirra and the Sweet Mother were synonymous, Aurobindo was in no doubt that they were one and the same. And yet the Divine Mother was simultaneously so much more than the four physical manifestations of phenomenal existence:

There are three ways of being of the Mother of which you can become aware when you enter into touch of oneness with the Conscious Force that upholds us and the universe. *Transcendent*, the original supreme Shakti, she stands above the worlds and links the creation to the ever-unmanifest mystery of the Supreme. *Universal*, the cosmic Mahashakti, she creates all these beings and contains and enters, supports and conducts all these million processes and forces. *Individual*, she embodies the power of these two vast arrays of her existence, makes them living and near to us and mediates between the human personality and the divine Nature.[10]

For Aurobindo, one's whole life should be dedicated in service to the divine feminine, submitting to her infinite grace and ineffable beauty:

There must be a total and sincere surrender; there must be an exclusive self-opening to the divine Power; there must be a constant and integral choice of the Truth that is descending, a constant and integral rejection of the falsehood of the mental, vital and physical Powers and Appearances that still rule the earth-Nature.

The surrender must be total and seize all the parts of the being. It is not enough that the psychic should respond and the higher mental accept or even the inner vital submit and the inner physical consciousness feel the influence. There must be in no part of the being, even the most external, anything that makes a reserve, anything that hides behind doubts, confusions, and subterfuges, anything that revolts or refuses [. . .]

All your life must be an offering and a sacrifice to the Supreme; your only object in action shall be to serve, to receive, to fulfil, to become a manifesting instrument of the Divine Shakti in her works. You must grow in the divine consciousness till there is no difference between your will and hers, no motive except her impulsion in you, no action that is not her conscious action in you and through you.[11]

Admitting that the path is neither instantaneous nor easy, Aurobindo outlines three distinct stages that can be recognized in the journey to the Absolute:

> Until you are capable of this complete dynamic identification, you have to regard yourself as a soul and body created for her service, one who does all for her sake [. . .] There must be no demand for fruit and no seeking for reward; the only fruit for you is the pleasure of the Divine Mother and the fulfilment of her work, your only reward a constant progression in divine consciousness and calm and strength and bliss [. . .]
>
> And afterwards you will realize that the divine Shakti not only inspires and guides, but initiates and carries out your works; all your movements are originated by her, all your powers are hers, mind, life and body are conscious and joyful instruments of her action, means for her play, moulds for her manifestation in the physical universe [. . .]
>
> The last stage of this perfection will come when you are completely identified with the Divine Mother and feel yourself to be no longer another and separate being, instrument, servant or worker, but truly a child and eternal portion of her consciousness and force. Always she will be in you and you in her; it will be your constant, simple and natural experience that all your thought and seeing and action, your very breathing or moving come from her and are hers. You will know and see and feel that you are a person and power formed by her out of herself, put out from her for the play and yet always safe in her, being of

her being, consciousness of her consciousness, force of her force, Ananda of her Ananda.[12]

By the time Aurobindo left his body, he believed his own mission had come to its rightful end, feeling satisfied he could leave Sweet Mother to take over responsibility for the work of enlightening humanity. She forged ahead during this period, establishing an International Centre of Education, as well as her own landmark project, the town of Auroville ("City of Dawn") just a few miles north of Puducherry, a place where the principles of Integral Yoga could be put into practice within a thriving community.

Mirra lived out her remaining days under strict self-discipline, following the same regime every day: in the morning, rising early at 4am, then giving *darshan* on the balcony of the ashram at 6am, followed by meditation, interviews with spiritual seekers and supervision of the distribution of alms. Later, in the afternoon, she supervised sports and children's games, then led evening meditation and gave *darshan* once more.

One night in 1969 she had an intense spiritual experience, after which she announced that there had been a descent of Superman-consciousness, the intermediary between human beings and the Supermind. In a vision reminiscent of Julian of Norwich's perception of the world as a tiny hazelnut (see Chapter 15), she said:

It was something very material, I mean it was very external – very external – and it was luminous, with a golden light. It was very strong, very powerful; but even so, its character was a smiling benevolence, a peaceful delight [. . .] very, very gentle, very smiling,

> *very benevolent* . . . My own impression was that of an
> immense personality . . . [and] the earth was small,
> small . . . like a ball . . . It gave the impression of a
> personal divinity . . . who comes to help, and so
> strong, so strong and at the same time so gentle, so
> all-embracing . . .[13]

Despite heavenly inspiration, Mirra's own physical health
was failing, and on 17 November 1973 she passed away at
the age of 95. For the next three days, her body lay in state
in the meditation room of the ashram, where thousands
of devotees paid their final respects.

Mirra Alfassa's legacy is of equal merit and profundity
to Aurobindo's. Unlike her spiritual companion's zest for
writing philosophical prose and poems, Mirra's own body
of work simply comprises transcripts of her speeches,
given in both French and English, which were recorded
on tape and transcribed by her loyal devotees. Her only
written work is *Prayers and Meditations*, which consists of
passages selected from her diary notes.

However, like Aurobindo, she was very thorough in
her expositions of Integral Yoga and her understanding
of nondual metaphysics. Always couched in her unique
words and suffused with the charm that only a French
woman can muster, she spoke on many subjects, including
science and religion, free will and reincarnation, illness
and health. The topic of art was also particularly close to
her heart, drawing on her vast experience as a visual artist.
Indeed, her creative work comprised many pencil sketches
and paintings of Aurobindo, including the ethereal *Divine
Consciousness Emerging from the Inconscient*, which depicts
his face and upper body emerging from a fiery swirl:

Art is nothing less in its fundamental truth than the aspect of beauty of the Divine manifestation. Perhaps, looking from this standpoint, there will be found very few true artists; but still there are some and these can very well be considered as Yogis. For like a Yogi an artist goes into deep contemplation to await and receive his inspiration. To create something truly beautiful, he has first to see it within to realize it as a whole in his inner consciousness; only when so found, seen, held within, can he execute it outwardly; he creates according to this greater inner vision. This too is a kind of yogic discipline, for by it he enters into intimate communion with the inner worlds.[14]

And on the nature of love, another theme she felt deeply passionate about, she said:

Love is a supreme force which the Eternal Consciousness sent down from itself into an obscure and darkened world that it might bring back that world and its beings to the Divine. The material world in its darkness and ignorance had forgotten the Divine. Love came into the darkness; it awakened all that lay there asleep; it whispered, opening the ears that were sealed, "There is something that is worth waking to, worth living for, and it is love!" And with the awakening to love there entered into the world the possibility of coming back to the Divine.[15]

Aurobindo and Mirra were not lovers in the physical sense but between them existed a dynamic relationship founded in mutual respect and love of the perennial wisdom. As

Aurobindo wrote one day in his diary: "The Mother and I are one and equal." Mirra confirmed this by also writing her own tribute: "Without him, I exist not; without me, he is unmanifest."[16]

Many other celebrated female mystics appeared in India during the 20th century – Anandamayi Ma, Anasuya Devi, Ammachi and Karunamayi, to name but a few. At least in the East, veneration of the sacred feminine, both in human form and as the creative principle, is finally very much alive and well.

CHAPTER TWENTY-TWO

SUFISM AND DIARIST IRINA TWEEDIE

It is difficult to believe,
unless one has experienced it,
that it is so glorious "not to be".

While Mira Alfassa was establishing recognition for the sacred feminine in India, belief in an immanent reality for many people was on shaky ground in the West. Modernist thinking had deconstructed all philosophical and religious beliefs into meaningless abstractions, culminating in Friedrich Nietzsche's famous maxim that God was effectively dead. However, in a climate where dogma and ideological ignorance were crumbling, new possibilities were arising. The pioneering spirit of women like Mirra enabled more and more women to search independently for their own salvation, to find the Truth for themselves beyond their domestic restraints.

The Russian-British diarist Irina Tweedie (1907–99) is yet another shining example of an independent Western woman taking a stand against the dictates of society in her quest for personal enlightenment, travelling to the sacred East to find her spiritual self. To read her autobiography is to be transported to India and experience almost directly the beauty and overwhelming majesty of living in a subcontinental wonderland:

> In the west the sun was setting in a sea of shimmering golden clouds. The whole world seemed to be illumined by this vivid gold, was transformed by it. I had to cross the *chowraha* [circus] to get to the baker's shop. Before entering, I stopped and turned and saw that right across the *chowraha* was a magnificent rainbow. So clear, vivid and bright, against the golden sky; and I must have walked right under it. I stood for a while, enchanted. There is a Russian saying that when one walks under a rainbow it means that if one has a wish or a desire it will be fulfilled. What an omen! My Master told me that my troubles are passing away. I don't think that I ever was so happy in my life ... with this special happiness never experienced before ...[1]

Aryanagar, the district where Irina stayed for two years, regularly visiting a Sufi Master, becomes a place where the mystery of the Absolute is directly revealed. Her diary entries, written between October 1961 and December 1966 while living in Aryanagar, London and then finally the Himalayas, take the reader on their own transcendental journey, so that they can experience the living presence of her Master and his wisdom for themselves.

With unashamed honesty, Irina records her thoughts and emotions as she embarks on her path of self-discovery. Her Naqshbandi Sufi Master, Bhai Sahib ("Elder Brother"), whom she also refers to as Guruji, is an enigmatic character – simultaneously cryptic, compassionate and aloof, not given to verbose discourses on the nature of reality. Nevertheless, Irina is deeply moved by his presence. In their first formal meeting, Bhai Sahib asks her, "Why did you come to me?" Irina's words come spilling forth:

"I want God," I heard myself saying, "But not the Christian idea of an anthropomorphic deity. I want the Rootless Root, the Causeless Cause of the Upanishads."
"Nothing less than that?" He lifted an eyebrow.[2]

Irina speaks very little of her past prior to visiting India. In the barest of detail, she reveals she was born in Russia, educated in Vienna and Paris, and eventually moved to England, where she was happily married to a naval officer. His death in 1954 caused a grief of such profundity that she sought solace in religion and philosophy, turning eventually to the Theosophical Society, which sadly failed to inspire her. Still experiencing an intense longing for freedom, she then felt compelled to travel to India.

Continuing to explain her reasons for coming to Bhai Sahib, she tells him of the theosophical belief that a guru is not necessary for liberation, as salvation is achievable through independent means:

"Not even in a hundred years!" he laughed outright. "It cannot be done without a Teacher!"
I told him that I did not know what Sufism was.
"Sufism is a way of life. It is neither a religion nor a philosophy. There are Hindu Sufis, Muslim Sufis, Christian Sufis. My Revered Guru Maharaj was a Muslim." He said it very softly, with a tender expression, his eyes dreamy and veiled. And then

I noticed something which in my excitement and eagerness I had not noticed before; there was a feeling of great peace in the room. He himself was full of peace. He radiated it; it was all around us and it seemed eternal. As if this special peace always was and always would be, forever . . .[3]

Immediately, Bhai Sahib instructs her to keep a diary of her experiences. *Daughter of Fire: A Diary of a Spiritual Training with a Sufi Master* meticulously records Irina's day-to-day existence (which was later abridged to a much shorter version, *Chasm of Fire: A Woman's Experience of Liberation Through the Teachings of a Sufi Master,* and published first). Charting her meetings and conversations with Bhai Sahib, her words are a visceral account of her frustrations and insights along the spiritual path.

At first, her entries tell of the sheer physical hardship of Indian life, which becomes an almost insurmountable obstacle – the smells and noise and chaos in temperatures well over 37°C (100°F). Provoked by her feisty and often quarrelsome character, Bhai Sahib is forced to break her attachment to the physical senses and her ongoing attitude of "poor me".

As a consequence, Irina is regularly asked to sit outside his house, often in the blinding dust or pouring rain, while welcoming other devotees into his home. He also demands that she hand over to him all of her income, as a test of her dependence on money. Her protestations are loud, and yet the Master knows it is for her own good, saying:

The world is for us as we create it: if you say there is a *bhut* [ghost] in the tree, then there will be a *bhut* for you. This is all *manas* [mind]. But what is *manas*? Nothing. *Manas* is *maya* [illusion]. You want everything but are not prepared to make sacrifices, to pay the price [. . .]

People are not prepared to give anything up. If you want to go anywhere you will have to take the train or the plane, you are expected to pay the fare, is it not so? Be always a friend of the Almighty and you *will never die*. Prayer should be done always, even in ordinary prayer; but of course the only *real* prayer is merging, *oneness* with God.[4]

Her heart responds to the essence of his words, but her mind is still reeling with anxiety and confusion. Her desire for permanent release evokes a tireless demand for her Master's assistance:

"Oh please help me! I am so confused!"

"Why should I?" He looked straight at me. "If I begin to help, you will ask again and again for help: how will you cross the stream? You must do it yourself, I will not help. If I do, you will get used to it and will never be able to do without my help. We all have to cross the stream alone. Don't you realize that this is the way? I am telling you, showing you the way. THE ONLY WAY. Why don't you realize that you are nothing? It means complete surrender. It takes time. It is not done in one day. It takes time to surrender."[5]

Bhai Sahib goes on to tell her that his method is the Way of the Silent Sufi. Dependent on the maturity of the devotee, practice can either be the path of *dhyana* (contemplative meditation in the mind) or the path of *tyaga* (complete renunciation in the heart). Although both paths ultimately lead to the same destination, the Teacher places greater emphasis on surrender:

> It is like love; it cannot be hidden. If I don't speak to you for days, you just sit. If I speak, you speak and never, never must you complain ... This is the door, the *only door* to the *King of the Heart*. What is surrender of the heart? You people do not even imagine. Not only Western people, I mean Indians too ... Learn to be *nothing*, this is the only way.[6]

Reiterating the teachings of all the great masters before him, expounding the mystical relationship between lover and Beloved, he continues:

> To say "I love you" is easy but to realize it is difficult. Here is hidden the mystery of the Realization of God or Truth. Because you have to realize one fact: "You are in my heart, you are everything, I am nothing." If you begin to realize that, then you really love, and your own self diminishes, the external things begin to lose all importance. The self, and everything else, remains with the Beloved from then on, and the Beloved remains with you permanently when there is no self anymore.[7]

In spite of his wise words, Irina's diary entries reveal the personal torment she endures, with no outlet for release. At night in the darkness, she sleeps badly, finding little respite. Her body starts to shake violently, her skin is weeping sweat. Then suddenly, with no warning, she is overwhelmed with carnal hunger:

Without the slightest indication that it may be coming, I was flooded with a powerful sexual desire. It was just the desire, for no object in particular, just the desire, *per se*, uncontrollable, a kind of wild cosmic force . . . I sat there helpless, shaking with fear . . . Good heavens, what was happening? Tried to listen, to *feel* from where this vibration came, where it was exactly. Then I knew; it was at the base of the spine, just above the anus. I could feel it there distinctly. It must be the *muladhara chakra* [psychic centre at the base of the spine]. I went ice-cold with terror . . . This was the *coup de grace*! I thought; he has activated the chakra at the base of the spine and left the kundalini energy there to . . . to what?

The most terrifying night of my life began. Never, not even in its young days had this body known anything even faintly comparable, or similar to this! This was not just desire; it was madness in its lowest, animal form; a paroxysm of sex-craving. A wild howling of everything female in me, for a male. The whole body was SEX ONLY; every cell, every particle, was shouting for it; even the skin, the hands, the nails, every atom . . .

Waves of wild goose-flesh ran over my whole body making all the hair stand stiff, as if filled with electricity. The sensation was painful, but the inexplicable thing was that the idea of intercourse did not even occur to me . . . The body was shaking, I was biting the pillow so as not to howl like a wild animal. I was beside myself; the craziest, the maddest thing one could imagine, so sudden, so violent.[8]

And she continues:

The body seemed to break under this force; all I could do was to hold it stiff, still and completely stretched out. I felt the over-stretched muscles full of pain as in a kind of cramp. I was rigid, I could not move. The mind was absolutely void, emptied of its content. There was no imagery; only an uncontrollable fear, primitive, animal fear and it went on for hours. I was shaking like a leaf . . . a mute, trembling jelly carried away by forces completely beyond any human control. A fire was burning inside my bowels and the sensation of heat increased and decreased in waves. I could do nothing. I was in complete psychological turmoil.

I don't know how long it lasted, don't know if I slept out of sheer exhaustion or if I fainted . . .

The whole body was shaking and trembling in the morning. The cup of tea tasted bitter. Felt like vomiting.[9]

Recalling the night's events, Bhai Sahib reassures her that this is all perfectly natural – it is indeed the awakening of kundalini energy in the base of the spine, the initiation of the soul's longing for union with God. Unlike men, her teacher continues, women are already well attuned to this mystical phenomenon:

Women, because they are nearer to Prakriti, are fertilized by the Divine Energy which they retain in their chakras and, because of this, very few practices are needed. Women are taken up through the Path of Love, for love is feminine mystery. Woman is the cup waiting to be filled, offering herself up in her longing which is her very being.[10]

Through the ensuing days and months, Irina is tossed upon the tidal waves of agony and ecstasy – for every drop of understanding, there is a backwash of unmitigated anguish. However, gradually a feeling of surrender arises within her and the feminine mystery starts to unfold.

Her devotion toward her beloved teacher also knows no bounds. Her gratitude is overwhelming, drowning her in a sea of love:

Deepest peace. And I nearly fall down when I salute him lately. And the feeling of nothingness before him represents such happiness. He will be resting, his eyes closed or open; and I sit, bent in two (a comfortable position for me in his presence) under the blow from the two fans; he and I alone somewhere, where nothing is but peace.

Lately it becomes increasingly lovely. Deep happiness welling from within. From the deepest depth . . . Also at home, when I think of him, it comes over me . . . soft, gentle. A bliss of non-being; not existing at all. It is difficult to believe, unless one has experienced it, that it is so glorious "not to be".[11]

The feeling of nothingness is taking over. Humiliation and pain are dissolving into an unshakeable experience of the Self:

Walking to his place amongst the busy morning traffic, the noise of children going to school, cows wandering aimlessly, rickshaws driving at greatest speed, dogs fighting and the sky covered with white clouds, I reflected that the feeling of Nothingness is not only now in his presence. It stays with me ... I feel like that before God, before life; it seems slowly to have become my very being.[12]

Irina treasured this experience in India for the rest of her life. Returning to London some years later and embarking on a series of lectures on Sufism at the Theosophical Society, she often became entranced with the memory of her beloved Master. Having taken a vow never to speak of anything other than her spiritual insights, her talks essentially became the record of a living tradition, imparted to all those eager to hear.

One day in the reading room of the British Library, Irina chanced upon a book about the metaphysics of Rumi by Khalifa Abdul Hakim, a Pakistani scholar. Reading it, she realized that the things Bhai Sahib and Rumi were saying were completely identical. Immediately, she went home and made two copies – one by hand, the other typed:

... there is only one way of rising from the lower to the higher stage and that is by assimilation of the lower into the higher ... [Rumi] believed that necessity is not only the mother of invention, it is the mother of creation as well. Even God would not have created the heaven and earth if He had not been urged by an irresistible inner necessity ... For Rumi ... life is nothing but a product of the will to live, and ever dissatisfied with the present equipment, life creates new desires, to fulfil which new organs come into existence.[13]

Irina retired from teaching publicly in 1992 but continued giving talks in her London home until her death on 23 August 1999. A black-and-white photographic portrait taken around this time shows a striking woman, with luminous eyes gazing peacefully into the distance. Speaking about the way of surrender to a student one day, she said:

Here again, the terrible paradox. Complete surrender, complete nothingness, "yes" to everything. This is the greatest power. I find this path is especially difficult for men, especially for the Western man because of the education, you know, the competition: "I am better than thou" in sport, in everything. For women, somehow it is easier. Guruji explains one place in the book [*The Chasm of Fire*], how a woman can reach Reality just by being a woman. So I'm very glad, and I said, "Oh, really, wonderful!" It's [actually] not like that. It is just as difficult for everybody. To men, I give many practices, women need only one practice: the detachment from worldly things. Because we by our very nature are attached to comfort, to children; because a woman has to bear children, she needs security. Women are attached to security. If a woman is prepared to give up security . . . because spiritual life is utmost insecurity, no-man's land, it's like walking on water, walking on air, you have nothing under your feet. It's a chasm of fire. Actually, the title, *Chasm of Fire* is from Gregory of Nyssa, the Christian mystic, a contemporary of St Augustine. He said,

"The path of love is like a bridge of hair across the chasm of fire." Of hair, you know. You walk on it; it falls, you fall into the fire . . . very insecure indeed.[14]

Irina Tweedie's final diary entries are made on solitary retreat in 1966 in the Himalayas, where she has reached the end of her journey. Three months have passed since Bhai Sahib left his physical body, after a series of heart attacks, and she is now reflecting on their relationship and the wisdom he has conferred. Who would have thought that a widow in her 50s could have endured so much suffering in the search for the ultimate understanding? However, through her surrender to the Path of Love all has finally been revealed. By the grace of her beloved Master, everything has merged into One:

The sunrise, the sunset, the garden, the people, the whole daily life seems outwardly the same. But the values have changed. The meaning underlying it all is not the same as before. Something which seemed intangible, unattainable, slowly, very slowly becomes a permanent reality. There is nothing but Him. At the beginning it was sporadic; later of shorter or longer duration, when I was acutely conscious of it. But now . . . The infinite, endless Him . . . Nothing else is there. And all the beauty of nature which surrounds me is as if only on the edge of my consciousness. Deep within I am resting in the peace of His Heart. The body feels so light at times. As if it were made of the pure, thin air of the snow peaks. This constant vision of the One is deepening and increasing in the mind, giving eternal peace.[15]

CHAPTER TWENTY-THREE
MODERNISM AND NOVELIST VIRGINIA WOOLF

Heaven be praised for solitude. Let me be alone.
Let me cast and throw away this veil of being,
this cloud that changes with the least breath . . .

Walking into the Visitor Centre at Charleston in Firle, East Sussex, the modernist home and studio of 20th-century artists Vanessa Bell and Duncan Grant, and location of the Bloomsbury Group's "experiments in living", one immediately sees a magnificent display cabinet of hand-decorated, ceramic dinner plates. Commissioned in 1932, the Famous Women Dinner Service chronicles powerful and notable women from antiquity to contemporary life.

Painted by the artists during their time at Charleston, there are 50 plates in the series, featuring Virginia Woolf (Vanessa Bell's sister), Vanessa herself and Duncan Grant, the only man in the collection. Also showcasing women who had subverted social mores within the context of their politics, sexuality or religious commitments, the dinner set is subdivided into Women of Letters, Queens, Beauties, and Dancers and Actresses. Included in the portraits are

Cleopatra, Makeda the Queen of Sheba, Sappho, Beatrice (Dante's muse), Helen of Troy, Elizabeth Tudor (Queen Elizabeth I), Christina Rossetti and Elizabeth Barrett Browning.

Less well known but similarly attractive to the avant-garde is Monk's House, the country retreat of Virginia Woolf and her husband Leonard, literally only a few miles away in the hamlet of Rodmell. An "unpretending", simple clapboard cottage with a garden and fruit-bearing orchard, Monk's House eventually became the Woolfs' permanent base, where the couple would read, write, garden and go for very long walks. More importantly, it was where Virginia found a sacred space, just as Irina Tweedie had done in the Himalayas, to be her authentic self.

It was also here that Virginia wrote many of her bestselling novels, including *Mrs Dalloway*, *To the Lighthouse*, *Orlando* and *The Waves*. In the ritual of daily routines and the quiet surroundings, Virginia found many moments of real happiness in her marriage with Leonard, in an existence also punctuated with crippling bouts of depression that would ultimately claim her life.

One of four children, Adeline Virginia Stephen (1882–1941) was born into an intellectual and artistic household in Kensington, London. Her father, Leslie Stephen, was the editor of the mighty *Dictionary of National Biography* and enjoyed a reputable standing in the literary world; her mother Julia Prinsep Stephen had been a Pre-Raphaelite model. As was the custom, her two brothers, Thoby and Adrian, went off to boarding school, leaving Vanessa and Virginia behind to be educated at home by their father, with full access to his extensive library. Both sisters soon exhibited their creative flair by writing and illustrating a weekly pamphlet, *Hyde Park Gate News*, full of stories about domestic life and all their illustrious visitors to the family home, as well as existential questions concerning the meaning of existence and whether everything around them was ultimately a dream.

Their stimulating childhood was soon to be dealt a series of shattering blows. The loss of their mother, half-sister Stella and then their father during their adolescent years would precipitate the first of Virginia's mental breakdowns. However, her erudite education gave Virginia the intellectual resources she needed to overcome her grief, at least for the immediate future. Coming of age in an agnostic household at the turn of the 20th century, when the very fabric of society was being called into question, enabled her to embrace her own philosophical beliefs, putting catastrophic events into some kind of meaningful perspective.

Indeed, lacking any formal Christian faith and believing emphatically that God did not even exist, Virginia was mystified when her friend, the poet T S Eliot, announced that he had converted to Anglo-Catholicism. And yet, Virginia's work was far from being the outpouring of an atheistic revolutionary proclaiming the nihilism of a godless universe. Rather, through her radical "stream of consciousness" technique she sought to encapsulate the thoughts, feelings and impressions of her inner world, which she believed were rooted in an interconnected pattern behind the "cotton wool" of everyday life. Through her skills as a writer, Virginia developed her narrative to reflect how our sense of self is in a constant state of flux and uncertainty, being something indefinable and ultimately unreal.

Her first short story "The Mark on the Wall" was printed in the collection *Monday or Tuesday* (1921) by the Woolfs' own Hogarth Press with wood-cut illustrations by Vanessa. It takes place in the mind of a woman sitting by a fire, while she meditates on the elusive and fragmentary nature of experience:

> I want to think quietly, calmly, spaciously, never to be interrupted, never to have to rise from my chair, to slip easily from one thing to another, without any sense of hostility, or obstacle. I want to sink deeper and deeper, away from the surface, with its hard separate facts. To steady myself, let me catch hold of the first idea that passes . . . Shakespeare . . . Well, he will do as well as another. A man who sat himself solidly in an armchair, and looked into the fire . . . A shower of ideas fell perpetually from some very high Heaven down through his mind . . .[1]

Her first two novels, published slightly earlier, *The Voyage Out* (1915) and *Night and Day* (1919), similarly explore the terrain of the inner world with its preoccupation with dreams and the nature of reality. More conventional in structure than her later works, both explore their protagonists' need for escaping the confines of religion and society, either through a sea voyage to South America or by examining the institution of marriage, in search of authenticity and living beyond the limits of self.

It would be in *Jacob's Room* (1922) where Virginia moved away from conventional forms of prose, experimenting with a more fluid approach to time, plot and character, as well as the formalities of language. Essentially a character study, the story of Jacob Flanders is told mainly through the perspectives of the women in his life in a series of shifting impressions, the overall effect leaving us wondering who exactly he, or indeed anyone, really is:

> It seems then that men and women are equally at fault. It seems that a profound, impartial, and absolutely just opinion of our fellow-creatures is utterly unknown. Either we are men, or we are women. Either we are cold, or we are sentimental. Either we are young, or growing old. In any case life is but a procession of shadows, and God knows why it is that we embrace them so eagerly, and see them depart with such anguish, being shadows. And why, if this and much more than this is true, why are we yet surprised in the window corner by a sudden vision that the young man in the chair is of all things in the world the most real, the most solid, the best known to us – why indeed? For the moment after we know nothing about him.[2]

As Virginia's work progressed, she would become increasingly absorbed in exploring established ideas surrounding personal identity and conscious reality, crystallized into what she called "moments of being", where life fleetingly shone in all its transcendental beauty through the illusory veil of existence.

In this way, her major novels reflect a radical departure from conventional literary forms in their compelling exploration of the nature of selfhood. *Mrs Dalloway* (1925), which was immortalized on screen in director Stephen Daldry's magnificent *The Hours* (2002) starring

Meryl Streep, Julianne Moore and Nicole Kidman, is a novel that centres around a June day in the life of Clarissa Dalloway, an upper-class woman in her 50s in post-World War I London, as she goes about town buying flowers for a party she will be holding later that day.

The book also weaves its way around the parallel story of a poet and war veteran, Septimus Warren Smith, who is suffering from shell shock and hallucinations of his dead companion from the Western Front. Before being committed to a psychiatric hospital, where he takes his own life by jumping out of a window, he sits in Regent's Park, lucidly taking note of the glory of the present moment in the "privacy of the soul":

Beauty, the world seemed to say. And as if to prove it (scientifically) wherever he looked at the houses, at the railings, at the antelopes stretching over the palings, beauty sprang instantly. To watch a leaf quivering in the rush of air was an exquisite joy. Up in the sky swallows swooping, swerving, flinging themselves in and out, round and round, yet always with perfect control as if elastics held them; and the flies rising and falling; and the sun spotting now this leaf, now that, in mockery, dazzling it with soft gold in pure good temper; and now and again some chime (it might be a motor horn) tinkling divinely on the grass stalks – all of this, calm and reasonable as it was, made out of ordinary things as it was, was the truth now; beauty, that was the truth now. Beauty was everywhere.[3]

Her next novel, *To the Lighthouse* (1927), continues Virginia's poetical, introspective narrative in a tale surrounding the Ramsay family and a group of friends on holiday in Scotland on the Isle of Skye, set just before and after World War I. Once again, the plot itself is minimal, with the focal point of attention being the metaphorical tower of light around which a maelstrom of dark thoughts and diaphanous feelings unfold. As she writes in her essay, *Modern Fiction* (1919), Virginia wanted to show how "an ordinary mind on an ordinary day" processes "a myriad impressions".

Functioning as an elegy for her dead parents and her childhood spent on blissful vacations in St Ives in Cornwall, the novel's essential preoccupation is with impermanence and the passing of time, in particular the paradox of how the present moment is simultaneously experienced as being insubstantial and yet suffused with wonder:

> What is the meaning of life? That was all – a simple question; one that tended to close in on one with years. The great revelation had never come. The great revelation perhaps never did come. Instead, there were little daily miracles, illuminations, matches struck unexpectedly in the dark; here was one.[4]

Momentary epiphanies illuminating a tumultuous life is a theme that Virginia explores through the character of Lily Briscoe, a single woman and amateur painter who struggles with questions of artistic self-worth and sense of identity. Piqued by the quip of a fellow guest who says that women have no ability for either painting or writing, Lily transcends her limiting views in a revealing moment of aesthetic insight – channelling Virginia's own struggles as a writer, as well as her sister's as a visual artist – with her portrait of the creative life anticipating *A Room of One's Own*:

> . . . she took her hand and raised her brush. For a moment it stayed trembling in a painful but exciting ecstasy in the air. Where to begin? – that was the question; at what point to make the first mark? One line placed on the canvas committed her to innumerable risks, to frequent and irrevocable decisions. All that in idea seemed simple became in practice immediately complex; as the waves shape themselves symmetrically from the cliff top, but to the swimmer among them are divided by steep gulfs, and foaming crests. Still the risk must be run; the mark made.[5]

For the Woolfs, art was an intrinsic aspect of their informal life at ramshackle Monk's House. While perhaps not as overtly aesthetically pleasing as Vanessa's Charleston, the interiors still exuded a quintessential charm, stacked high with books and vinyl records, as well as decorated with pictures, furnishings and ceramics produced by many of their Bloomsbury artist friends, such as the painters Duncan Grant, Roger Fry and Angelica Garnett (Vanessa's daughter), potter Quentin Bell (Vanessa's son) and pieces made by Vanessa herself. Indeed, her oil portrait of Virginia, which currently hangs in the dining room, arrestingly captures her sister's pensive, melancholic nature, her arms folded in quiet defiance upon her desk.

Even the Woolfs themselves turned their hands to producing beautiful works of art by printing many of Leonard and Virginia's earliest essays and novels, illustrated by Vanessa, through their Hogarth Press. Teaching themselves to use the small hand-press machine from the accompanying instruction manual was an unmitigated success, giving Virginia the opportunity to write exactly what she wanted without having to pander to the whims and demands of editors and publishers. Moreover, the attention required for typesetting, printing and bookbinding proved to be an effective treatment for headaches, something Virginia suffered from throughout her entire life.

It is *The Waves* (1931) that would become Virginia's crowning literary achievement, a novel distilling all her existential ideals into one compellingly beautiful, impressionistic narrative. Described by the author as a "playpoem" and shying away from a conventional plot and dialogue, it follows the intertwined lives of six friends from childhood to adulthood, with the book itself being divided into nine sections. Each of these sections, like a dramatic soliloquy echoing the rhythm of a gentle tide, corresponds to a time of day and a period in the lives of the characters.

The familiar themes are all here – beauty, death, the nature of self – but they are developed to their most dazzling and experimental, utilizing to full effect Virginia's original use of interior monologue to drive the prose along. Ingeniously, the inner mind of one protagonist seemingly shifts and blends with all the others, creating a communal consciousness, ebbing and flowing upon the central assumption that our identity is essentially a fiction.

The opening of the book, one of ten italicized interludes describing the lie of the sea, harks back to the beginning of creation and the tradition of witnessing the birth of a mythological world from a shimmering expanse of water. Interestingly, Virginia likened the act of writing itself to a rhythm, flowing like a wave as it breaks and tumbles in the mind:

The sun had not yet risen. The sea was indistinguishable from the sky, except that the sea was slightly creased as if a cloth had wrinkles in it. Gradually as the sky whitened a dark line lay on the horizon dividing the sea from the sky and the grey cloth became barred with thick strokes moving, one after another, beneath the surface, following each other, pursuing each other, perpetually.

As they neared the shore each bar rose, heaped itself, broke and swept a thin veil of white water across the sand. The wave paused, and then drew out again, sighing like a sleeper whose breath comes and goes unconsciously. Gradually the dark bar on the horizon became clear as if the sediment in an old wine bottle had sunk and left the glass green. Behind it, too, the sky cleared as if the white sediment there had sunk, or as if the arm of a woman couched beneath the horizon had raised a lamp and flat bars of white, green and yellow spread across the sky like the blades of a fan. Then she raised her lamp higher and the air seemed to become fibrous and to tear away from the green surface flickering and flaming and in red and yellow fibres like the smoky fire that roars from a bonfire. Gradually the fibres of the burning bonfire were fused into one haze, one incandescence which lifted the weight of the woollen grey sky on top of it and turned it to a million atoms of soft blue. The surface of the sea slowly became transparent and lay rippling and sparkling until the dark stripes were almost rubbed out. Slowly the arm that held the lamp raised it higher and then higher until a broad flame became visible; an arc of fire burnt on the rim of the horizon, and all round it the sea blazed gold.[6]

The novel then charts the solitary paths each character is destined to follow, periodically coming together with the others to share their experiences of living – education, work, being in nature, relationships – with the death of their mutually esteemed friend Percival lending a melancholic undertone to their final meeting. It is the last, ninth section that is Virginia's *pièce de résistance*, where the protagonist, Bernard, in a summing up of who he believes himself to be, delivers a homily on the meaning of existence indirectly suggesting that his own mind and those of his companions are merely multiple expressions of oneself.

In a resounding climax, deconstructing his identity and the very medium of language, he concludes that being alone is where peace ultimately resides:

"Heaven be praised for solitude! I am alone now. That almost unknown person has gone, to catch some train, to take some cab, to go to some place or person whom I do not know. The face looking at me has gone. The pressure is removed. Here are empty coffee-cups. Here are chairs turned but nobody sits on them. Here are empty tables and nobody any more coming to dine at them tonight.

"Let me now raise my song of glory. Heaven be praised for solitude. Let me be alone. Let me cast and throw away this veil of being, this cloud that changes with the least breath, night and day, and all night and all day. While I sat here I have been changing. I have watched the sky change. I have seen clouds cover the stars, then free the stars, then cover the stars again. Now I look at their changing no more. Now no one sees me and I change no more. Heaven be praised for solitude that has removed the pressure of the eye, the solicitation of the body, and all need of lies and phrases [. . .]

"How much better is silence; the coffee-cup, the table. How much better to sit by myself like the solitary sea-bird that opens its wings on the stake. Let me sit here for ever with bare things, this coffee-cup, this knife, this fork, things in themselves, myself being myself."[7]

Bernard also recognizes how life is a cycle with its eternal renewal, its perpetual rise and fall, culminating again in the loss of self:

"And in me too the wave rises. It swells; it arches its back. I am aware once more of a new desire, something rising beneath me like the proud horse whose rider first spurs and then pulls him back. What enemy do we now perceive advancing against us, you whom I ride now, as we stand pawing this stretch of pavement? It is death. Death is the enemy. It is death against whom I ride with my spear couched and my hair flying back like a young man's, like Percival's, when he galloped in India. I strike spurs into my horse. Against you I will fling myself, unvanquished and unyielding, O Death!"

The waves broke on the shore.[8]

The spectre of death is a presence that lurks ominously within Virginia's writing as well as in her own life, which was plagued with crippling bouts of anxiety and depression, rendering her frequently bedridden and culminating in her first suicide attempt by overdose of sleeping pills shortly after marrying Leonard. Forever the artist, she used these moments of despair to her advantage, citing that "madness is terrific" because it heightened her creative awareness, as outlined in her revelatory essay *On Being Ill* (1926):

Considering how common illness is, how tremendous the spiritual change that it brings, how astonishing, when the lights of health go down, the undiscovered countries that are then disclosed, what wastes and deserts of the soul a slight attack of influenza brings to view, what precipices and lawns sprinkled with bright flowers a little rise of temperature reveals, what ancient and obdurate oaks are uprooted in us by the act of sickness, how we go down into the pit of death and feel the waters of annihilation close above our heads and wake thinking to find ourselves in the presence of the angels and the harpers when we have a tooth out and come to the surface in the dentist's armchair and confuse his "Rinse the mouth – rinse the mouth" with the greeting of the Deity stooping from the floor of heaven to welcome us [...]

In illness words seem to possess a mystic quality. We grasp what is beyond their surface meaning, gather instinctively this, that and the other – a sound, a colour, here a stress, there a pause – which the poet, knowing words to be meagre in comparison with ideas, has strewn about his page to evoke, when collected, a state of mind which neither words can express nor the reason explain. Incomprehensibility has an enormous power over us in illness – more legitimately, perhaps, than the upright will allow.[9]

Illness, death and loss of self were not the only themes Virginia explored in her writing. Paradoxically, and perhaps of even greater importance, was her preoccupation with the rights of women and the value of female friendship, her radical views making her the doyenne of the feminist movement in her celebration of the feminine self.

Indeed, her novel *Orlando* (1928) was dedicated to her one-time lover and close friend, Vita Sackville-West, writer, gardener and grande dame of majestic Sissinghurst Castle in the neighbouring county of Kent. In this "biography" of an aspiring poet and aristocrat, the titular protagonist travels through time from the Elizabethan age to the modern era, meeting illustrious figures from English literary history, first as a man and then as a woman. By giving Orlando a gender-shifting, multiple-selves identity, Virginia addresses a key concept close to her heart on the nature of being female:

Different though the sexes are, they intermix. In every human being a vacillation from one sex to the other takes place, and often it is only the clothes that keep the male and female likeness, while underneath the sex is the very opposite of what it is above. Of the complications and confusions which thus result everyone has had experience; but here we leave the general question and note only the odd effect it had in the particular case of Orlando herself.[10]

In a sumptuous film adaption of *Orlando* (1992) by Sally Potter starring Tilda Swinton, the theme of how women are defined by their sartorial appearance and beauty is brought to the fore. Moreover, echoing Sigmund Freud's declaration that the human psyche is essentially bisexual, exploring gender boundaries meant that *Orlando* would become a seminal text for subsequent generations of feminists, particularly in modern times where the debate has encompassed what being male or female actually even means.

In October 1928, Virginia was invited to deliver lectures at Newnham and Girton Colleges, which were the only women's colleges in Cambridge at that time, in order to explore these very issues. Centred around the topic of women and fiction, the talks were revised, extended and published the following year as *A Room of One's Own* (1929). A partially fictionalized narrative, Virginia assesses the importance specifically of 19th-century female novelists – George Eliot, Jane Austen, Charlotte Brontë, all of whom, incidentally, are included in the Famous Women Dinner Service – and the state of English literature, finishing her thesis by exhorting women everywhere to take up the pen, making the book one of the most important feminist tracts on the nature of writing of the 20th century.

After declaring from the outset that a woman must have money and a room of her own if she is to write fiction, in a remarkable passage Virginia brings together all the major ideas that preoccupied her thinking, not least familiar issues relating to moments of being and the unifying flow of reality:

> At this moment, as so often happens in London, there was a complete lull and suspension of traffic. Nothing came down the street; nobody passed. A single leaf detached itself from the plane tree at the end of the street, and in that pause and suspension fell. Somehow it was like a signal falling, a signal pointing to a force in things which one had overlooked. It seemed to point to a river, which flowed past, invisibly, round the corner, down the street, and took people and eddied them along, as the stream at Oxbridge had taken the undergraduate in his boat and the dead leaves. Now it was bringing from one side of the street to the other diagonally a girl in patent leather boots, and then a young man in a maroon overcoat; it was also bringing a taxi-cab; and it brought all three together at a point directly beneath my window; where the taxi stopped; and the girl and the young man stopped; and they got into the taxi; and then the cab glided off as if it were swept on by the current elsewhere. [11]

She goes on to draw together her views on the gender divide and how the two may be mentally united:

The sight was ordinary enough: what was strange was the rhythmical order with which my imagination had invested it; and the fact that the ordinary sight of two people getting into a cab had the power to communicate something of their own seeming satisfaction. The sight of two people coming down the street and meeting at the corner seems to ease the mind of some strain, I thought, watching the taxi turn and make off. Perhaps to think, as I had been thinking these two days, of one sex as distinct from the other is an effort. It interferes with the unity of the mind. Now that effort had ceased and that unity had been restored by seeing two people come together and get into a taxi-cab. The mind is certainly a very mysterious organ, I reflected, drawing my head in from the window, about which nothing whatever is known, though we depend upon it so completely. [12]

Virginia then continues:

What does one mean by "the unity of the mind"?, I pondered, for clearly the mind has so great a power of concentrating at any point at any moment that it seems to have no single state of being. It can separate itself from the people in the street, for example, and think of itself as apart from them, at an upper window looking down on them. Or it can think with other people spontaneously, as, for instance, in a crowd waiting to hear some piece of news read out. It can think back through its fathers or through its mothers, as I have said that a woman writing thinks back through her mothers. Again if one is a woman one is often surprised by a sudden splitting off of consciousness, say in walking down Whitehall, when from being the natural inheritor of that civilization, she becomes, on the contrary, outside of it, alien and critical. Clearly the mind is always altering its focus, and bringing the world into different perspectives. But some of these states of mind seem, even if adopted spontaneously, to be less comfortable than others. In order to keep oneself continuing in them one is unconsciously holding something back, and gradually the repression becomes an effort. But there may be some state of mind in which one could continue without effort because nothing is required to be held back.[13]

Ever deeper she penetrates into the very heart of her line of thinking about the conciliatory nature of the present moment, echoing Simone de Beauvoir's sentiments on brotherhood:

And this perhaps, I thought, coming in from the window, is one of them. For certainly when I saw the couple get into the taxi-cab the mind felt as if, after being divided, it had come together again in a natural fusion. The obvious reason would be that it is natural for the sexes to cooperate. One has a profound, if irrational, instinct in favour of the theory that the union of man and woman makes for the greatest satisfaction, the most complete happiness. But the sight of the two people getting into the taxi and the satisfaction it gave me made me also ask whether there are two sexes in the mind corresponding to the two sexes in the body, and whether they also require to be united in order to get complete satisfaction and happiness? And I went on amateurishly to sketch a plan of the soul so that in each of us two powers preside, one male, one female; and in the man's brain the man predominates over the woman, and in the woman's brain the woman predominates over the man. The normal and comfortable state of being is that when the two live in harmony together, spiritually cooperating. If one is a man, still the woman part of the brain must have effect; and a woman also must have intercourse with the man in her. Coleridge perhaps meant this when he said that a great mind is androgynous.[14]

In 1934, with the funds from Virginia's writing, the Woolfs demolished the old toolshed at the end of the garden, which she had been using as a writing room, and replaced it with a new weatherboarded lodge with French windows and a small brick patio, affording privacy and tranquility to think. Unconventionally, she would sit inside in an armchair with a plywood board across her knees to write her prolific output of letters, diary entries, essays and two further novels, *The Years* (1937) and *Between the Acts* (1941), composing them in various shades of ink – greens, blues and purples, the latter being the colour she particularly preferred for her voluminous correspondence. Later in the day, she would sit at her desk, typing up and editing her morning's work.

In spite of her idyllic life at Monk's House – the beautiful garden and stunning landscapes, the tender care of a loving husband and a room of her own to fulfil a satisfying literary career – Virginia continued to suffer debilitating bouts of depression. London had been badly blitzed and many of their friends and loved ones had been killed at home and abroad. Coupled with the lingering fear of possible German occupation, the Woolfs made a pact that if they were ever invaded by Hitler, they would kill themselves in the garage.

The seeds of suicide already sown, Virginia inevitably shifted toward taking the next fateful step. On the morning of 28 March 1941, she put on her coat, took her walking stick and went quickly up the garden path to the top gate leading out onto the Downs and the River Ouse, where she put a large stone in her pocket and waded into the water in one final bid for peace.

In her three heartbreaking suicide notes (two for Leonard, one for Vanessa), she writes of the terror of going mad again: "I begin to hear voices, and I can't concentrate."[15] Leonard found the letters in the upstairs sitting room at one o'clock that afternoon, when he went to listen to the news on the radio. He rushed to the river but could only find her abandoned walking stick. Her body was found downstream three weeks later.

Virginia was cremated in Brighton; her ashes were then buried by Leonard under the two elm trees in the garden that they had christened Virginia and Leonard (which have sadly been felled), marked with a stone tablet and engraved with the final, sacred lines of *The Waves*: "Against you I will fling myself, unvanquished and unyielding, O Death! *The waves crashed on the shore.*"

EPILOGUE

Virginia Woolf was not the only woman to sacrifice her own life, precipitated by inner turmoil. A few decades earlier, in June 1913, suffragette Emily Wilding Davison threw herself in front of the King's horse at Epsom Derby, dying four days later from her injuries without ever regaining consciousness. Even though her intentions are unknown, we can guess that her motive was probably wanting to draw attention to the cause of female emancipation that she felt so passionate about – as an active member of the Women's Social and Political Union, she had even spent time in prison for her feminist beliefs.

I am not advocating anyone take action as drastic as Emily's, and yet we should be in awe of a woman who stood up for what she believed. Thankfully, today there are many who nobly and publicly champion the rights of underrepresented and dispossessed women to achieve educational and financial independence, as well as afford them protection from sexual and domestic abuse.

However, for some of us, perhaps a more understated response is welcome. In summing up our journey together through the sacred feminine testimony of so many inspirational writers, visionaries and mystics, I would like to return to Virginia, a woman whose legacy I feel more intensely every single day.

In the concluding remarks of *A Room of One's Own*, compiled in her writing shed at Monk's House in East Sussex, she reflects upon what piece of advice she can leave for her women readers. In her typically sardonic, self-effacing manner, she offers very little in terms of a rallying call to arms; rather, she returns to fundamentals, and stresses how vital it is to be authentic and embrace the very essence of who we truly are:

> Here I would stop, but the pressure of convention decrees that every speech must end with a peroration. And a peroration addressed to women should have something, you will agree, particularly exalting and ennobling about it. I should implore you to remember your responsibilities, to be higher, more spiritual; I should remind you how much depends upon you, and what an influence you can exert upon the future [. . .] When I rummage in my own mind I find no noble sentiments about being companions and equals and influencing the world to higher ends. I find myself saying briefly and prosaically that it is much more important to be oneself than anything else.[1]

Such is the hallmark of all the extraordinary women presented here, from Mesopotamian priestess Enheduanna right through to Virginia Woolf. Despite, even because of, harrowing and difficult circumstances, a belief in oneself above all else gives us – both men and women alike – the courage to live an authentic life and the strength to follow our destinies, whatever the price to be paid.

ACKNOWLEDGEMENTS

It is vital that I acknowledge my indebtedness and unreserved gratitude to the following authors and their respective texts, which have formed the mythological, literary and philosophical foundations of *The Sacred Feminine Through the Ages*: S Abhayananda, *History of Mysticism: The Unchanging Testament*; Anne Baring and Jules Cashford, *The Myth of the Goddess: Evolution of an Image*; and Serinity Young, *An Anthology of Sacred Texts by and about Women*.

I would also like to express my thanks to all the publishers who have given permission to use quotations from their authors' material, details of which are cited at the end of the book (see Permissions).

Finally, I want to acknowledge the amazing women in my life: first and foremost, my beautiful mother, who has always been a constant source of love, support and companionship; and second, Anne Corkhill, Stella Konsta, Suzanne Page and Indira Paramanandam, trusted allies and confidantes on this extraordinary journey called life.

ABOUT THE AUTHOR

Paula Marvelly read English at Royal Holloway College, University of London, and European Studies at Selwyn College, University of Cambridge. She is creator and editor of The Culturium (theculturium.com), an online platform dedicated to exploring the interface between spirituality and the cultural arts. She lives in Sussex.

NOTES AND REFERENCES

Prologue

1 *A Room of One's Own*, Virginia Woolf, p.108.

1. Mesopotamia and Priestess Enheduanna

1 *Inanna, Lady of Largest Heart, Poems of the Sumerian High Priestess, Enheduanna*, Betty De Shong Meador, p.94.

2 Ibid., pp.122, 125, 128.

3 Ibid., p.174.

2. Ancient Egypt and Queen Hatshepsut

1 *Egyptian Mysteries: New Light on Ancient Knowledge*, Lucie Lamy, quoted in *The Myth of the Goddess: Evolution of an Image*, Anne Baring and Jules Cashford, p.255.

2 Ibid., pp.261–2.

3 "Hymn VII", from *Hymns to Isis in Her Temple at Philae*, L Zabkar, quoted in *The Divine Feminine: Exploring the Feminine Face of God Around the World*, Andrew Harvey and Anne Baring, p.50.

4 *Ancient Egyptian Literature: A Book of Readings, Vol 2, The New Kingdom*, Miriam Lichtheim, quoted in *An Anthology of Sacred Texts by and about Women*, Serinity Young, p.132.

5 Ibid., pp.132–3.

6 *Royal Sarcophagi of the XVIII Dynasty,* W C Hayes, quoted in *Hatshepsut: The Female Pharaoh*, Joyce Tyldesley, p.86 (Tyldesley uses the alternative spelling).

3. Hinduism and Sage Vak

1 "Hymn of Creation", Rigveda, X, cxxix, 1–5, quoted in *History of Mysticism: The Unchanging Testament*, S Abhayananda, pp.24–6.

2 Rigveda, X, cxxv, quoted in *Great Women of India*, Swami Madhavananda and Ramesh Chandra Majumdar (eds.), pp.131–2.

3 "Devi Upanishad", quoted in *The Divine Feminine: Exploring the Feminine Face of God Around the World*, Andrew Harvey and Anne Baring, p.158.

4 "Brihadaranyaka Upanishad", *The Thirteen Principal Upanishads*, Robert Ernest Hume (trans.), quoted in *An Anthology of Sacred Texts by and about Women*, Serinity Young, pp.274–5.

5 *The Laws of Manu*, G Bühler (trans.), quoted in Ibid., p.277.

4. Judaism and Queen of Sheba Makeda

1 (NRSVA) Bible Gateway online, Sirach, 1:2–10.

2 Ibid., Sirach, 25:24.

3 (NRSV) Logos Bible Study online, Wisdom of Solomon, 6:12–16.

4 Ibid., Wisdom of Solomon, 8:2–5.

5 Ibid., Proverbs, 8:1–17.

6 *Women in Praise of the Sacred: 43 Centuries of Spiritual Poetry by Women*, Jane Hirshfield (ed.), p.13.

7 Ibid., p.14.

8 "The Song of Solomon", *Poetry for the Spirit: An Original and Insightful Anthology of Mystical Poems*, Alan Jacobs (ed.), pp.4–5.

9 Ibid., p.6.

10 Ibid., p.14.

5. Ancient Greece and Lyrist Sappho

1   *The Symposium*, Plato, Christopher Gill (trans.), pp.47–9.

2   "Hymn to the Earth: Mother of All", P B Shelley (trans.), quoted in *Poetry for the Spirit: An Original and Insightful Anthology of Mystical Poems*, Alan Jacobs (ed.), p.17.

3   Homeric "Hymn to Athena", Jules Cashford (trans.), quoted in *The Myth of the Goddess: Evolution of an Image*, Anne Baring and Jules Cashford, p.343.

4   Homeric "Hymn to Aphrodite", Jules Cashford (trans.), quoted in *Harvest*, 1987, quoted in Ibid., p.349.

5   "Poem 1", *Sappho Poems and Fragments*, Stanley Lombardo (trans.), p.1.

6   "Poem 6", Ibid., p.6.

7   "Poem 54", Ibid., p.54.

8   "Poem 62", *Sappho: Poems and Fragments*, Josephine Balmer (trans.), p.56.

9   "Poem 106", Ibid., p.80.

6. Indian Buddhism and Mother of the Buddha Mahapajapati

1   *Dhammapada*, XI, Babbitt, quoted in *History of Mysticism: The Unchanging Testament*, S Abhayananda, pp.73–4.

2   Adaptation of *Cullavagga*, X, 1, 1–4, quoted in *The First Buddhist Women: Translations and Commentary on the Therigatha*, Susan Murcott, pp.15–16.

3   Ibid., pp.18–19.

4   Ibid., pp.33–4.

5   Ibid., pp.65–6.

6   Ibid., pp.87–8.

7   Ibid., p.196.

7. Gnosticism and Disciple Mary Magdalene

1 *An Anthology of Sacred Texts by and about Women*, Serinity Young, p.63.

2 (NRSVA) Bible Gateway online, Ephesians, 5:22–24.

3 Ibid., I Corinthians, 14:34–35.

4 Ibid., I Timothy, 2:8–15.

5 *The Thunder: Perfect Mind*, quoted in *The Nag Hammadi Library*, James M Robinson (ed.), pp.297–8.

6 *Trimorphic Protennoia*, quoted in Ibid., p.513.

7 *The Gospel of Mary Magdalene*, Jean-Yves Leloup (trans.), p.25.

8 Ibid., p.27.

9 Ibid., p.27.

10 Ibid., p.25.

11 Ibid., p.25.

12 Ibid., p.37.

13 Ibid., p.39.

14 Ibid., p.37.

8. Chinese Buddhism and Nun Hui-hsü

1 *Visuddhi-Magga*, XIII, in *Buddhism in Translations*, Henry Clarke Warren (trans.), quoted in *An Anthology of Sacred Texts by and about Women*, Serinity Young, p.308.

2 *Women in Buddhism: Images of the Feminine in the Mahayana Tradition*, Diana Paul, quoted in Ibid., p.322.

3 *The Journey to the West*, Anthony C Yu (trans.), quoted in *The Goddesses' Mirror: Visions of the Divine from East and West*, David Kinsley, pp.25–6.

4 *The Position of Woman in Early China According to the Lieh Nü Chuan: The Biographies of Eminent Chinese Women*, Albert Richard O'Hara, quoted in *An Anthology of Sacred Texts by and about Women*, Serinity Young, p.361.

5 *Lives of the Nuns: Biographies of Chinese Buddhist Nuns from the Fourth to Sixth Centuries*, Kathryn Ann Tsai (trans.), p.15.

6 Ibid., p.15.

7 Ibid., p.18.

8 Ibid., p.24.

9 Ibid., p.39.

10 Ibid., pp.52–3.

11 Ibid., p.57.

12 Ibid., p.83.

13 *Original Teachings of Chan Buddhism*, Chang Chung-yuan, quoted in *History of Mysticism: The Unchanging Testament*, S Abhayananda, p.219.

14 *Studies in Shinto Thought*, Muraoka Tsunetsugu, Delmer M Brown and James T Araki (trans.), quoted in *The Goddesses' Mirror: Visions of the Divine from East and West*, David Kinsley, p.71.

9. Sufism and Mystic Rabia al-Adawiyya

1 *Bezels of Wisdom*, Ibn Al-'Arabi and R W J Austin (trans.), quoted in *An Anthology of Sacred Texts by and about Women*, Serinity Young, p.119.

2 *Tazkirat al-Awliya*, Attar, quoted in *Muslim Women Mystics*, Margaret Smith, p.21.

3 *Doorkeeper of the Heart: Versions of Rabia*, Charles Upton, p.58.

4 Ibid., p.31.

5 Ibid., p.2.

6 Ibid., p.9.

7 Ibid., p.11.

8 Ibid., p.6.

9 Ibid., p.66.

10 "Love in Absence", *Rumi: Poet and Mystic*, Reynold A Nicholson (trans.), quoted in *An Anthology of Sacred Texts by and about Women*, Serinity Young, p.120.

11 "The Love of Woman", *Rumi: Poet and Mystic*, Reynold A Nicholson (trans.), quoted in Ibid., p.120.

12 *Doorkeeper of the Heart: Versions of Rabï'a*, Charles Upton, p.61.

10. Tantric Buddhism and Lama Yeshe Tsogyal

1 *Buddhist Texts Through the Ages*, Edward Conze (ed.), quoted in *An Anthology of Sacred Texts by and about Women*, Serinity Young, p.327.

2 Ibid., p.327.

3 *The Origin of the Tara Tantra*, Jo-Nan Taranatha and David Templeman (ed. and trans.), quoted in Ibid., p.331.

4 "Hymn to Tara", Vagisvarakirti, quoted in *The Divine Feminine: Exploring the Feminine Face of God Around the World*, Andrew Harvey and Anne Baring, p.145.

5 *The Yoga of Knowing the Mind, and Seeing the Reality, which is Called Self-Realization*, Padma-Shambhava, in *The World of the Buddha*, Lucien Stryck (ed.), quoted in *History of Mysticism: The Unchanging Testament*, S Abhayananda, p.85.

6 *Lady of the Lotus-Born: The Life and Enlightenment of Yeshe Tsogyal*, Gyalwa Changchub, Namkhai Nyinpo and Padmakara Translation Group (trans.), pp.94–5.

7 Ibid., pp.21–2.

8 Ibid., pp.23–4.

9 Ibid., pp.139–40.

10 Ibid., p.91.

11 Ibid., p.141.

12 Ibid., pp.145–6.

13 Ibid., pp.176–7.

14 Ibid., p.164.

15 *Tibetan Yoga and Secret Doctrines*, W Y Evans-Wentz (ed.), quoted in *An Anthology of Sacred Texts by and about Women*, Serinity Young, p.337.

16 Ibid., p.337.

11. Hinduism and Poet Andal

1 *Devi-Mahatmya: The Crystallization of the Goddess Tradition*, Thomas B Coburn, quoted in *An Anthology of Sacred Texts by and about Women*, Serinity Young, p.303.

2 Ibid., p.300.

3 *Padma Purana*, Sanskrit Safire online.

4 *Classical Hindu Mythology: A Reader in the Sanskrit Puranas*, Cornelia Dimmitt and J A B van Buitenen (trans. and ed.), quoted in *An Anthology of Sacred Texts by and about Women*, Serinity Young, p.302.

5 *Devi-Mahatmya: The Crystallization of the Goddess Tradition*, Thomas B Coburn, quoted in Ibid., p.301.

6 *The Ramayana* of *Valmiki*, Hari Prasad Shastri (trans.), quoted in Ibid., p.293.

7 *The Mahabharata, Vol 2: The Book of the Assembly Hall, The Book of the Forest*, J A B van Buitenen (trans. and ed.), quoted in Ibid., p.286.

8 *The Geeta: The Gospel of the Lord Shri Krishna*, Shri Purohit Swami (trans.), IV:9–11, pp.24–5.

9 Ibid., VI:26–8, pp.32–3.

10 Ibid., IX:13–19, p.43.

11 *Srimad Bhagavatam*, Kamala Subramaniam (trans.), p.375.

12 *The Yoga of Spiritual Devotion: A Modern Translation of the Narada Bhakti Sutras*, Prem Prakash (trans.), 1–6, pp.6, 8, 9, 11, 14, 17.

13 Ibid., 51–5, pp.96–7, 100–2.

14 Ibid., 28–30, pp.55–7.

15 Ibid., 82, p.147.

16 *Andal: Tiruppavai*, P S Sundaram (trans.), 1, p.3.

17 Ibid., 29, p.31.

18 Ibid., 30, p.32.

19 *Andal: Nachiyar Tirumozhi*, P S Sundaram (trans.), I:8, p.42.

20 Ibid., V:7, p.83.

21 Ibid., VI:4, p.90.

22 Ibid., XI:2–3, pp.124–5.

23 Ibid., XIII:10, p.149.

12. Christianity and Abbess Hildegard of Bingen

1 *The Consolation of Philosophy of Boethius*, H R James (trans.), I:I., The Project Gutenberg online.

2 Ibid., II:IV.

3 Ibid., III:XII.

4 *La Vita Nuova*, Dante Alighieri and Dante Gabriel Rossetti (trans.), p.1.

5 *Hildegard of Bingen: Selected Writings*, Mark Atherton (trans.), p.3.

6 *Women Writers of the Middle Ages: A Critical Study of Texts from Perpetua to Marguerite Porete*, Peter Dronke, p.145.

7 Ibid., p.168.

8 *Hildegard of Bingen: Selected Writings*, Mark Atherton (trans.), p.91.

9 *Hildegard of Bingen: Scivias*, Mother Columba Hart and Jane Bishop (trans.), p.109.

10 Ibid., p.124.

11 *Hildegard of Bingen: Selected Writings*, Mark Atherton (trans.), p.171.

12 Ibid., pp.172–3.

13 *Women Writers of the Middle Ages: A Critical Study of Texts from Perpetua to Marguerite Porete*, Peter Dronke, p.175.

14 Ibid., p.176.

15 *Hildegard of Bingen: Selected Writings*, Mark Atherton (trans.), p.122.

13. Taoism and Immortal Sister Sun Bu-er

1 *Ways to Paradise: The Chinese Quest for Immortality*, Michael Loewe, quoted in *An Anthology of Sacred Texts by and about Women*, Serinity Young, p.392.

2 *The Eight Immortals of Taoism: Legends and Fables of Popular Taoism*, Kwok Man Ho and Joanne O'Brien (ed. and trans.), quoted in Ibid., p.395.

3 *Lao Tsu: Tao Te Ching*, Gia-Fu Feng and Jane English (trans.), 1, p.3.

4 Ibid., 6, p.8.

5 Ibid., 20, p.22.

6 *Chuang Tze*, quoted in *History of Mysticism: The Unchanging Testament*, S Abhayananda, p.67.

7 Ibid., p.68.

8 "The Jade Woman of Greatest Mystery", *History of Religion*, Edward H Schafer, quoted in *An Anthology of Sacred Texts by and about Women*, Serinity Young, p.383.

9 *Seven Taoist Masters: A Folk Novel of China*, Eva Wang (trans.), quoted in Ibid., p.387.

10 Ibid., p.389.

11 *Immortal Sisters: Secret Teachings of Taoist Women*, Thomas Cleary (trans. and ed.), p.48.

12 Ibid., p.7.

13 Ibid., p.22.

14 Ibid., p.38.

15 Ibid., p.45.

14. Christianity and Beguine Marguerite Porete

1 *The "Summa Theologica" of St. Thomas Aquinas, Part I*, Fathers of the English Dominican Province (trans.), quoted in *An Anthology of Sacred Texts by and about Women*, Serinity Young, p.69.

2 *Meister Eckhart: Selected Writings*, Oliver Davies (trans.), p.258.

3 Ibid., p.108.

4 Sermon 27, *Meister Eckhart: A Modern Translation*, Raymond B Blackney (trans.), quoted in *History of Mysticism: The Unchanging Testament*, S Abhayananda, p.281.

5 Sermon 52, *Meister Eckhart: The Essential Sermons, Commentaries, Treatises and Defense*, Edmund Colledge and Bernard McGinn (trans.), quoted in Ibid., pp.281–2.

6 *Marguerite Porete: The Mirror of Simple Souls*, Ellen Babinsky (trans.), p.79.

7 Ibid., pp.192–3.

8 Ibid., p.193.

9 Ibid., p.129.

10 Ibid., p.129.

11 Ibid., p.195.

12 Ibid., p.200.

13 Ibid., p.201.

14 *Mechthild of Magdeburg: The Flowing Light of the Godhead*, Frank Tobin (trans.), p.40.

15 Ibid., p.39.

16 Ibid., p.62.

17 Ibid., p.111.

18 Ibid., pp.53–4.

19 Ibid., p.49.

20 Ibid., pp.96–7.

21 *Hadewijch: The Complete Works*, Mother Columba Hart (trans.), p.280.

22 Ibid., p.66.

23 *Visions and Longings: Medieval Women Mystics*, Monica Furlong, pp.107–8.

24 *The Malleus Maleficarum of Heinrich Kramer and James Sprenger*, Montague Summers (trans.), quoted in *An Anthology of Sacred Texts by and about Women*, Serinity Young, p.79.

25 Ibid., pp.79–80.

15. Christianity and Anchorite Julian of Norwich

1 *Thomas à Kempis: On the Love of God*, S Abhayananda (ed.), quoted in *History of Mysticism: The Unchanging Testament*, S Abhayananda, p.294.

2 *The Cloud of Unknowing: The Classic of Medieval Mysticism*, Evelyn Underhill (ed.), p.16.

3 *Richard Rolle: The English Writings*, Rosamund S Allen (trans. and ed.), quoted in *Women and Mystical Experience in the Middle Ages*, Frances Beer, p.129.

4 *Anchoritic Spirituality: Ancrene Wisse and Associated Works*, Anne Savage and Nicholas Watson (trans.), pp.189–90.

5 *Julian of Norwich: Revelations of Divine Love*, Elizabeth Spearing (trans.), "The Short Text", p.5.

6 Ibid., "The Short Text", p.6.

7 Ibid., "The Short Text", pp.10–11.

8 Ibid., "The Long Text", p.137.

9 Ibid., "The Long Text", p.138.

10 Ibid., "The Short Text", p.7.

11 Ibid., "The Short Text", p.12.

12 Ibid., "The Long Text", p.80.

13 Ibid., "The Long Text", p.139.

14 Ibid., "The Short Text", p.8.

15 Ibid., "The Short Text", p.10.

16 Ibid., "The Long Text", p.179.

16. Hinduism and Bhakta Mirabai

1 *Jnaneshvar: The Life and Works of the Celebrated 13th Century Indian Mystic-Poet*, S Abhayananda (trans.), quoted in *History of Mysticism: The Unchanging Testament*, S Abhayananda, pp.270–3.

2 *The Song of the Goddess: The Devi Gita: Spiritual Counsel of the Great Goddess*, C Mackenzie Brown (trans.), pp.45, 47.

3 Ibid., pp.53–4.

4 Ibid., p.63.

5 *Lalla: Naked Song*, Coleman Barks (trans.), p.19.

6 Ibid., p.42.

7   Ibid., p.54.

8   Ibid., p.21.

9   *Love Song of the Dark Lord: Jayadeva's Gitagovinda*, Barbara Stoler Miller (trans. and ed.), p.112.

10 Ibid., pp.123–4.

11 *Mirabai: Ecstatic Poems*, Robert Bly and Jane Hirshfield (versions), p.6.

12 *For Love of the Dark One: Songs of Mirabai*, Andrew Schelling (trans.), p.23.

13 *Mirabai: Ecstatic Poems*, Robert Bly and Jane Hirshfield (versions), p.57.

14 *For Love of the Dark One: Songs of Mirabai*, Andrew Schelling (trans.), p.30.

15 "On the Acquisition of Dharma, Artha and Kama", *The Kama Sutra of Vatsyayana*, Richard Burton (trans.), Sacred Texts online.

17. Neoplatonism and Carmelite Teresa of Avila

1   *Corpus Hermeticum*, XI & XII, Walter Scott (trans. and ed.), quoted in *The Fall of Sophia: A Gnostic Text on the Redemption of Universal Consciousness*, Violet MacDermot, p.54.

2   *Spenser's The Faerie Queene*, Book I, IV:28–34 (my spelling), George Armstrong Wauchope (ed.), The Project Gutenberg online.

3   *The Tempest*, Act IV, scene 1, William Shakespeare, the Complete Works of Shakespeare online.

4   "The Garden", 5–6, *Andrew Marvell: The Complete Poems*, Elizabeth Story Donno (ed.), p.101.

5   "De sapientia", I, *Unity and Reform: Selected Writings of Nicholas de Cusa*, John P Dolan (ed.), quoted in *History of Mysticism: The Unchanging Testament*, S Abhayananda, p.309.

6   *Luther's Works, Volume 1: Lectures on Genesis, Chapters 1–5*, Jaroslav Pelikan (ed.), quoted in *An Anthology of Sacred Texts by and about Women*, Serinity Young, p.85.

7   Ibid., p.85.

8   *St. John of the Cross: The Dark Night of the Soul*, David Lewis (trans.),
     Poetry Foundation online.

9   "The Ascent of Mount Carmel", *The Collected Works of John of the
     Cross*, Kieran Kavanaugh and Otilio Rodriguez (trans.), quoted
     in *History of Mysticism: The Unchanging Testament*, S Abhayananda,
     p.321.

10   *The Life of Saint Teresa of Avila by Herself*, J M Cohen (trans.), p.74.

11   Ibid., p.125.

12   Ibid., p.127.

13   *The Way of Perfection: Teresa of Avila*, E Allison Peers (trans.), pp.65–
     6.

14   Ibid., p.199.

15   *Teresa of Avila: The Interior Castle*, Kieran Kavanaugh and Otilio
     Rodriguez (trans.), p.35.

16   Ibid., p.37.

17   Ibid., p.93.

18   Ibid., p.179.

18. Judaism and Mystic Grace Aguilar

1   "The Royal Crown", *Selected Religious Poems of Solomon Ibn Gabi-
     rol*, Israel Zangwill (trans.) and Israel Davidson (ed.), quoted in
     History of Mysticism: The Unchanging Testament, S Abhayananda,
     p.247.

2   *Zohar*, Gershom Scholem, quoted in Ibid., p.250.

3   *Zohar*, Daniel C Matt (trans.), quoted in *An Anthology of Sacred
     Texts by and about Women*, Serinity Young, p.31.

4   *Grace Aguilar: Selected Writings*, Michael Galchinsky (ed.), pp.225–
     6.

5   Ibid., pp.248–9, p.255.

6   Ibid., p.183.

7   Ibid., p.191.

8   Ibid., pp.198, 200.

19. Transcendentalism and Poet Emily Dickinson

1   *Arthur Schopenhauer: The World as Will and Representation*, E F J Payne (trans.), Vol. I, § 3, pp.7–8.

2   Ibid., Vol. I, § 68 p.390.

3   *The Norton Anthology of Poetry*, Margaret Ferguson, Mary Jo Salter and Jon Stallworthy (eds.), p.729.

4   "Confluents", Christina Rossetti, *Poetry for the Spirit: An Original and Insightful Anthology of Mystical Poems*, Alan Jacobs (ed.), p.337.

5   *Aurora Leigh*, Elizabeth Barrett Browning, Ibid., pp.280–1.

6   *A Vindication of the Rights of Women*, Mary Wollstonecraft, The Project Gutenberg online.

7   #959, quoted in *The Life of Emily Dickinson*, Richard B Sewall, p.328.

8   #280, *Emily Dickinson*, Helen McNeil (ed.), p.15.

9   #642, Ibid., p.64.

10   #550, quoted in *The Life of Emily Dickinson*, Richard B Sewall, pp.458–9.

11   #593, *Emily Dickinson*, Helen McNeil (ed.), pp.56–7.

12   *The Life of Emily Dickinson*, Richard B Sewall, pp.514–15 (I have retained Emily's original spelling).

13   Ibid., pp.518–19.

14   #817, Ibid., p.693.

15   #721, *Emily Dickinson*, Helen McNeil (ed.), p.70.

20. Hinduism and Holy Mother Sarada Devi

1   *The Gospel of Sri Ramakrishna*, Swami Nikhilananda (trans.), quoted in *History of Mysticism: The Unchanging Testament*, S Abhayananda, p.362.

2   Ibid., p.363.

3   Ibid., p.367.

4   Ibid., p.368.

5   *The Gospel of Sri Ramakrishna*, Swami Nikhilananda (trans.), quoted in *The Return of the Mother*, Andrew Harvey, p.61.

6   *Women Saints East and West*, Swami Ghanananda and Sir John Stewart-Wallace (eds.), pp.102–3.

7   Ibid., p.109.

8   *The Holy Mother, Being the Life of Sri Sarada Devi, Wife of Sri Ramakrishna and Helpmate in His Mission*, Swami Nikhilananda, p.214.

9   Ibid., p.235.

10 Ibid., p.319.

11 Ibid., p.237.

12 *Great Women of India*, Swami Madhavananda and Ramesh Chandra Majumdar (eds.), p.537.

13 Ibid., p.538.

21. Integral Yoga and Sweet Mother Mirra Alfassa

1   *Simone de Beauvoir: The Second Sex*, H M Parshley (trans. and ed.), p.633.

2   Ibid., p.687.

3   *The Mother: A Short Biography*, Wilfried, p.3.

4   Ibid., pp.5–6.

5   Ibid., p.10.

6   Quoted in *The Spiritual Tourist*, Mick Brown, pp.151–2.

7   *The Mother*, Aurobindo, quoted in *The Return of the Mother*, Andrew Harvey, p.127.

8   *The Mother: A Short Biography*, Wilfried, p.18.

9   Ibid., p.54.

10 *The Mother*, Aurobindo, quoted in *The Return of the Mother*, Andrew Harvey, p.135, italics added.

11 *The Mother*, Aurobindo, quoted in *Great Women of India*, Swami Madhavananda and Ramesh Chandra Majumdar (eds.), p.84.

12 *The Mother*, Aurobindo, quoted in Ibid., pp.84–5.

13 *The Mother: A Short Biography*, Wilfried, p.93.

14 *The Mother's Vision*, The Mother, pp.385–6.

15 Ibid., pp.188–9.

16 *The Mother: A Short Biography*, Wilfried, p.58.

22. Sufism and Diarist Irina Tweedie

1 "25 June", *The Chasm of Fire: A Woman's Experience of Liberation Through the Teachings of a Sufi Master*, Irina Tweedie, p.191.

2 "3 October", Ibid., p.12.

3 "3 October", Ibid., p.13.

4 "27 November", Ibid., p.42.

5 "8 June", Ibid., p.104.

6 "8 June", Ibid., p.105.

7 "9 March", Ibid., pp.77–8.

8 "20 January", Ibid., pp.57–8.

9 "20 January", Ibid., p.58.

10 "7 January", Ibid., p.150.

11 "30 June", Ibid., p.191.

12 "24 July", Ibid., p.194.

13 *The Metaphysics of Rumi*, Khalifa Abdul Hakim, quoted in *The Taste of Hidden Things: Images on the Sufi Path*, Sara Sviri, p.193.

14 Interview Golden Sufi Center, California, quoted in *Women of Sufism, A Hidden Treasure: Writings and Stories of Mystic Poets, Scholars & Saints*, Camille Adams Helminski, p.274.

15 "8 November", *The Chasm of Fire: A Woman's Experience of Liberation Through the Teachings of a Sufi Master*, Irina Tweedie, p.201.

23. Modernism and Novelist Virginia Woolf

1 "The Mark on the Wall", *Monday or Tuesday*, Virginia Woolf, A Celebration of Women Writers, University of Pennsylvania online.

2 *Jacob's Room*, Virginia Woolf, p.70.

3   *Mrs Dalloway*, Virginia Woolf, p.68–9.

4   *To The Lighthouse*, Virginia Woolf, p.181.

5   Ibid., p.178.

6   *The Waves*, Virginia Woolf, pp.3–4.

7   Ibid., pp.212–13.

8   Ibid., p.214.

9   *On Being Ill: An Essay on Illness, On Loneliness, Vulnerability and Privilege in Illness*, Virginia Woolf, pp.7–8, 23.

10 *Orlando: A Biography*, Virginia Woolf, p.133.

11 *A Room of One's Own*, Virginia Woolf, p.95.

12 Ibid., p.95.

13 Ibid., pp.95–6.

14 Ibid., pp.96–7.

15 Open Culture online.

Epilogue

1   *A Room of One's Own*, Virginia Woolf, p.109.

BIBLIOGRAPHY

Primary Sources and Critical Texts

Abhayananda, S, *History of Mysticism: The Unchanging Testament* (Watkins Publishing, London, 2002)

Alighieri, Dante and Rossetti, Dante Gabriel (trans.), *La Vita Nuova* (Ellis and Elvey, London, 1899), The Project Gutenberg online

Armstrong, Karen, *A History of God* (Vintage, London, 1993)

Atherton, Mark (trans.), *Hildegard of Bingen: Selected Writings* (Penguin, London, 2001)

Babinsky, Ellen (trans.), *Marguerite Porete: The Mirror of Simple Souls* (Paulist Press, Mahwah (NJ), 1993)

Balmer, Josephine (trans.), *Sappho: Poems and Fragments* (Bloodaxe Books, Newcastle upon Tyne, 1992)

Baring, Anne and Cashford, Jules, *The Myth of the Goddess: Evolution of an Image* (Penguin, London, 1993)

Barks, Coleman (trans.), *Lalla: Naked Song* (Maypop Books, Athens, 1992)

Barnstone, Aliki and Barnstone, Willis (eds.), *Women Poets from Antiquity to Now* (Schocken Books, New York, 1992)

Beer, Frances, *Women and Mystical Experience in the Middle Ages* (The Boydell Press, Woodbridge, 1998)

Bly, Robert and Hirshfield, Jane (versions), *Mirabai: Ecstatic Poems* (Beacon Press, Boston, 2004)

Bolton, Chelsea Luellon, *Mother of Writing* (Chelsea Bolton, 2023)

Briggs, Julia, *Virginia Woolf: An Inner Life* (Harcourt, Orlando, 2005)

Brooks, Miguel F (trans.), *Kebra Nagast* (The Red Sea Press, New Jersey, 2002)

Brown, C Mackenzie (trans.), *The Song of the Goddess: The Devi Gita: Spiritual Counsel of the Great Goddess* (State University of New York Press, New York, 2002)

Brown, Mick, *The Spiritual Tourist* (Bloomsbury, London, 1998)

Burton, Richard (trans.), *The Kama Sutra of Vatsyayana* (1883), Sacred Texts online

Busby, Margaret (ed.), *Daughters of Africa: An International Anthology of Works and Writings by Women of African Descent from the Ancient Egyptian to the Present* (Ballantine Books, New York, 1992)

Cahill, Susan (ed.), *Wise Women: Over 2000 Years of Spiritual Writing by Women* (W W Norton & Co, New York, 1996)

Campbell, Joseph, *The Hero with a Thousand Faces* (Fontana Press, London, 1993)

Changchub, Gyalwa and Nyinpo, Namkhai and Padmakara Translation Group (trans.), *Lady of the Lotus-Born: The Life and Enlightenment of Yeshe Tsogyal* (Shambhala, Boston, 2002)

Chittick, William, *Sufism: A Short Introduction* (Oneworld, Oxford, 2003)

Cleary, Thomas (trans. and ed.), *Immortal Sisters: Secret Teachings of Taoist Women* (North Atlantic Books, Berkeley, 1996)

Cohen, J M (trans.), *The Life of Saint Teresa of Avila by Herself* (Penguin, London, 1957)

Davies, Oliver (trans.), *Meister Eckhart: Selected Writings* (Penguin, London, 1994)

Dronke, Peter, *Women Writers of the Middle Ages: A Critical Study of Texts from Perpetua to Marguerite Porete* (Cambridge University Press, Cambridge, 1996)

Eliot, T S, *Collected Poems: 1909–1962* (Faber and Faber, London, 1963)

Ellis, Ralph, *Solomon: Falcon of Sheba* (Edfu Boks, Cheshire, 2002)

Feng, Gia-Fu and English, Jane (trans.), *Lao Tsu: Tao Te Ching* (Vintage Books, New York, 1989)

Ferguson, Margaret, and Salter, Mary Jo and Stallworthy, Jon (eds.), *The Norton Anthology of Poetry* (Norton, New York, 1996)

Flinders, Carol Lee, *Enduring Grace: Living Portraits of Seven Women Mystics* (HarperSanFrancisco, New York, 1993)

Ford-Grabowsky, Mary (ed.), *Sacred Voices: Essential Women's Wisdom Through the Ages* (HarperSanFrancisco, New York, 2002)

Furlong, Monica, *Visions and Longings: Medieval Women Mystics* (Mowbray, London, 1996)

Galchinsky, Michael (ed.), *Grace Aguilar: Selected Writings* (Broadview Press, Ontario, 1993)

Ghanananda, Swami and Stewart-Wallace, Sir John (eds.), *Women Saints: East and West* (Vedanta Press, Hollywood, 1979)

Gilbert, R A, *The Elements of Mysticism* (Element, Shaftesbury, 1991)

Giles, Mary, *The Feminist Mystic and Other Essays on Women and Spirituality* (Crossroad, New York, 1985)

Gill, Christopher (trans.), *The Symposium*, Plato (Penguin, London, 1999)

Godman, David (ed.), *Padamalai: Teachings of Sri Ramana Maharshi Recorded by Muruganar* (David Godman, Boulder, 2004)

Griffith, Ralph (trans.), *The Hymns of the Rig Veda* (Motilal Banarsidass Publishers, Delhi, 1995)

Guillaumont, A, *The Gospel According to Thomas* (Leiden, 1976)

Hart, Mother Columba (trans.), *Hadewijch: The Complete Works* (Paulist Press, Mahwah (NJ), 1980)

Hart, Mother Columba and Bishop, Jane (trans.), *Hildegard of Bingen: Scivias* (Paulist Press, Mahwah (NJ), 1990)

Harvey, Andrew, *The Return of the Mother* (Frog, Berkeley, 1995)

Harvey, Andrew and Baring, Anne, *The Divine Feminine: Exploring the Feminine Face of God Around the World* (Conari Press, Berkeley, 1996)

Helminski, Camille Adams, *Women of Sufism, A Hidden Treasure: Writings and Stories of Mystic Poets, Scholars & Saints* (Shambhala, Boston, 2003)

Hinnells, John R, *Who's Who of Religion* (Penguin Reference, London, 1991)

Hirshfield, Jane, *Women in Praise of the Sacred: 43 Centuries of Spiritual Poetry by Women* (Harper Perennial, New York, 1994)

Hoeller, Stephan, *Jung and the Lost Gospels* (Quest Books, Illinois, 1989)

Jacobs, Alan (ed.), *Poetry for the Spirit: An Original and Insightful Anthology of Mystical Poems* (Watkins Publishing, London, 2002)

_____(trans.), *The Principal Upanishads* (O Books, London, 2003)

James, H R (trans.), *The Consolation of Philosophy of Boethius* (Elliot Stock, London, 1897), The Project Gutenberg online

James, William, *The Varieties of Religious Experience* (Touchstone, New York, 1997)

Jantzen, Grace, *Julian of Norwich: Mystic and Theologian* (SPCK, London, 2000)

Jung, Carl Gustav, *Aspects of the Feminine* (Routledge, London, 2003)

Kavanaugh, Kieran and Rodriguez, Otilio, *Teresa of Avila: The Interior Castle* (Paulist Press, Mahwah (NJ), 1979)

King, Karen L, *The Gospel of Mary of Magdala: Jesus and the First Woman Apostle* (Polebridge Press, Santa Rosa, 2003)

Kinsley, David, *The Goddesses' Mirror: Visions of the Divine from East and West* (State University of New York Press, Albany, 1989)

Leloup, Jean-Yves (trans.), *The Gospel of Mary Magdalene* (Inner Traditions, Rochester (VT), 2002)

Lombardo, Stanley (trans.), *Sappho Poems and Fragments* (Hackett Publishing, Indianapolis, 2002)

MacDermot, Violet (trans.), *The Fall of Sophia: A Gnostic Text on the Redemption of Universal Consciousness* (Lindisfarne Books, Great Barrington (MA), 2001)

Madhavananda, Swami and Majumdar, Ramesh Chandra (eds.), *Great Women of India* (Advaita Ashrama, Kolkata, 2001)

Madigan, Shawn (ed.), *Mystics, Visionaries & Prophets: A Historical Anthology of Women's Spiritual Writings* (Fortress Press, Minneapolis, 1998)

Masset, Claire, *Virginia Woolf at Monk's House* (National Trust, 2018)

McGill, Bernard (ed.), *Meister Eckhart and the Beguine Mystics* (Continuum, New York, 1994)

McNeil, Helen (ed.), *Emily Dickinson* (Everyman, London, 2004)

Meyer, Marvin (ed.), *The Gospels of Mary Magdalene* (HarperSanFrancisco, New York, 2004)

Miller, Barbara Stoler (trans. and ed.), *Love Songs of the Dark Lord: Jayadeva's Gitagovinda* (Columbia University Press, New York, 1997)

Mosse, Kate, *Warrior Queens & Quiet Revolutionaries: How Women (Also) Built the World* (Mantle, London, 2022)

Mother, The, *The Mother's Vision: Selections from Questions and Answers* (Sri Aurobindo Ashram, Pondicherry, 2002)

Murcott, Susan, *The First Buddhist Women: Translations and Commentary on the Therigatha* (Parallax Press, Berkeley, 1991)

Neumann, Erich, *The Origins and History of Consciousness* (Princeton University Press, Princeton, 1973)

(NRSVA) Bible Gateway & (NRSV) Logos Bible Study online

Nicholson, D H S and Lee, A H E, *The Oxford Book of Mystical Verse* (Clarendon Press, Oxford, 1932)

Nikhilananda, Swami, *The Holy Mother, Being the Life of Sri Sarada Devi, Wife of Sri Ramakrishna and Helpmate in His Mission* (Ramakrishna Vivekananda Centre Press, New York, 1962)

Noffke, Suzanne (trans.), *Catherine of Siena: The Dialogue* (Paulist Press, Mahwah (NJ), 1980)

Pagels, Elaine, *Adam, Eve and the Serpent* (Vintage Books, New York, 1989)

———*The Gnostic Gospels* (Penguin, London, 1990)

Parshley, H M (trans. and ed.), *Simone de Beauvoir: The Second Sex* (Jonathan Cape, London, 1956)

Paulsell, Stephanie, *Religion Around Virginia Woolf* (The Pennsylvania State University Press, University Park, 2019)

Payne, E F J (trans.), *Arthur Schopenhauer: The World as Will and Representation* (Dover Publications, New York, 1969)

Peers, Allison (trans.), *The Way of Perfection: Teresa of Avila* (Dover, Mineola, 2012)

Picknett, Lynn, *Mary Magdalene* (Robinson, London, 2003)

Prakash, Prem (trans.), *The Yoga of Spiritual Devotion: A Modern Translation of the Narada Bhakti Sutras* (Inner Traditions International, Rochester (VT), 1998)

Ricks, Christopher (ed.), *Andrew Marvell: The Complete Poems* (Penguin, London, 1985)

Robinson, James M (ed.), *The Nag Hammadi Library* (Harper, SanFrancisco, 1990)

Rossetti, Dante Gabriel (trans.), *La Vita Nuova: Dante Alighieri* (Dover Publications, New York, 2001)

Savage, Anne and Watson, Nicholas (trans.), *Anchoritic Spirituality: Ancrene Wisse and Associated Works* (Paulist Press, Mahwah (NJ), 1991)

Schelling, Andrew (trans.), *For the Love of the Dark One: Songs of Mirabai* (Hohm Press, Prescott (AZ), 1998)

Sewall, Richard, *The Life of Emily Dickinson* (Harvard University Press, Cambridge, 1980)

Shong Meador, Betty de, *Inanna, Lady of Largest Heart, Poems of the Sumerian High Priestess, Enheduanna* (University of Texas Press, Austin, 2000)

Smith, Margaret, *Muslim Women Mystics: The Life and Work of Rabi'a and Other Women Mystics in Islam* (Oneworld, Oxford, 2001)

———*Studies in Early Mysticism in the Inner and Middle East* (Oneworld, Oxford, 1995)

Spearing, Elizabeth (trans.), *Julian of Norwich: Revelations of Divine Love* (Penguin, London, 1998)

Story Donno, Elizabeth (ed.), *Andrew Marvell: The Complete Poems* (Penguin, London, 1985)

Subramaniam, Kamala, *Srimad Bhagavatam* (Bharatiya Vidya Bhavan, Mumbai, 1993)

Sundaram, P S (trans.), *Andal: Tiruppavai, Nachiyar Tirumozhi* (Ananthacharya Indological Research Institute, Mumbia, 1987)

Sviri, Sara, *The Taste of Hidden Things: Images on the Sufi Path* (The Golden Sufi Centre, Inverness, 1997)

Swami, Shri Purohit (trans.), *The Geeta: The Gospel of the Lord Shri Krishna* (Faber and Faber, London, 1965)

Teasdale, Wayne, *The Mystic Heart: Discovering a Universal Spirituality in the World's Religions* (New World Library, Novato, 2001)

Tharu, Susie and Lalita, K (eds.), *Women Writing in India: 600 BC to the Present, Vol I* (The Feminist Press, New York, 1991)

Tobin, Frank (trans.), *Mechthild of Magdeburg: The Flowing Light of the Godhead* (Paulist Press, Mahwah (NJ), 1998)

Tsai, Kathryn Ann, *Lives of the Nuns: Biographies of Chinese Buddhist Nuns from the Fourth to Sixth Centuries* (University of Hawaii Press, Honolulu, 1994)

Tweedie, Irina, *The Chasm of Fire: A Woman's Experience of Liberation through the Teachings of a Sufi Master* (Element, Tisbury, 1979)

Tyldesley, Joyce, *Daughters of Isis: Women of Ancient Egypt* (Penguin, London, 1995)

———*Hatchepsut: The Female Pharaoh* (Penguin, London, 1998)

Umansky, Ellen and Ashton, Dianne (eds.), *Four Centuries of Jewish Women's Spirituality: A Sourcebook* (Beacon Press, Boston, 1992)

Underhill, Evelyn, *Mysticism: The Nature and Development of Spiritual Consciousness* (Oneworld, Oxford, 1993)

———(ed.), *The Cloud of Unknowing: The Classic of Medieval Mysticism* (Dover, New York, 2003)

Upton, Charles, *Doorkeeper of the Heart: Versions of Rabia* (Pir Press, New York, 2003)

Verez, Gwenaël, *The Search for the Divine Mother* (Divine Cool Breeze Books, Lulu.com, 2021)

Wauchope, George Armstrong (ed.), *Spenser's The Faerie Queene* (The MacMillan Company, New York, 1903), The Project Gutenberg online

Wilfried, *The Mother: A Short Biography* (Sri Aurobindo Society, Pondicherry, 2005)

———*The Mother's Vision: Selections from Questions and Answers* (Sri Aurobindo Ashram, Pondicherry, 2002)

Wollstonecraft, Mary, *A Vindication of the Rights of Women*, The Project Gutenberg online

Woolf, Virginia, *A Room of One's Own* (Penguin, London, 2000)

———*How Should One Read a Book?* (Renard Press, London, 2021)

———*Jacob's Room* (Vintage, London, 2022)

———*Monday or Tuesday* (Harcourt, Brace and Company, New York, 1921), A Celebration of Women Writers, University of Pennsylvania online

———*Mrs Dalloway* (Vintage, London, 2020)

———*On Being Ill: An Essay on Illness, On Loneliness, Vulnerability and Privilege in Illness* (Renard Press, London, 2022)

———*Orlando: A Biography* (Vintage, London, 2020)

———*The Waves* (Vintage, London, 2020)

———*To The Lighthouse* (Vintage, London, 2022)

Young, Serinity, *An Anthology of Sacred Texts by and about Women* (Pandora, London, 1993)

Texts Cited in Secondary Sources

Abdul Hakim, Khalifa, *The Metaphysics of Rumi* (The Ripon Printing Press, Lahore, 1933)

Abhayananda, S, *Thomas à Kempis: On the Love of God* (Atma Books, Washington, 1992)

————*Jnaneshvar: The Life and Works of the Celebrated 13th Century Indian Mystic-Poet* (Atma Books, Washington, 1989)

Allen, Rosamund S (trans. and ed.), *Richard Rolle: The English Writings* (Paulist Press, Mahwah (NJ), 1988)

Aurobindo, Sri, *The Mother* (Sri Aurobindo Ashram, Pondicherry, 1928)

Austin, R W J (trans.), *The Bezels of Wisdom* (Paulist Press, Ramsey, 1980)

Babbitt, Irving (trans.), *Dhammapada* (New Directions, New York, 1965)

Bary, W Theodore de, et al., *Sources of Chinese Tradition* (Columbia University Press, New York, 1964)

Baynes, Cary F (trans.), *The I Ching or Book of Changes* (Princeton University Press, Princeton, 1967)

Blackney, Raymond B, *Meister Eckhart: A Modern Translation* (Harper Torchbooks, New York, 1941)

Bloomfield, Maurice, *Hymns of the Atharva Veda* (Motilal Banarsidass, Delhi, 1964)

Bowie, Fiona and Davies, Oliver, *Beguine Spirituality* (SPCK, London, 1989)

Bühler, G (trans.), *The Laws of Manu* (Motilal Banarsidass, Delhi, 1964)

Buitenen, J A B van (ed. and trans.), *The Mahabharata, 2 Vols: The Book of the Assembly Hall, The Book of the Forest* (University of Chicago Press, Chicago, 1975)

Chung-yuan, Chang, *Original Teachings of Ch'an Buddhism* (Pantheon Books, New York, 1975)

Coburn, Thomas B, *Devi-Mahatmya: The Crystallization of the Goddess Tradition* (Motilal Banarsidass, Delhi, 1984)

Colledge, Edmund and McGinn, Bernard, *Meister Eckhart: The Essential Sermons, Commentaries, Treatises and Defense* (Paulist Press, New York, 1981)

Conze, Edward (ed.), *Buddhist Texts through the Ages* (Harper & Row, New York, 1964)

Das, Nilima (ed.), *Glimpses of the Mother's Life, Vols 1 & 2* (Sri Aurobindo Ashram, Pondicherry, 1978, 1980)

Dimmitt, Cornelia and Buitenen, J A B van, *Classical Hindu Mythology: A Reader in the Sanskrit Puranas* (Temple University Press, Philadelphia, 1978)

Dolan, John P (ed.), *Unity and Reform: Selected Writing of Nicholas de Cusa* (University of Notre Dame Press, Notre Dame, 1962)

Evans-Wentz, W Y, *Tibetan Yoga and Secret Doctrines* (Oxford University Press, London, 1967)

Fathers of the English Dominican Province (trans.), *The "Summa Theologica" of St. Thomas Aquinas* (Burns Oates & Washbourne, London, 1912)

Hallo, William W and Van Dijk, J J A, *The Exaltation of Inanna* (Yale University Press, New Haven, 1968)

Hayes, W C, *Royal Sarcophagi of the XVIII Dynasty* (Princeton University Press, Princeton, 1935)

Ho, Kwok Man, and O'Brien, Joanne, *The Eight Immortals of Taoism: Legends and Fables of Popular Taoism* (Penguin, New York, 1990)

Hume, Robert Ernest (trans.), *The Thirteen Principal Upanishads* (Oxford University Press, London, 1931)

Iyengar, K R Srinivasa, *On The Mother: The Chronicle of a Manifestation and Ministry* (Sri Aurobindo Ashram Publications Department, Pondicherry, 1978)

Kavanaugh, Kieran and Rodriguez, Otilio (trans.), *The Collected Works of John of the Cross* (ICS Publications, Washington, 1973)

Lamy, Lucie, *Egyptian Mysteries: New Light on Ancient Knowledge* (Thames & Hudson, London, 1981)

Langdon, Stephen, *Sumerian and Babylonia Psalms* (Libraire Paul Geuthner, Paris, 1909)

Lewis, David (trans.), *St. John of the Cross: The Dark Night of the Soul* (Thomas Baker, London, 1908)

Lichtheim, Miriam, *Ancient Egyptian Literature: A Book of Readings, Vol 2, The New Kingdom* (University of California, Berkeley, 1976)

Loewe, Michael, *Ways to Paradise: The Chinese Quest for Immortality* (George Allen and Unwin, London, 1979)

Mackenzie, D A, *Myths of Babylonia and Assyria* (Gresham Publishing, London, 1915)

Matt, Daniel C (trans.), *Zohar: The Book of Enlightenment* (Paulist Press, New York, 1982)

Mother, The, *Collected Works of the Mother, 17 Vols* (Sri Aurobindo Divine Life Trust, Pondicherry, 1978)

Nicholson, Reynold A (ed.), *Rumi: Poet and Mystic* (Allen and Unwin, London, 1950)

Nikhilananda, Swami (trans.), *The Gospel of Sri Ramakrishna* (Ramakrishna-Vivekananda Center, New York, 1942)

O'Hara, Albert Richard, *The Position of Woman in Early China According to the Lieh Nü Chuan: The Biographies of Eminent Chinese Women* (Mei Ya Publications, Taiwan, 1971)

Paul, Diana, *Women in Buddhism: Images of the Feminine in the Mahayana Tradition* (University of California Press, Berkeley, 1985)

Pelikan, Jaroslav (ed.), *Luther's Works: Lectures on Genesis* (Concordia, Saint Louis, 1958)

Roberts, Rev A, Donaldson J and Clarke T, *The Ante-Nicene Christian Library* (Continuum International Publishing, Edinburgh, 1892)

Scholem, Gershom (ed.), *Zohar: The Book of Splendour* (Schocken Books, 1949)

Scott, Walter (ed.), *Hermetica: The Ancient Greek and Latin Writings Which Contain Religious or Philosophic Teachings Ascribed to Hermes Trismegistus* (Shambhala, Boston, 1985)

Shastri, Hari Prasad (trans.), *The Ramayana of Valmiki* (Shanti Sadan, London, 1959)

Smith, Daniel (trans.), *Selections from the Vedic Hymns* (University of California Press, Berkeley, 1968)

Stryck, Lucien (ed.), *The World of the Buddha* (Doubleday, New York, 1968)

Summers, Montague (trans.), *The Malleus Maleficarum of Heinrich Kramer and James Sprenger* (Dover Publications, New York, 1971)

Taranatha, Jo-Nan and Templeman, David (ed. and trans.), *The Origin of the Tara Tantra* (Library of Tibetan Works and Archives, Dharamshala, 1981)

Tsunetsugu, Muraoka, *Studies in Shinto Thought*, Brown, Delmer M and Araki, James T (trans.) (Ministry of Education, Japan, 1964)

Thurman, Robert (trans.), *The Holy Teaching of Vimalakirti: A Mahayana Scripture* (Pen State University Press, 1976)

Waley, Arthur, *The Analects of Confucius* (Vintage Books, New York, 1989)

Wang, Eva, *Seven Taoist Masters: A Folk Novel of China* (Shambhala, Boston, 1990)

Warren, Henry Clarke, *Buddhism in Translations* (Atheneum, New York, 1962)

Yu, Anthony C, *The Journey to the West* (University of Chicago Press, Chicago, 1983)

Zabkar, Louis V, *Hymns to Isis in Her Temple at Philae* (University Press of New England, Hanover, 1988)

Zangwill, Israel (trans.) and Davidson, Israel (ed.), *Selected Religious Poems of Solomon Ibn Gabirol* (Jewish Publication Society, Philadelphia, 1974)

PERMISSIONS

Every care has been made to trace copyright holders. The author would expressly like to thank the following publishers, who have given permission to reproduce their material in *Women of Wisdom* (2005) and its reissue, *The Sacred Feminine Through the Ages* (2024).

Advaita Ashrama: *Great Women of India*, Madhavananda, Swami and Majumdar, Ramesh Chandra (eds.) (2001)

Alderman Electronic Library: *The Consolation of Philosophy*, Boethius (2005)

Ananthacharya Indological Research Institute: *Andal: Tiruppavai, Nachiyar Tirumozhi*, Sundaram, P S (1987)

Asian Humanities Press: *Women in Buddhism: Images of the Feminine in the Mahayana Tradition*, Paul, Diana (1985)

Atma Books: *Jnaneshvar: The Life and Works of the Celebrated 13th Century Indian Mystic-Poet*, Abhayananda, S (1989); *Thomas à Kempis: On the Love of God,* Abhayananda, S (1992)

Avadhuta Foundation: *Padamalai: Teachings of Sri Ramana Maharshi Recorded by Muruganar*, Godman, David (2004)

Beacon Press: *Mirabai: Ecstatic Poems*, Bly, Robert and Hirshfield, Jane (2004)

Bharatiya Vidya Bhavan: *Srimad Bhagavatam*, Subramaniam, Kamala (1993)

Bloodaxe Books: *Sappho: Poems and Fragments*, Balmer, Josephine (1992)

Boydell & Brewer: *Women and Mystical Experience in the Middle Ages*, Beer, Frances (1998)

Brill Academic Publishers: *The Gospel According to Thomas*, Guillaumont, A (1976)

Broadview Press: *Grace Aguilar: Selected Writings*, Galchinsky, Michael (1993)

Bruno Cassirer: *Buddhist Texts Through the Ages*, Conze, Edward (1964)

Cambridge University Press: *Women Writers of the Middle Ages: A Critical Study of Texts from Perpetua to Marguerite Porete*, Dronke, Peter (1996)

Columbia University Press: *Sources of Chinese Tradition*, Bary, W Theodore de (1964); *Love Songs of the Dark Lord: Jayadeva's Gitagovinda*, Miller, Barbara Stoler (1997)

Conari Press: *The Divine Feminine: Exploring the Feminine Face of God Around the World*, Harvey, Andrew and Baring, Anne (1996)

Concordia Publishing House: *Luther's Works: Lectures on Genesis*, Pelikan, Jaroslav (1958)

Continuum Books: *Summa Theologica of St Thomas Aquinas*, Fathers of the Dominican Province (1912); *The Ante-Nicene Christian Library*, Roberts, Rev A, Donaldson, J and Clarke, T (1892)

Dover Publications: *Arthur Schopenhauer: The World as Will and Representation*, Payne, E F J (1969); *The Malleus Maleficarum of Heinrich Kramer and James Sprenger*, Summers, Montague (1971); *The Cloud of Unknowing: The Classic of Medieval Mysticism*, Underhill, Evelyn (2003)

Faber and Faber: *The Geeta: The Gospel of the Lord Shri Krishna*, Swami, Shri Purohit (1965)

Golden Sufi Center: Irina Tweedie interview

Greenwood Publishing: *Studies in Shinto Thought*, Brown, Delmer M and Araki, James T (1964)

Gresham Publishing: *Myths of Babylonia and Assyria*, Mackenzie, D A (1915)

Hackett Publishing: *Sappho Poems and Fragments*, Lombardo, Stanley (2002)

HarperCollins Publishers: *Buddhist Texts Through the Ages*, Conze, Edward (1964); *Women in Praise of the Sacred: 43 Centuries of Spiritual Poetry by Women*, Hirshfield, Jane (1994); *Ways to Paradise: The Chinese Quest for Immortality*, Loewe, Michael (1979); *Rumi: Poet and Mystic*, Nicholson, Reynold A (1950); *The Nag Hammadi Library*, Robinson, James (1990); *The Chasm of Fire*, Tweedie, Irina (1979)

Harvard University Press: *The Life of Emily Dickinson*, Sewall, Richard (1980); *Buddhism in Translation*, Warren, Henry Clarke (1962)

Holm Press: *For the Love of the Dark One: Songs of Mirabai*, Schelling, Andrew (1998)

ICS Publications: *The Collected Works of St. John of the Cross*, translated by Kieran Kavanaugh and Otilio Rodriguez Copyright © 1964, 1979, 1991 by Washington Province of Discalced Carmelites ICS Publications 2131 Lincoln Road, N.E. Washington, DC 20002-1199 U.S.A. www.icspublications.org

Inner Traditions: *The Gospel of Mary Magdalene*, Leloup, Jean-Yves (2002); *The Yoga of Spiritual Devotion: A Modern Translation of the Narada Bhakti Sutras*, Prakash, Prem (1998)

Jewish Publication Society: *Selected Religious Poems of Solomon Ibn Gabirol*, Zangwill, Israel (1974)

Karnac Books: *Harvest: Journal for Jungian Studies*

Libraire Paul Geuthner: *Sumerian and Babylonia Psalms*, Langdon, Stephen (1909)

Library of Tibetan Works and Archives: *The Origin of the Tara Tantra*, Taranatha, Jo-Nan and Templeman, David (1981)

Lindisfarne Books: *The Fall of Sophia: A Gnostic Text on the Redemption of Universal Consciousness*, MacDermot, Violet (2001)

Maypop Books: *Lalla: Naked Song*, Barks, Coleman (1992)

Mei Ya Publications: *The Position of Woman in Early China According to the Lieh Nü Chuan: The Biographies of Eminent Chinese Women,* O'Hara, Albert Richard (1971)

Metropolitan Museum of Art: *Bulletin of the Metropolitan Museum of Art*

Motilal Banarsidass Publishers: *Devi-Mahatmya: The Crystallization of the Goddess Tradition,* Coburn, Thomas B (1984)

New Directions Publishing: *Dhammapada,* Babbitt, Irving (1965)

North Atlantic Books: *Immortal Sisters: Secret Teachings of Taoist Women,* Cleary, Thomas (1996)

O Books: *The Principal Upanishads,* Jacobs, Alan (2003)

Oneworld Publications: *Muslim Women Mystics: The Life and Work of Rabi'a and Other Women Mystics in Islam,* Smith, Margaret (2001); *Mysticism: The Nature and Development of Spiritual Consciousness,* Underhill, Evelyn (1993)

Oxford University Press: *The Laws of Manu,* Bühler, G (1886); *Tibetan Yoga and Secret Doctrines,* Evans-Wentz, W Y (1967); *The Thirteen Principal Upanishads,* Hume, Robert Ernest (1931)

Paulist Press: *The Bezels of Wisdom,* Austin, R W J (1980); *Marguerite Porete: The Mirror of Simple Souls,* Babinsky, Ellen (1993); *Meister Eckhart: The Essential Sermons, Commentaries, Treatises and Defense,* Colledge, Edmund and McGinn, Bernard (1981); *Hadewijch: The Complete Works,* Hart, Mother Columba (1980); *Hildegard of Bingen: Scivias,* Hart, Mother Columba and Bishop, Jane (1990); *Teresa of Avila: The Interior Castle,* Kavanaugh, Kieran and Rodriguez, Otilio (1979); *Zohar: The Book of Enlightenment,* Matt, Daniel C (1982); *Anchoritic Spirituality: Ancrene Wisse and Associated Works,* Savage, Anne and Watson, Nicholas (1991); *Mechthild of Magdeburg: The Flowing Light of the Godhead,* Tobin, Frank (1998)

Penguin: *Hildegard of Bingen: Selected Writings,* Atherton, Mark (2001); *The Myth of the Goddess: Evolution of an Image,* Baring, Anne and Cashford, Jules (1993); *The Life of Saint Teresa of Avila by Herself,* Cohen, J M (1957), *Meister Eckhart: Selected Writings,* Davies, Oliver

(1994); *Plato: The Symposium*, Gill, Christopher (1999); *The Eight Immortals of Taoism: Legends and Fables of Popular Taosim,* Ho, Kwok Man and O'Brien, Joanne (1990); *Julian of Norwich: Revelations of Divine Love*, Spearing, Elizabeth (1998)

Parallax Press: Reprinted from *The First Buddhist Women: Trans lations and Commentary on the Therigatha* (1991) by Susan Murcott with permission of Parallax Press, Berkeley, California. www.parallax.org

Penn State University Press: *The Holy Teaching of Vimalakirti: A Mahayana Scripture*, Thurman, Robert (1976)

Pir Press: *Doorkeeper of the Heart: Versions of Rabia*, Upton, Charles (2003)

Princeton University Press: *The I Ching or Book of Changes*, Baynes, Cary F (1967)

Ramakrishna-Vivekananda Center of New York: *The Gospel of Ramakrishna*, Nikhilananda, Swami (1985); *Holy Mother*, Nikhilananda, Swami (1962)

Random House: *The World of the Buddha*, Stryck, Lucien (Doubleday, 1968); *Original Teachings of Chan Buddhism*, Chung-yuan, Chang (Pantheon, 1975); *The Way of Perfection: Teresa of Avila*, Peers, Alison (Image, 2004); *Zohar: The Book of Splendour*, Scholem, Gershom (Schocken Books, 1949)

Renard Press: *On Being Ill: An Essay on Illness, On Loneliness, Vulnerability and Privilege in Illness*, Woolf, Virginia (2022)

Shambhala Publications: *Lady of the Lotus Born: The Life and Enlightenment of Yeshe Tsogyl*, Changchub, Gyalwa and Nyinpo, Namkhai and Padmakara Translation Group (2002); *Seven Taoist Sisters: A Folk Novel of China*, Wang, Eva (1990)

Shanti Sadan: *The Ramayana of Valmiki*, Shastri, Hari Prasad (1959)

Simon and Schuster: *The Analects of Confucius*, Waley, Arthur (1989)

SPCK: *Beguine Spirituality*, Bowie, Fiona and Davies, Oliver (1989)

Sri Aurobindo Society: *The Mother*, Aurobindo (1928); *The Mother: A Short Biography*, Wilfried (2005); *The Mother's Vision: Selections from Questions and Answers,* The Mother (2002)

State University of New York Press: *The Song of the Goddess: The Devi Gita: Spiritual Counsel of the Great Goddess*, Brown, C Mackenzie (2002)

Temple University Press: *Classical Hindu Mythology: A Reader in the Sanskrit Puranas*, Dimmitt, Cornelia and Buitenen, J A B van (1978)

Thames and Hudson: *Egyptian Mysteries: New Light on Ancient Knowledge*, Lamy, Lucie (1981)

Theosophical Publishing House: *Jung and the Lost Gospels*, Hoeller, Stephan (1989)

University of California Press: *Ancient Egyptian Literature: A Book of Readings, Vol 2, The New Kingdom,* Lichtheim, Miriam (1976); *Selections from the Vedic Hymns*, Smith, Daniel (1968); *Women in Buddhism: Images of the Feminine in the Mahayana Tradition*, Paul, Diana Y (1985)

University of Chicago Press: *History of Religion*, Schafer, Edward H (1978); *The Journey to the West*, Yu, Anthony C (1983); *The Mahabharata, 2 Vols: The Book of the Assembly Hall, The Book of the Forest*, Buitenen, J A B van (1975)

University of Hawaii Press: *Lives of the Nuns: Biographies of Chinese Buddhist Nuns from the Fourth to Sixth Centuries*, Tsai, Kathryn Ann (1994)

University of Notre Dame: *Unity and Reform: Selected Writing of Nicholas de Cusa*, Dolan, John P (1962)

University of Texas Press: *Inanna: Lady of Largest Heart, Poems of the Sumerian High Priestess, Enheduanna*, Shong Meador, Betty de (2000)

University Press of New England: *Hymns to Isis in Her Temple at Philae*, Zabkar, Louis V (1988)

Van Pelt-Dietrich Electronic Library: "Dark Night of the Soul", St John of the Cross (2005)

Vintage Books: *Lao Tsu: Tao Te Ching*, Feng, Gia-Fu and English, Jane (1989); *The Analects of Confucius*, Waley, Arthur (1989)

Watkins Publishing, *History of Mysticism: The Unchanging Testament*, Abhayananda, S (2002); *Poetry for the Spirit: An Original and Insightful Anthology of Mystical Poems*, Jacobs, Alan (ed.) (2002)

Yale University Press: *The Exaltation of Inanna*, Hallo, William W and Van Dijk, J J A (1968)

INDEX